For Pan

Jerry 7-1-2019

Paterson Boy

Paterson Boy

My Family and Other Strangers: A Memoir in Twenty-Eight Stories

JERRY VIS

Rare Bird Books
Los Angeles, Calif.

THIS IS A GENUINE RARE BIRD BOOK

PUBLISHED IN ASSOCIATION WITH DRAGONFLY BOOKS & MEDIA

A Rare Bird Book | Rare Bird Books
453 South Spring Street, Suite 302
Los Angeles, CA 90013
rarebirdbooks.com

A Rare Bird Book | Rare Bird Books
Subsidiary Rights Department,
453 South Spring Street, Suite 302,
Los Angeles, CA 90013.

Set in Janson
Printed in the United States

10 9 8 7 6 5 4 3 2

Publisher's Cataloging-in-Publication data
Names: Vis, Jerry, author.
Title: Paterson Boy: My Family and Other Strangers,
A Memoir in Twenty-Eight Stories / Jerry Vis.
Description: Trade Paperback Edition | A Genuine Rare Bird Book |
New York, NY; Los Angeles, CA: Rare Bird Books, 2018.
Identifiers: ISBN 9781947856622
Subjects: LCSH Vis, Jerry—Childhood. | Vis, Jerry—Family. | Paterson (NJ)—
Biography. | Paterson (NJ)—Social life and customs. | BISAC BIOGRAPHY &
AUTOBIOGRAPHY / Personal Memoirs
Classification: LCC F144.P4 .V57 2018 | DDC 974.9/23/921—dc23

Dedication

For my wife Betty Lou who never tired of my stories and insisted I write them down—in longhand at the time—for Jenny, my daughter who created the ritual of holiday retellings, and Tristan who never ran out of new friends that had to be included. And finally, for my son, Ben, who bought me a laptop and said, "Now get serious."

Contents

Prologue

"Of course life is trouble, only death is not."
—*Zorba the Greek*

IS A MEMOIR AN attempt to bring order to the chaos of memory? Or is it, in reality—now there is a funny word—quite the opposite?

"Start over, Daddy." I had interrupted a bedtime story near its end. This was typical of my dreamy five-year-old son, Benjamin. Which was appropriate. At least from his point of view. If ever he was interrupted, which happened often because he spoke with such deliberation, he would have to start over, not continue, but start over.

I had been telling a story about The Snow Fort War, a monumental battle waged when I was in fourth grade—the expurgated version. I don't know why I switched from storybooks to memories then. It didn't have the desired effect of putting my children to sleep. Instead I had to answer questions. Jenny, the oldest, preferred made-up stories that resumed every night, which, unlike memories, were free to wander anywhere. But occasionally she too would ask to hear the others.

There's nothing like your own children for an audience. I told these stories so often then they seem like someone else's memories. But my kids never tired of them. Of course any deviation or omission brought on instantaneous and indignant correction. It's a short, wonderful period in your life as a parent when your children actually want to hear what you have to say. Though I remembered myself at that same age, listening to my parents talk about their childhoods. It always conjured up feelings of foreignness or alien beings. Were they really once children?

As time went by, a late third addition to the family, Tristan, revitalized the whole bedtime storytelling ritual, instigated by his older siblings and my wife.

As my children grew older they began asking for stories at family events—holidays, birthdays—and I had to comply. Even at unexpected moments, as when schoolmates were at our house, even when company was invited for dinner. Most awkward.

Totally unknown teenagers would come through the kitchen door and ask to hear the ghost story or a cave story or the sledding story. It seemed unimaginable that anyone would want to listen to such stuff. I felt it was right up there with that most boring of requirements, looking at endless pictures of someone's wedding. My life in 1940s Paterson, New Jersey, was ordinary, blue collar, uneventful. Not a life of drama. No social upheavals, no overt family violence, just standard boy adventures. Good and bad stuff. Not terrible. Not wonderful.

Most holidays I faced with considerable trepidation, knowing that my wife would insist that I fulfill this imagined responsibility. Had I no say in this matter? Evidently not. Even as of this last Christmas I was prevailed upon by my youngest child, now twenty-eight years old, to tell the story of The Snow Fort War again. He wanted beautiful Ola, from Poland, the love of his life, to hear this story. I suggested we go to another room. My intent was to winnow down the audience. There were two dozen relatives and friends at the dining table. It took me several minutes to excuse myself. I walked into the other room expecting only two people to be present. Tristan, Ola, and five of their friends were waiting. I perversely decided to tell a different story, about being given away when two months of age, the unedited version no one had ever heard before.

What has happened to these stories over the years, perhaps from so many tellings, or boredom, or early onset Alzheimer's, is a transmogrified fleshing out. That's a little disingenuous. I have found though, that the first recollection of a memory is like a road trip without directions. Only the general destination is known. But in time, repeated trips open up the landscape of the mind, flooding that place where memories lie with realizations and connections seemingly improbable at first. Not exaggerations. Nuances.

In 1978, my family and I started visiting Monhegan Island in the summer, reached by ferry, and about ten miles out in the Atlantic from the nearest coast. I usually spent the time painting. But one year, feeling at loose ends, and at my wife's suggestion—well a bit stronger than that—I decided to scribble some of these stories down in pocket size spiral notebooks.

"I told everyone that you're writing down your childhood memories. Why don't you read them to us later?" This was a setup job by my wife. There were several people from New Jersey staying with us. What choice did I have? I read the stories. When the stay was over I brought the notebooks home and immediately misplaced them in the attic. That was thirty years ago.

The storytelling has diminished since then. The children are grown, my life less demanding. I was rummaging around in the attic with the intent of putting things in order, never a very useful activity, and rediscovered the notebooks. They were in poor shape. The pencil scrawl barely legible. At about the same time Benjamin gave me a laptop to bring me up to speed in the world. In reality it was so he and my wife Lou, could prod me to rewrite these stories. For posterity. I gave up and gave in.

And in the midst of giving in a peculiar thing happened. As I began to rewrite the stories, I remembered more details. As I remembered more, I started to understand the people of my childhood. They ceased being cartoon characters. They became humanized, dimensional, connected, and yes, nuanced, as did my childhood.

"How do you remember all that," was the response of Tristan and Ola and their friends. "Is it true? Is it real?"

"Yes. Relatively," I said slyly with no intention of explaining further. I've lived long enough to realize that truths are usually arbitrary and reality is whatever we think it is. But I assure you, to the best of my mental ability, these stories are true and real.

1

How I Learned Not To Cry
Ages 2 Months–8 Years

Is it possible that life is a magical journey of misdirection?

Don't take it serious.
It's so mysterious.
You work.
You save.
You worry so.
But you can't take your dough
when you go, go, go.

—"Life Is Just a Bowl of Cherries,"
written by Lew Brown

A S AN ADULT I have gotten a job so often in the town I moved away from, I am considering working my way backward. Plus, I had to start this journey before pampers were created. When I was eight I saved someone's life.

"It's gonna' be so hot today. Let's go up to Lakeside swimming." That was Mary.

"Sounds good to me," I said. It was a Saturday morning and the forecast was for humid weather in the mid to upper nineties. We went by ourselves. We didn't have enough money for the bus so we walked fifteen blocks up to the top of Haledon Avenue to the Lakeside Swim Club. We got there at ten in the morning. The lake was already impossibly crowded, too crowded to swim, so we went off to find a place away from the sardine crush. The only open area was a part of this small lake that had a natural, though unpleasant mud bottom.

Mary was wading through hip-deep water ahead of me. Her back toward me when she stepped on something, stopped, and pulled it to the surface, then screamed and swirled away through the murky water. Not sure what had caused her to scream, I moved forward, groped about on the muddy bottom, and found what could only be a body. Mary was now facing me, a good distance away. Both hands were squeezed tight to her temples, her fingers tangled in her hair. I just knew it was a boy, that he wasn't large, about my same age, before I ever pulled him up to the surface.

"He's dead," I thought as I brought him back up. His body had the feel of flaccid, uncooked meat. His face was puffy, deep purple, his tongue swollen and protruding from his mouth. I watched water drain from his unblinking eyes facing into the white-hot sun.

I remember that day. Not the indifferent day, but the snap shots entered in my mental album, and why and how I felt then, or feel now, or anytime I think about it.

We've all heard people say, "I remember the time…" or some such thing. But we don't. We don't remember time. If we could, we could say, with absolute certainty what the date and time was for any memory. In reality, most of our lives are a forgotten blur within a few moments of their passing. But occasionally, when something significant happens, we create those snapshots in the mind that, without regard for time or place, become a living thing again, to be enjoyed or wept over.

When I was a young teenager I used to go spelunking. There was a cave we called the Big Mack Cave. This was before McDonald's hamburgers. My friends and I gave it that name because it could have held a half dozen big Mack tractor-trailer trucks. One day I found a small tunnel in the side of the large entry room of this cave that I crawled into on my hands and knees. After about fifty feet I had to keep my head down as the tunnel reduced in height. At one hundred feet I was flat on my stomach. Another one hundred feet farther on I had to keep my head sideways and my arms straight out in front of me to narrow my shoulders. I cannot explain what compelled me to continue but it never occurred to me to resist the urge to move forward. I never felt any fear or concern. I do vaguely recall that I had done something like this before, also head first, although that prolonged journey had begun in a posterior position in the womb. Some things in life are just irresistible. A few yards farther on the tunnel terminated. There was a pile of chicken bones and feathers in front of me. Why? What brought them there? It had to be a small animal, a predator, a red fox looking for a safe place, just its size, to eat its kill. Within a few inches of the chicken bones was a small grapefruit-size hole that I shined my flashlight through. Beyond was an enormous inaccessible space. A strong breeze moving through the hole told me there was an opening to the sky somewhere, mysteriously out of sight. The breeze had kept me moving ahead, suggesting bigger and better adventures to be had. It took me fifteen minutes to get to the end of this tunnel and over two hours to wriggle out. It was only at that point that I realized my self-made dilemma. There was a rush of panic as my first movements snagged my pants and shirt on jagged rocks, bunching them up, filling them with red clay and gravel. I lay still for a few moments to beat down the terror. I had no choice but to ignore the dirt and gravel and concentrate on how to move. My arms were useless. Only wriggling my body and using the tips of my toes to pull against the tunnel floor allowed me to inch backward. At times I had to shut off my light, close my eyes and lay still to calm myself enough to continue. When I was nearly out I felt someone tie a rope to my ankles and pull me out the last few yards. I lay there too exhausted to move or even thank my worried, angry friends.

I imagine that's what it's like to grow old, only you don't get a second turn. You can't wriggle your way back out if you don't like where you ended up or count on someone being there with a rope to pull you back. Of course there are days in life that are better than others, which if you're short sighted, can make you feel smug and self-satisfied. And then there are the bad ones. The ones that make you feel incredulous if you're very self-confident, or depressed and sorry for yourself if you're unrealistic. But the truth is we are, mostly, propelled by irresistible forces beyond our control. When we're young, we think life has a purpose, and perhaps it does. But if it does—and the jury is out on this one—it's most likely not the one we thought it should be.

I was just a bit short of two months old. It was late April 1939 in Paterson, New Jersey, and I had been crying for some time. I guess in retrospect it was quite self-indulgent of me, but really, after three constricting days of labor anyone would be cranky. As I just mentioned, I had tried to back butt first into the world. So I cried a lot, for the entire first two months of my life. In reality I shouldn't have complained. Compared with the demands I placed on my mother, I got off relatively easy.

My poor mother was terrified of childbirth, for good reason as it turned out. But still I had my issues too. I mean, put yourself in my place. I couldn't believe I had been born to start life as a Stoic, and I refused to take my birth trauma lying down. My dilemma didn't end with my protracted ejection from the birth canal. Everyday there were layers upon layers of additional constrictions.

For instance, the first time I went to my great uncle Phil's butcher shop I was packaged like a sausage with two layers of unmentionables, one of which crinkled and made me feel wet, then a tee shirt, a nightie, a bunting with built in booties, mittens, and hood, a bonnet, swaddled in a sheet, two blankets and of course my mother's own hand-crocheted coverlet in squares of pink and blue, (talk about hedging your bets) after which I was wedged into a carriage and wheeled out of doors into a clear blue, warm spring day. Too, too hot, too constricted and quite gassy. To say the least, I was very unhappy when we reached the shop a block away.

On entering the butcher shop my mother attempted to tell her uncle what she wanted. "I'd like one (WHAAAAAAA) of (YAAAAAAAAAH) meat (WAAA WAAA) please," said Roselyn with accompaniment from me. That's her name. Roselyn, not Rose Lynn. She gets very miffed if you call her Rose Lynn.

"God, this was so annoying," I said to myself. (I was two months old and already I was calling for the help of a deity.) I couldn't tell what we were doing there and neither could my great uncle Phil.

Phil was a man of few words. His brother, my grandfather was the same. They kept their own counsel. And while it seemed to be one of the predominate traits of the men in the family, in time it drove everyone else mad. After the third attempt by my mother to place an order over my indignant wails proved futile, Great Uncle Phil attempted to speak. It was at that precise moment, when our eyes met for the first time, over the white porcelain, glass fronted deli case, that I had my first insightful, if not prescient moment—outside the uterus that is. It started as a tingle in my stomach that spread upward into the back of my mouth. It differed subtly from indigestion. My eyes grew wide. Something in the primal recesses of my mind insisted that I pay attention to my inner voice.

Now, I don't know what your first ah-ha moment was like. I guess glimpsing the future, like any other ability can vary, but my suspicions about coming events have usually been long on apprehension and short on usefulness. But then this was a first time for me so I went with it. *Nothing good is going to come of this visit.* I tried to make eye contact with my mother but her eyes were as swollen and red as mine.

Great Uncle Phil moved to the end of the cabinet, cupped his hands about his mouth and yelled to Roselyn, "Hey kid." It was the forties and "Kid" was a gruff term of endearment gleaned from some Humphrey Bogart film, except in my great uncle's case it was most likely how he thought of his niece. "Hey kid, why don't you pick him up?" he shouted over the noise that I was still drilling into their sanity.

"Meat...chop meat...a pound," repeated Roselyn, not sure what her uncle had said.

Exhausted from screaming, I let out one last, dwindling "WAAAAAA".

"What's wrong with you? Don't you know how to keep him quiet?" It was Great Uncle Phil again, taking advantage of the lull.

As I said, Phil was a man of few words. Not the strong silent type but the snarly impatient sort. He had been standing behind a counter for the better part of his adult life, waiting for something special to come through the door of his shop to give his life some kind of unique meaning. This exhausted young woman, with her bawling child, didn't quite measure up. Especially since they were only relatives. It was at that very moment when my eyes met his over the deli cabinet that I knew my life was about to change forever. But since I wasn't sure how, I let forth with another squall and fell silent as I paused to gulp in a deep replenishing breath.

Roselyn said tearfully, "Since you think you know what to do you can have him," and she turned and walked out the door, leaving me behind. It suddenly looked like I might be Great Uncle Phil's unique something that had just come through the door. In the gap of their angry silence my own stillness so startled me that I missed that very prescient moment I knew was coming.

As the bell on the door sounded, announcing my mother's departure, I refocused on Phil's bald head. His face was closely shaved with a wispy fringe of graying hair at the temples. We stared at each other without moving, which in my swaddled condition only required I keep my mouth shut. Well, now I knew what all the prescience was about, but if this ability was going to be useful to me in the future I'd have to achieve better lead time between the sensation and the event and it would also help if I could get out of all these sweaty layers too.

Soooo! I guess she's abandoned me to my great, laconic uncle Phil. I don't know how long we stared at each other over the deli case, an hour, maybe two. Could that be? It seemed an immeasurable time in my sixty-first day of life.

After a while he walked out of the shop, making me the winner of my very first staring contest, and disappeared upstairs to his apartment. The bell on the door rang. I looked over to see if it was my derelict mother coming back to reclaim me. I got all puckered up to cry, not having understood the bit about overdoing things, and realized I didn't recognize the person looming over my carriage. The stranger uttered some unintelligible baby drivel, then turn away when Phil reentered the store. "Nice baby. So well behaved, and calm. Whose baby is she?" said the customer.

Damnable coverlet. It looks more pink than blue.

"Yeah. Right," said GUP. GUP was an acronym I created for Great Uncle Phil that eventually got transformed into Guppy because he had the habit of working his lips in and out like a fish whenever he was irritated.

"He's my niece's baby," his lips pulsing in and out. "She walked out. Just left him here 'bout an hour or two ago."

I was right. It was a couple of hours!

"He's a boy? He's so cute. Really! A boy?" Her attitude smacked of chauvinism. My lips began to twitch in and out. *Oh no! The same family gene.*

"If it's a boy, why's she got him wrapped up in a pink coverlet? You say she just left him here?"

"You wanna buy something or not?" snarled GUP. Phil was not succeeding at getting his lips under control.

After the women left, Phil's wife, Granma Hazel, came down from their apartment and stood next to Phil on her toes to stare at me over the deli case. I stretched my eyelids back to see her but she was too short and we couldn't make eye contact. She was called Granma Hazel not because she was somebody's Grandma. It was what everyone called her. No one ever called her Hazel. Not her husband, not even the customers, always Granma Hazel, as if she were the wizened, maternal caregiver of the universe, which she was, excluding the care of babies as I was soon to discover.

Another chunk of time passed and no one moved and no one spoke, at least not to me. They left me lying in my carriage, isolated a safe distance away with the added benefit of their deli case barricade. I could hear them whispering about their future lives together without me in the store. There was little I could do. While I lay there I began to sense how my smelliness was obliterating the odor of fresh sawdust Phil had spread on the wooden floor of the butcher shop and simultaneously became fascinated with the distorted reflection of the tin ceiling and hanging lights in the glass front of the deli case and whatever part of their conspiratorial heads were visible over the case. I must confess, my growing awareness of the sensual postpartum life of smells and sounds and sights, and also eavesdropping, was gaining my interest over crying and being too hot and too wet.

Granma' Hazel stood up on her toes and tried to peer over the top of their protective barricade and for the first time I just about got a glimpse of her eyebrows.

"Tell me again. Then what happened?"

"Well," said Phil, "she was complaining a lot about her kid—not a gruff term of endearment this time—and I told her to handle it."

"And then?" Hazel had moved to the end of the deli case and was peering around the white porcelain corner for a better view of me.

"She started yelling at me! She got crazy."

With a dramatic air of incredulity and personal offense Hazel snorted, "I could hear her through the floor upstairs!"

Phil went on, "She was yelling, and the kid was screaming, and she ran out the door."

"Did she say anything else?"

"Yeah...." Phil had reached his allotted quota of words on this subject, if not for the entire day and stopped there.

"Well what?" Hazel yelled. After years of pulling information out of her husband she had a short fuse. "Well..." he cleared his throat, and he and I made eye contact again over the deli case, "she said if I knew so much about babies I could keep him."

The words struck me with such force I forgot I was feeling gassy again.

She didn't just abandon me, she gave me away!

"That's it. I'm gonna call Edna," said Granma Hazel. She turned and went to the back room where the phone was.

Edna was Roselyn's best friend and just another irritant for me. She thought that having children was tantamount to keeping a passel of pigs in the living room. Edna's thin-lipped arrival at the store delighted all concerned but me. Phil, now euphoric at the prospect of being rid of me turned loquacious and told the whole ugly story about my mother's immature, disrespectful, self-indulgent, disrespectful, emotionally out of control, irresponsible, disrespectful behavior. He was really on a good roll, especially in regard to her disrespectfulness, but it did not elicit the sympathy he needed from Edna. Edna bristled.

"Just a minute, Phil. She's been under a terrible strain. She had a difficult ten-month pregnancy. Then three days a' labor because of that primitive old-fashioned doctor's ideas about natural childbirth. I mean, these are modern times. Nobody needs to suffer anymore! It near killed her! And then the baby's head looked like a football from being stuck three days in delivery and he's been crying for two months straight whenever he's awake." As Edna paused for a breath, Phil and this time Hazel too slipped into guppy mode. "And do you know what?" Edna continued. "She never wanted to have a baby. She was so terrified of having one. Made Bill promise not to get her pregnant."

Phil was not happy with the direction of this conversation. He felt cheated of the sympathy that was surely his due. And even worse, his discomfort was beginning to trump his indignation. "If she was so set on not having kids why'd she have one?" Phil was flat out snarly now. "No self-control, huh?"

The idea of crying instead of eavesdropping was starting to appeal to me again.

"OK, Mr. Know-It-All! I promised not to tell, but you deserve this. Bill cut tiny holes in the end of his condoms. That's how she got pregnant!

"Oh my God!" said Phil."

"Oh my God!" said Hazel.

Oh my God! I thought this was just going to be another ordinary day.

Great Uncle Phil went gray, turned quickly and disappeared into the meat locker at the rear of the store. He came back with a paper wrapped package. "Here. Bring this to my niece. It's one of my best steaks. No charge."

Edna grabbed the large steak and dropped it into the carriage on top of me, knocking the air out of me making it difficult to resume crying, and said, "You know what? This is the first time I've ever seen this kid awake and not crying!" She turned and wheeled me out the door. The bell rang and the carriage dropped abruptly off the stone step in front of the store. We turned right and bounced briskly over the irregular slate sidewalk, then crossed North Straight Street and continued on North Main for another few houses.

Roselyn had made it as far as the front stoop of the two family house where she lived. She was sitting there tear streaked, looking dejected with her elbows on her knees and her chin resting on the palms of her hands.

"You forget something'?" Edna chided.

"I didn't even hear you coming'," said Roselyn. "Hey! He's not crying."

"I know," said Edna, "that uncle of yours must be a marvel of a man, an' look!

He gave you one of his best steaks. Free. Just to make you feel better. Can you believe it? Shall I cook it up as a treat just for us?"

"OK," sighed Roselyn, "But please, no onions. The smell might make him cry," she added. A feeble explanation.

It was ungodly hot that day at the Lakeside Swim Club. The water so jammed with people it was impossible to do more than bob about. I held the drowned boy, nearly my same size, in my arms and started to wade toward the beach. Mary and I were yelling for help but the clamor from so many people drowned out our voices. When we reached the shore Mary ran ahead to get the lifeguard. He jumped down from his stand, ran down the beach, grabbed the boy and began to work on him. Suddenly the lake drained of people and formed a circle of voyeurs. Here was the drama of life and death.

Mary and I looked silently at each other. We had had enough. She pointed at the water and without a word we decided to go swimming in a lake that was exclusively ours to use.

That same evening the paper had a feature article on the front page about the young boy that nearly drowned at Lakeside and the mystery person that had saved his life. My mother notified the paper that her son was the mystery person and the next day there was a follow up article on my part in the rescue. A few days after that, a policeman arrived at my house wanting to know if I had tried to drown the boy.

"After all," the policeman responded to my mother's objections, "it does seem very strange to us that he went back into the water right away and didn't talk to anyone." He looked over at me. I noticed that his right hand was resting on his revolver. I knew that this concerned me but it took me several moments to respond.

"I don't know," I said meekly. "It was so hot. I just had go back in. I can't stand being hot."

Despite what you may think about my illicit conception and chronic complaining, we're all perfect little beings at birth. It's what comes afterward, when we realize we're required to live in an imperfect world, that the game begins. Lakeside Swim Club has since been filled in and replaced by a supermarket. The designation "Swim Club" was to provide a way to keep non-whites out.

2

The Clothes Pole Affair

or How I Relearned How To Cry

Before any Doubting Thomas's get started out there, you should know it is possible to recall an event that happened when you were only two. One day, for no apparent reason, at the age of forty, or fifty, while reminiscing with my mother, I described the Paterson, NJ, apartment we lived at that time of the close pole incident. We moved from the house shortly after my second birthday.

Starting with your back to the street, on the second floor of this wood frame house, there was a largish front room with my parents' bedroom off to the right. From that front room there was a single step down to a short hall with a bathroom to the left, and to the right the door to the front hall stairs. Next was a large square kitchen which I described perfectly to her—I'll not burden you with those details—and then my room off to the left. My crib stood against the wall common to the stairway hall. Behind the kitchen was a large porch. I even remember where the ironing board stood in the kitchen that day, which I'll get to eventually.

My mother agreed. I had perfect recall of the entire apartment as well as the events of that day. You could ask her if you don't believe me. She wouldn't lie, except she died in 2004.

THE CLOTHES POLE INCIDENT occurred at 185 North Main Street where my family lived for the first two years of my life. They had a rental apartment on the second floor, with a large porch that ran across the back of the house and doubled as my outdoor play area. There was a backyard but its use was exclusively for the first floor tenants, off-limits to my family. In the rear left corner of that backyard was a two-story wooden clothes pole to which the four surrounding houses had their clotheslines attached, a standard arrangement in pre dryer days. Since all four were two family houses it meant that there were eight clotheslines attached to the pole. One day my mother came home from shopping to find the pole collapsed with all her clean laundry on the ground and the neighbor's clotheslines, pulled from their houses, tangled in hedges, draped across picket fences, and the surrounding backyards. The pole had rotted out. My father talked to the landlord who said he would provide a new pole, and if my father would install the pole he would take something off the rent. My father agreed to that task, though this was impossible for one man to handle, so he went around to all our neighbors to enlisted their help.

The new pole was delivered to the backyard a few days later. He dug out the stump, removed all the clothesline reels from the old pole and waited for the promised help to arrive. When the pole collapsed it came to rest against our second floor porch railing where it stayed for a couple of weeks as he waited for the procrastinating neighbors' promised help.

My giant playpen was the whole back porch, which provided protection from the hot sun and the chilling rain and contained everything a two-year-old child could want or need—safety, security, diverting colorful toys, quick access to food, an attentive mother nearby and a view on the wider world beyond the railing. I realize it doesn't seem reasonable that a two-year-old should experience feelings of disquiet about anything other than dampish diapers or the next bit of food. But I was disquieted. We all start to feel disquieted at some point in life. I was just precocious.

Even though I had a nice large porch to play in the siren call of dirt to my boy brain found me looking longingly through the railing at the yard below.

It was a memorable occasion the day I spied the tip of the pole above the railing of my prison. It escapes me now, but somehow, some way, I got up to the top of the railing and with legs akimbo, slid naked to the ground. (My modern mother had decided that not wearing a diaper while on the porch would bring about an awareness of certain bodily functions.) I don't remember the fireman's maneuver that brought me to the backyard but I do recall lying on my back in the warm dirt, staring silently up into the sky for maybe five seconds until the awareness of my new and unexpected circumstances got my attention. I guess I began to scream.

Again, Edna, ever the stalwart best friend to my mother Roselyn, and rescuer of me from my great uncle Phil's butcher shop, that Edna, rushed down to my aid. At this point I was standing, legs spread, trying to see what had happened to those parts of my anatomy that had never garnered any awareness on my part beyond the discomfort of diaper rash. She brought me back upstairs to the kitchen where I was laid upon the kitchen table for inspection. The table proved to be too low. They moved me from the cold Formica tabletop to the ironing board, with comfy padding and at a better height for Edna and my mother to pluck splinters out of those unseemly areas of my tiny two-year-old body. It was a long operation. This part I have never been able to recall, thank goodness, but it sounds like there were enough pieces to make a toddler-sized cross of pain. Of course, this all transpired in the days before Hula Hoops, rock 'n' roll, trips to the moon and it would seem, the existence of emergency rooms. What possible reason could those two women have had for not bringing me to the hospital, or giving me some baby aspirin?

"It was awful," my mother informed me years later. Oh I'll bet! "You screamed for hours and hours." The poor things, and no earplugs to be had I suppose. "Even when we put you in your crib and closed the door we heard you carry on," she concluded with some, embarrassed laughter, "Tee, hee, hee, tee, hee!"

I know this was somewhat a situation of my own making—minimally—but would it have hurt them to show some serious medical consideration for my condition? Oh sure, they're really lucky that I didn't instantly become a misogynist. Well I ask you? And did my father really need to wait to take down that pole? I could've been killed!

I tell you, relating this affair has been so exhausting I think I need a nap. Maybe I should go outside and lay in the dirt.

Though I was off to a fast start the first two months of my life, learning how to complain, nothing incredible happened on that learning curve until I chose to leave the porch. That's when I truly understood what it meant to have a body. That is, I learned where my body ends and the world begins and that I should take nothing for granted, including safe landings. That's painfully confusing when you're only two. Later would have been more to my liking.

My college friend Murphy, an enigmatic guy, used to say, "Don't miss it if you can." This experience had been a "Don't miss it if you can" moment in my life. Good prep for the future.

3

Trees

Ages 3–8

My journey to understand the difference between religion and spirituality began at the age of three.

IN 1942, BEFORE MY third birthday we moved from 185 to 99 North Main Street. There were no trees in our yard, none on the street, none in the yards around us. But, we had a Rose of Sharon tree in front of our house, a tree in name only. It was a spindly weedy looking thing with gloriously silly outsized pink blossoms in the summer. Maybe it was eight feet high, totally. At the age of three it was all that I could handle. A little more than two feet above the ground the tree divided into two parts making a comfortable and easy place to sit to look out over the front yard fence at the mystery beyond. The tree became a friend, a helpmate in those first attempts to understand a wider world. Why I was drawn to trees, even from that earliest age, is unclear to me even now. Perhaps it was a child's simple curiosity, or a primal memory from an ancient life in the forest, an imprint of God's handy work or a memory of that trip down the clothes pole.

Maybe it was the repetitive dream I had. It started when we moved to 99 North Main Street and went on until I was seven. I was born February 24—six months before Germany invaded Poland in 1939. Sometime in early '42 I started to have, what I can only imagine, was a dream synchronistic with then unknown events thousands of miles away.

I was in a disorganized, tired group of about thirty men and boys stumbling along a dirt track through a thick isolated forest. Prodded along by men in uniform, we emerged from the woods into a large grassy clearing. Everyone was dressed in black. The men wore long unbuttoned overcoats and broad brimmed fedoras. I was the youngest male and was wearing black pants with suspenders, black shoes and a blousy white shirt. The air was chilly. I could see everyone's breath. I was holding the hand of the man next to me. I didn't know him and he didn't speak to me. No one spoke nor made a sound. We just did what we were told. The men in uniforms were shouting instructions and shoving us into a single line along the edge of a bank. I looked longingly at the trees beyond the far side of the clearing. As I stood there at the end of the row I imagined myself walking off into the calm protection of the forest. None of the soldiers, for that is what they were, made eye contact with anyone as they set up machine guns and began to shoot. I was hit and thrown backward off the bank into a large freshly dug pit. I lay there with a searing hot pain in the pit of my stomach as other bodies began to fall nearby and on top of me. I knew I was dying, but then I floated up out of the pit, walked past the firing soldiers toward the distant, tranquil trees. But, alarmingly they seemed to recede from me so that I could not reach them. Somehow I knew wanted me to reach them, to become one with them. But I kept getting smaller and the grassy clearing wider, and the beckoning of the trees fainter.

And then, as always, I awoke screaming. Years later—I might have been in my late teens—for no explicable reason, I remembered this recurring dream and asked my mother about it. She said it was true. I did have such nightmares starting at the age of three. Sometimes twice a week I would awaken her with my screams. She would come into my room and try to comfort me. Hold me until I fell asleep again.

When I was seven and allowed to cross our street alone, I was sent to a new Italian deli down on the corner of Stout Street and North Main. Italians were new to our Anglo/Dutch neighborhood. Very exotic. We began to buy things at their very foreign shop, and though my parents abhorred their use of smelly garlic, we grew to like the food.

Just around the corner from North Main, on Stout, a largish tree had taken root between the slate sidewalk and the curb. I had seen it from the bus we took to town, but until I was allowed to cross the street by myself, I could never get near it. I wasn't thinking of the tree as I crossed the intersection of Stout Street. I was doing an errand for my mother and lost in my own thoughts. The tree was a mere peripheral flash, more like a resurrected memory, as I stood waiting to cross to the deli. Ah yes, that's the tree I've seen from the bus. I checked the street for traffic. The traffic cleared. I crossed the street, but instead of going to the store I found myself going down Stout Street to the tree. This was not an impulse born of curiosity. It was a compelling need, as if an unseen switch had been thrown by an unseen hand sending me to another time and place. I've no rational explanation. I was only seven and hadn't yet been conditioned to stay on task. Perhaps I did approach the tree out of a seven-year-old's inquisitiveness. It was the only sizable tree anywhere in the neighborhood, but I don't believe that's what drew me.

The tree was in front of the second house from the corner on the left side of the street looking toward the river. Its circumference was larger than my arms could surround by more than twice. The bark was deeply rutted between rough gray ridges. Feathery spear shaped leaves grew along slender branches that moved easily in a breeze and made whispering sounds. It was growing in a narrow three-foot space and the sidewalk had been made uneven by the tree's roots pushing up and out from beneath. On the other side two large roots had overlapped both the curb and the sidewalk creating a bowl shaped space between them against the trunk. I circled the tree slowly several times looking up into its branches and the seven-year-old in me thought, "climb this tree," but instead I sat down on the dirt and squeezed in as tightly as I could against the two large roots and the trunk and the earth. It was so comfortable, a perfect fit, and I could watch the traffic and the people around me going about their business. I knew I was supposed to do something, get something at the deli, but I couldn't stir myself. There was a feeling in my chest from the moment I put my back against the trunk, an amazing shiver, which began in my legs along the roots, moved into the base of my spine, then up between my shoulders into the back of my neck, to the top of my head until my entire body felt one with the tree, and invisible just a few feet from the busyness of the street, as if I had become the eyes of this ignored willow. I was the tree. The sounds of the street disappeared, the movements of the things around me became curious and unfamiliar and distant as though seen through a telescope. So peaceful, so very peaceful. It had been this sensation, the peace, that had drawn me to the trees in my dream.

When I arrived home my mother said she was just about to send out the Coast Guard to look for me, which was her typical reproach for this, my all too common behavior.

I didn't visit the tree on a regular basis. My other life, the business of growing up, took over, so I didn't feel a need. I didn't really think about it either, unless I had to go to the deli on the corner of Stout Street. Even then it was always like a recollection. There's my tree friend. I'd go and sit between the roots and feel completely safe.

Only once did someone stop to speak to me, an old man, Italian I believe. He came out of the deli, walked diagonally across the street directly to where I was sitting and asked, "Why have 'a you been 'a sitting for such a long 'a time 'a gainst that 'a tree?" Without any hesitation I told him how it made me feel. He nodded at me knowingly then said, "That's 'a good. You 'a know that it's a willow 'a tree. They're very 'a special. For t'ousand years people have 'a used willow for 'a headaches, and 'a fever and 'a stomach 'a pains."

"Really? Stomach pains?!" I asked. *The pains from my nightmare that woke me up? Those stomach pains?* I knew the answer as I formed the question in my mind. I never had that dream again.

Every Saturday my mother and I traveled to her parents' store in West Paterson to help them because it was their busiest day. In their backyard was a Linden tree, a handsome tree, but off limits to me. "Too dangerous to climb," was the general opinion. Not really, just grown-ups on autopilot. But down by the river, just before the Hillary Street Bridge, was Willow Way, a dirt lane along the Passaic River. It's paved today, and lined with buildings on the river side, but then there were few houses and the area between the road and the river was open and wild and lined with numerous willows. My friend Tippy O'Neal lived in the second house on the right. His father had an auto repair shop in their garage in the backyard. He wore blue-and-white striped coveralls and a striped railroad cap. He never spoke to us unless we played in the driveway. Then he would come to the door of the garage and quietly ask us not to play there because a car might come into the drive unexpectedly. So we stayed out in front of the house in the dirt lane by a giant willow tree that was in front of his house. Tippy was my age, though a bit taller than me. His father never spoke directly to me and I never saw Tippy's mother that I can recall, or the inside of his house. Whenever I got to their kitchen door Tippy would always magically appear. They had a good size yard with a vegetable garden behind the house and though Tippy's father worked on cars there was never any auto debris or cars about the property. The tan colored house was a bit shabby, in need of paint. Yet it felt good there, special and snug and protected under their giant willow.

Saturday mornings there always began the same way. Tippy and I would chase each other around, play fighting and wrestling. Slowly other children from the lane would appear and join in, both boys and girls, mostly seven to ten years old, but some even younger, all running around chasing each other, wrestling, until someone would say, "Let's start the game," which meant there were enough kids there to begin. In my neighborhood boys and girls never played together. I had to keep my friendship with Mary, my neighbor, separate from the boys I knew. And five-year-olds? They were babies. But at Tippy's everyone could play.

The game centered on the willow. It wasn't the only willow on Willow Way but it was the biggest. It made Tippy's house look like a fairy tale illustration, and it made the space around it feel magical. There seemed to be an energy that radiated out like a protective cloak that defined an area for our game that was bigger than the tree's crown, a circle that I now realize must have been defined by the spreading roots. And though I can't recall anyone of us saying this, we all sensed that going beyond that invisible edge would be out of bounds. It was like being in a sphere of pristine peace, with the leafy canopy above and the roots spread out below. And nothing of the outside world intruded to dispel the unspoken giddy magic we all felt.

The game had no name. It just began with everyone leaning a hand against the tree. The last person to jump away from the tree was "it". It was a progressive form of tag, with everyone caught staying tagged until everyone was chasing the last untagged person. Both your hands had to touch someone for them to be tagged. The tree was home base, but no more than two kids could be there at a time to rest. When a third touched home, the first one had to leave. As more and more kids were tagged it became impossible to go to or leave the tree. So, everything that happened within the game brought all of us under the spreading branches, our zone of safety and uncertainty.

I loved this game. Everyone did, though we couldn't always play. It depended on the number of kids that showed up—the more kids the more fun and excitement.

One Saturday morning we had been playing for several hours. Everyone was worn out. We were sitting under the tree, some were leaning against it, some against the porch, and we were arguing about starting another game. It was ruining the morning's fun. Then I had an idea. I told them about my tree on Stout Street and how it made me feel.

"Let's try it? All of us." said someone.

"Yes, let's all lean our backs against the tree and see what happens," I said.

There were twelve children there that day and we all leaned our bodies, legs and heads against that huge tree, every inch of every part of us that could touch the tree, so that we made a complete circle with everyone's shoulders touching. I don't know how long we all were there. It didn't seem to matter, but I was certain everyone felt the same something I felt, giddiness as though my whole, entire being was happy. And when we stopped no one made a sound, no one laughed, or ran or tried to play or did anything that would break the connection to the vibrant life of the tree. We looked at each other in a quiet knowing way then left for home.

It was another fine Saturday morning. I had just finished cutting the lawn and doing chores at my grandparents' store, so I walked down to the river to find Tippy. As usual I stood outside his back door. He didn't appear. I called but got no response.

"He's not here." His father had come out of the garage for a smoke. "He's down under the bridge."

I found him in the cool shade of the Hillary Street Bridge, on the riverbank, staring into the water, trying to catch minnows with a big tin can.

"What's happening?" I asked. There was something strange about him. He didn't say hello. Just, "You wanna see something'?"

"Sure. What?"

He stood up, set the can of minnows down on the riverbank, and started back toward the house. I caught up to him just as we reached the stoop by the kitchen door. *Maybe he's going to take me inside.* But instead he crouched down and tried to open the sloped, wooden cellar door next to the kitchen stoop. It was heavy so I helped him with it. Rough stone steps led down to a dirt floor. The opening was small. We had to duck down to enter the cellar. The ceiling was low. The walls were made of rough cut stone. There were two small windows that admitted a trickle of light. The air was damp and moldy. Still blinded by the bright sunlight, unable to find my way, I asked, "What are we doing down here?"

Tippy didn't say anything. He found the pull chain on a solitary bare bulb and pointed off into the dim back left corner at the front of the house.

"What is it Tippy?" It was still too dark to see.

"Come closer."

I moved up next to him. There seemed to be a jumble of pipes and hoses where he had pointed.

"Well?" I said not understanding.

"Can't you see? It's the roots? From our tree."

"Tree roots?" The tangle of pipes and hoses suddenly transformed themselves like a trick puzzle. "Yes. Oh wow! I see them now." The roots from the willow filled about a quarter of the basement. They came in through the stone foundation, some as big around as dinner plates. They had dislodged whole sections of the foundation wall then branched out in all directions and sizes. Some reached up to the ceiling.

Others burrowed down into the dirt floor, others were wrapped around forgotten things stored in the cellar.

"They're gonna cut down the tree. My father told me it's destroyin' our house."

"When?" I was alarmed.

"I don't know. Soon. Real soon."

We didn't play that day. We went back to the river and sat on the bank. It was a few months before I was back at my grandparents' place. From their back porch I could always see the willow, which filled the sky over the roof of Tippy's father's garage. I wasn't really thinking about the tree until I looked toward his house. The sky was empty.

In the next instant I was off the porch and running toward Willow Way. Tippy came out just as I got to the back door. We stood there looking at the giant stump of the willow. Every branch, leaf, and twig were gone. What remained was the six-foot diameter, fifteen-foot tall stump. A mangled, ugly, amputated remnant that had defeated the best efforts of the tree cutter's saws. Neither of us said anything. We walked out past the amputated willow to the river and followed it downstream to find a place to sit. Away from his house.

That spring I hadn't been to the Italian deli on the corner of Stout Street for quite a while. We were having spaghetti for supper and my mother asked me to get some Italian bread. Just before I crossed the street to the store I looked down the block to see my tree. It was gone. Cut almost flush to the curb and sidewalk. There were sawhorses blocking the entrance to the street and several men in gray overalls raking up the last bit of debris.

"What have you done to the tree?" I said to the man raking up around the stump. He didn't respond.

"Why'd you cut it down? It was the only tree around here!"

He glanced at me but kept raking. The sound of the metal rake scratching away at the macadam set my teeth on edge, like finger nails on a blackboard.

"It was a wonderful tree! I always sat against it. It made me feel good. Why'd you kill it?"

"Really?" He glanced over at me, "Kill it? It's only a tree. Besides, it was getting into the water pipes under the road." He picked up the last of the scraps and removed the sawhorses blocking the street. He and the rest of the crew put their tools in the truck and drove off. I walked over to the stump and stepped up onto it wondering if I would still feel the magical bonding. I looked down at my feet. A clear thin watery fluid was oozing up and beading around my sneakers. Whatever I had felt at one time wasn't happening. *It'll happen. It'll just take longer.* So I stood there until I started to daydream, until I forgot why I was there at all.

When I walked in the back door my parents were sitting at the kitchen table eating. "Where were you and where's the bread?" My mother was vexed. I didn't know what to say. It felt like my dream, never able to reach the safety of the trees, except I wasn't sleeping.

"What's wrong with you? You've been gone over an hour."

"I guess I forgot." It was a lame thing to say. I knew it would make her angry. I didn't care.

Sometimes the most trivial of occurrences can have a profound, lasting effect.

At the age of three I would have been delighted to miss that repetitive nightmare. "It's only a dream," I was assured by my mother for years. I couldn't articulate it then but I knew that dream was truly about something real. The dream was synchronistic with the killing of the Jews in Europe. And it was personal. I was painfully shot. I was called to safety by the forest. I never reached the trees. It seemed both literal and symbolic. Karl Jung says the best interpreter for a dream is the dreamer. I have no inkling what that dream meant or what the connection was to the two willows on a literal level. But on an intuitive, non-verbal level, it was an intense feeling of consuming fear, a need to connect to the living planet and then an extraordinary feeling of peace, terminated by a reality of rude loss. It was, I knew, prophetic.

I've never doubted those three disparate events were connected. There was a mysterious responsibility I sensed that was mine. Thus began my inner life of introspection, and my ultimate decision to become an artist, all because of a dream.

4

Aunt Tyne

Ages 6–20

My early childhood was so very, very smooth—smooth as glass. What I learned at my aunt's house—life is not smooth. And it may not ever, ever be smooth, so make the best of it. It's the wrinkles in life that memories are made from.

I WAS SITTING IN my favorite spot on the small concrete stoop in front of my grandparents' butcher shop in West Paterson, patient as a cat before a mouse hole, waiting to catch a glimpse of a train as it slipped soundlessly along the crest of the gentle hill behind the wooden houses three blocks away. If there was a lull in street traffic you could hear it coming, steam whistle sounding at road crossings as it approached the city of Paterson. Most times it would appear in the narrow solitary space between the houses, silent as a mist shrouded ghost, if the wind was from the wrong direction. It would have been so much better if I could have gone up the hill to sit by the tracks and wait, but age six, I was informed every time I asked, was just too young.

It was a pristine day when I saw the best train ever possible. The sky, a Walt Disney vacant blue, the morning air, seductively mild, gave no hint of the blistering heat to come as the sun in its transit over the gable roof would nudge the store's shadowy edge toward me on the cool concrete stoop where I sat protected from its glare. Saturdays were the busiest day of the week. Most people did their major food shopping on that day, which kept Roselyn, my mother, and her mother Ada, busy helping customers with groceries, while John, my Grandfather, worked at the butcher block behind the meat counter. My mother and I took two buses through Paterson in order to arrive at the store no later than eight o'clock. It was a small mom-and-pop operation by today's standards, but in the early forties, before supermarkets and shopping centers, that's all there was unless someone was willing to take a bus downtown. Paterson was filled with all sorts of specialty food markets—Italian, Irish, Jewish, Armenian—but without a car, and most people didn't own cars then, getting everything home was difficult. If things slowed momentarily at the store, Roselyn would box up call-in orders that her father would deliver to customers' homes when they closed the shop at six. There wasn't much for me to do but try to stay out of the way, which was the reason I was sitting on the stoop watching trains. It used up some of the time in a long, boring day.

It had been my grandfather that pointed out the trains to me. Told me that they came often.

"How high can you count?"

"Mmmm, over a hundred, I think."

"You'll need to go higher than that," he said. "There are some really, really big trains, all the time. Specially on Saturdays."

He told me his highest count was 125. "See if you can see one that's longer, and tell me what you see on them." So my grandparents didn't mind that I sat there, even though it made it somewhat difficult for customers to enter and leave the store. Occasionally a customer would stop to talk to me. Typically, they would begin, "What are you doing' there?" And typically, I would reply, "Nothing," without looking up. I tried not to sound rude, but I really had more important things to do than talk to a sweaty adult on a hot summer day. I was after all, watching for the longest train in the world. The railroad ran behind a row of gable-roofed houses jammed along the crest of the hill. Only one narrow space between their picket fenced silhouettes, was large enough to see each train car for counting. If I turned to talk to some kindly grownup because I was a cute little boy sitting so nicely on the cement step, or some miscreant nuisance in their way, I might miss a complete count of the longest train that surely had to be the very next one. I even went so far as to believe I could make myself invisible, a technique I developed at the age of three, and was always surprised and irritated when this veil of invisibility didn't work. But I couldn't risk one moment of distraction to look away from that solitary space on the edge of the hill. As the weeks went by I did see some longish trains, but knew there had to be a longer one out there somewhere on its way toward Paterson. It was just sheer good luck that I saw the very beginning of the longest train ever, because someone trying to leave the store banged into me with the new screen door that swung out over the stoop. Startled, I looked up at the woman as she began, "I didn't see you there. You alright?" I started to slide out of the way along the edge of the stoop to let her pass when I spotted steam billowing up behind the houses out of the corner of my eye.

"OK," I answered but turned away as the first engine slipped into that special space, followed by seven more with their coal tenders. *Maybe. Maybe this is it, the longest train ever!* I had once seen a train with four engines and 150 cars loaded with army trucks stacked belly to back, like a conga line of copulating dogs. I knew that was only pretty good, not likely the best ever longest train. But pretty good.

"Where're they going'?" I had asked my grandfather.

To the war, I was told. I knew about the war with the Krauts and the Japs. That was the only thing the grown-ups talked about. Families had small Sons-In-Service flags in their windows to show how many men they had in the war. The flags had a blue star for each member in the military, inside a rectangle of white with a wide border of red. My aunt Tyne had one in her window only hers had just a single gold star in the center.

This train did turn out to be the longest train ever in the world. I just knew it! The effort of counting just half the cars left my eyes wet and burning even though I was still inside the shadow cast by the store. I dared not blink. Several boxcars followed after the eight engines and their coal tenders. Then came a ribbon of flat cars carrying olive drab tanks, two to each car, with their gun turrets facing backward followed by several more engines and tenders, then more flat cars of olive brown fighter planes with their wings pinched back like beagle's ears, to fit the size of the flatcars, and finally several cabooses. When the end of the train came I didn't want to look away. There had been nearly two hundred fifty engines, and tenders, with flatcars of tanks and planes on their way to that war in Europe. I had seen newsreels in the movies, saw fighter planes diving down to shoot at truck convoys and tank battles in the North African dessert. How many tanks and planes did that take?

It was during the previous summer of '44 that my mother and I started to visit Great Aunt Tyne once a week. Tyne was her Dutch family's nickname for her. She was my Grandma Ada's sister. Her very old but well cared for three-story brick house was near the center of downtown Paterson and I think the only house on Ryerson Alley. Since we lived but a few blocks away on the other side of the Passaic River, we always walked there over the Main Street Bridge. The house was squeezed tight up against the sidewalk, about three feet from the curb on this very narrow street. There was neither room for a front garden nor even one step, to the entrance in the front hall. The door opened straight in off the slate sidewalk. I can recall the uncomfortable feeling of apprehension I had standing in that narrow space, in the hot sun, waiting for the door to open. When it did we seemed to be sucked into the vacuum of a cold, darkened entrance hall, so dark it took your sight away. The windows next to the front door permitted no light to enter the house and were forever smothered by dark green blackout shades because of the war. Not that the Germans would likely bomb Paterson. The hall lights were never allowed.

By the time greetings between Roselyn and Tyne were concluded my eyes adjusted to the dim light that reached us from the far end of the long hall that led to the kitchen. The floor was wide-planked and on the right, a few feet from the front door, was a staircase to the equally dark second floor. Beyond and beneath these stairs was the door to the cellar. On the left near the entry was a door that led into the front room, and farther along the hall on that same side, was a second door. Always closed. The first door was usually closed too, except once when we were let in the door stood open. My great uncle, a lawyer, used this front room as his office. When I looked through the open door I saw him, or someone I assumed was my great uncle, seated at a desk in front of the windows in this unlit room, like an escapee from a Dickens tale, silhouetted by the scant light oozing around the drawn blackout shades. He neither spoke nor moved.

The kitchen at the end of the hall was spacious, as blindingly bright as the hall was dark. It was perhaps fifteen by thirty feet and ran at right angles to the hall and the only room in the otherwise silent darkened house that seemed alive and welcoming. All along the back wall was a bank of French doors, with a view of a beautifully lush, formal, brick walled garden. On the kitchen wall was a large, ancient fireplace, once meant for cooking. It was half again my height and three times my length. In front of the fireplace, dominating the center of the room, was a refractory table with twelve ladder-back chairs. To the right were the working bits of the kitchen—stove, sink, two worktables, ice box. And above, in the high ceiling, were several translucent wire-glass skylights, which cleansed everything in the room with golden-white sunlight. And then there were the canaries. Eight cages on stands, each with a diminutive golden orange bird. Two more cages stood near the French doors in a Tarzan-like jungle of huge potted plants, enough to fill my bedroom. On the wall to the left of the fireplace was a really large cuckoo clock with weights on chains that nearly reached the floor, each hour the cuckoo emerged to flap its wings and spin around while the clock bonged resonantly and chirped sweetly.

In addition to my mother, there were usually five or so other women invited for tea and buttered Irish soda biscuits with raisins. They clustered around one end of the table with Aunt Tyne at its head. Most of the women were Tyne's age except for my mother and another woman that I learned was Tyne's oldest daughter, Barbara.

I was ever the only child, with little to occupy me. Of course I did make the rounds of the canaries, which took no notice of me. But what I really wanted to do was explore the house, to see the mysterious rooms above and the cellar below.

So one day I tried. All the women seemed engrossed in conversation. I was somewhat nervous about my great uncle, perpetually ensconced in his front room, but I thought if I was quiet and moved slowly, I could make it up the stairs without his notice. I leaned against the kitchen wall by the hall door and waited for the conversation among the women to become animated. I eased unnoticed through the doorway and braved the inky hall to the foot of the stairs, where I froze across from my uncle's partly open door that framed him at his desk. *Why is he sitting there like that in the dark? Always in the dark.*

"Where do you think you're going?" said my aunt. "Come back before you disturb your uncle." Pointing down the hall, she continued, "Don't you ever leave that kitchen again without permission." I was unable to break my view of my uncle through that sliver of space, as she began pulling me down the hall.

Visit after visit was the same. I disliked the black hall, ran past the front room door whenever it was open, and then, once in the kitchen, set about making canary sounds at each cage. The canaries never ever responded, nor did the women sitting at the long table seem to notice that I often circled quietly around the table sniffing them. There was the familiar mixture of perfume and makeup but also an underlying musky human smell, which repelled me but at the same time was irresistible. What was it? I decided that the sweet, musky odor was blend of their sweaty legs and their seamed silk stockings.

Tea usually took place mid-afternoon. I never noticed if the women were the same from week to week. They all seemed to look alike in their veiled hats and frilly dresses, open-toed, high-heeled shoes and white gloves, so formal and excessive for that informal room.

The sameness of these gatherings never varied but once. Aunt Tyne asked everyone to come in the morning. We were still there, at noon, when the cuckoo clock began its measured toning of the hour. Not the expected twelve times for noon, but twenty-four times. Bong-cuckoo, bong-cuckoo, bong-cuckoo, bong-cuckoo, and on and on, bringing all talk in the room to a halt, except the eternally silent canaries, who began frantically flying about their cages and singing as though they had lost their little bird brains. I too, unable to control myself, ran squealing in delight around the room as if I had also lost my mind.

"Stop," my mother said. "You're making too much noise. You're going to fall and dirty your clothes." *What? This is the only fun I ever have in this house.* It was beyond fun; it was memorable.

The clock stopped its manic chiming and the birds returned to their usual state of arrogant indifference. Their silence seemed directed specifically at me.

"You're also disturbing your uncle," said Tyne as she turned toward my mother. "I've been meaning to tell you Roselyn, don't dress your son in that army suit anymore. It is upsetting to your uncle."

Upsetting to my uncle? Did he know I was alive?

It was the style then, during the war, to dress little boys in military uniforms. I loved mine. I had a sailor's suit and an army officer's suit with the cap and shoes to match. It was exciting to feel a part of all the important grown up wartime things. It was part of the reason for watching the trains. Not just to see how long they were but to look for the trains with weapons.

Our visits went on for several years. The war was over and I was now in grammar school, so I only went there in the summer, and even then very seldom. I had grown old enough to be off on my own with my friends. But my memories of those earlier visits persisted—of their peculiarity and what I tried to piece together later.

Most memories appear like bright sparks, isolated and random, flying up into a dark vacuum of forgotten moments. But less frequently, others, like those from my visits to Aunt Tyne's house, occur with such a vivid wholeness of atmosphere, sights, sounds and smells, that I can see that five-year-old me dressed in that crisp Army suit, my hand in my mother's as we turned off of lower Main Street on to Ryerson Alley, the day always cloudless and hot. We're crowded against the brick house, our backs to the narrow street, the hall, musty, cool and dark, unwelcoming, my plumpish aunt in a matronly dress and string of pearls, my ominous uncle silent and immobile at his desk in the dark, the door to the room down the hall closed, the songless canaries, waiting for the clock to strike, and the women, as always, odoriferous and white gloved, sitting in the golden light of the kitchen, drinking their tea from thin china cups, static, unchanging, attentive.

On one singular visit, the second door down the hall on the left, nearest the kitchen, was partly open. Of all the times we had visited Aunt Tyne's house I had never been upstairs, never been allowed to leave the kitchen. That partially open door drew me like a puppy in a pet store window. I waited until the women had settled into their tea and biscuits and gossipy conversation to slip from the kitchen into the front hall and slide with my back tight to the stairway wall until I was across from the partially open door. I was counting on the darkness of the hall and the brightness of the kitchen to conceal my movements. I checked the kitchen. No one seemed to notice I was missing. It must have been particularly interesting gossip that was working in my favor that afternoon. I leaped across the hall through the doorway into what could have been a closet but wasn't. As my eyes adjusted to the dimness I saw there was a floor lamp to my right. I found the pull chain. The space was filled with things I had never seen before. Next to the lamp was a floor model radio. Ours, at home, was small and sat on a table in the living room. Alongside the radio was a Victrola record player, a big one, also a floor model with a large speaker covered on the front with gold speckled cloth. The rear wall of the room was lined floor to ceiling with shelves. There was also a wing chair, a table, and lamp. Crowded into the other half of this room, up against the shelves, was a piano. The room was windowless and cramped. The shelves were filled with thin boxes. As I walked toward them I noticed a partially open door behind the wing chair that led into the darkened front room. My great uncle was sitting behind his desk. I expected him to scold me but he didn't move. He had never spoken to me, nor I to him. Still, no movement. I had never even seen him in the light. *Is he dead? He must be able to see me standing here in the light.* I could hear his quick rhythmic gasp of air and soft explosive exhale: aa-taa, aa-taa, aa-taa, aa-taa. A hand fell upon my shoulder and I heard the fearsome sound of my aunt's regal voice.

"Would you like to see the piano?"

Her soft words whispered next to my ear confused me, struck the fear of God in me.

"Just don't touch it. It might disturb your uncle."

She led me away from the open door toward the glistening black piano. I had expected her to yank me back into the kitchen.

"Is it a player piano?" I knew it wasn't but that was the only type I had ever seen.

"It's a baby grand." She opened the top for me to look inside. "Would you like to hear a record?"

The shelves were filled with sheet music folios and boxed record sets. I pulled a box from its shelf and opened it.

"That's organ music," she informed me. "Would you like to hear it?"

"Huh?"

"Would you like to hear those records, Jerry?"

"Yes?" I said tentatively.

As we walked to the Victrola she paused to close the door to the front room. "We mustn't disturb him," she said again.

"Why does he always sit in the dark?"

"It helps him think. Now let me help you do this." She showed me how to hold the records by their edges, never slide them against each other, and how to stack them on the changer. "When these two records have played you will need to turn them over to finish the music."

She set the volume and asked me not to play it louder. I sank to the floor in front of the Victrola and listened. I had expected her to scold me. Instead she introduced me to a larger, unknown, wonderful world.

When it was time to leave she asked me, "Did you enjoy the Bach piece?" And without pause she said, "This was a special time, Jerry. You won't be able to do this again."

It was several months before we returned to Aunt Tyne's house. I believe it was the start of summer vacation. As we entered the front door the sunlight from the street followed us in through the now shadeless windows. Morning light flowed in through the uncovered windows behind my uncle's desk as well. No one was in the room. I turned questioningly from the doorway toward my aunt but she and my mother were already in the kitchen. I ran to catch up but stopped short at the end of the hall. On the cellar door just before the kitchen was a shiny new padlock. I thought I heard something. I put my ear to the door. There were muffled sounds of voices and something like a door slamming and furniture being pushed about. On our walk home I asked my mother why the door had a lock on it and who was in the cellar?

"Oh, I think your aunt rented out a cellar apartment."

I knew she was lying. The cellar was totally below the ground and windowless.

Each visit that summer I listened at the cellar door. Sometimes there was nothing to hear, sometimes there was screaming. Loud screaming. Anguished screaming. I ran into the kitchen "I hear screaming! In the cellar!" All the chatter stopped as the women turned toward me. Some looked nervously back at Tyne.

"Aunt Tyne, who's screaming in the cellar?" The screams continued. *Was I the only one that heard them?* I looked franticly from face to face.

She stared at me. The only sound in the kitchen, the staccato ticking of the clock. Then with a forced smile on her face said, "Would you like to visit the music room again?" As she started to rise she continued, "Of course you would. You need something to do don't you?"

"Well, Mother, I'm glad someone had the courage to ask about those sounds. Tell us all. Why is there a lock on the door?" It was my aunt's daughter, who was one of the tea women that day.

Aunt Tyne stopped part way to the hallway and glared at her daughter. We started to move again when a door near the garden end of the room opened and a young woman in a wheel chair entered.

"You alright dear?" said Tyne, turning to this new person.

"Yes. It was so quiet. Then I heard loud voices. Why were there loud voices?"

To me she looked grown up but she was probably in her late teens. Polio had crippled her and limited her ability to speak easily.

"Oh! It's nothing, nothing." interrupted Aunt Tyne, "I was just taking your cousin Jerry here into the music room to listen to some of your records, dear. You don't mind do you? Why don't you go back to your bedroom? You'll be more comfortable there."

Great Aunt Tyne and Great Uncle Richard had had four children. My only recollection of of them is from that one day, for I never saw any of them after the visits stopped except for Pat. Pat was the eldest son. He was not living at home then. He occasionally showed up, unwanted, at our house on North Main Street. Barbara was the second oldest, about my mother's age. I'm not sure about her name. She always seemed angry. And the youngest daughter, Ada I think her name was, I only saw that one time. And then there was Mike, the youngest son. I never saw Mike.

It wasn't until near the end of that same summer that we visited again.

"Come with me. I want to show you something upstairs." It was so out of character for my great aunt to voluntarily speak to me that I was both frightened and intrigued. I followed her up the forbidden stairs to the second floor and then on up to the third. In the faint light at the top of the stairs was a narrow landing, off of which were three bedroom doors: one toward the front of the house, one to the back and one in the middle which was Mike's room. On that small landing was an illuminated glass-topped stand. On the stand, inside the glass case, was an exquisitely made wood model of a sailing ship, about eighteen inches long by eighteen inches tall. The small bulb in the top of the case cast the only light on the landing, the stairs and the magical ship.

"Do you know what ship this is?"

The detail was amazing, no matter how minute, perfectly made. The unfurled sails looked filled with wind, the figurehead at the bow carefully carved. Every detail perfectly painted. And I wanted it.

"It's the Mayflower, the ship the Pilgrims came on." She paused as I continued to study the ship. " Did you ever meet my son? No. I guess not. Well, Mike made it when he was about fifteen. I have a feeling Mike would like you to have it. You're a lot like him. Maybe when you're a little older you could take it home…"

"Mother! Mother where are you? We're going to start without you." It was her daughter down below at the foot of the stairs.

Aunt Tyne's behavior toward me was confusing, severe and indifferent, then like that day on the third floor, kindly.

Another year passed before we were at the house again. My mother and I had been invited for lunch. It was, as it always seems in my memory, a bright blue day. The dark green shades were drawn in the hall again, also in the front room. My great uncle was still absent. The music room door was shut but the pad lock on the cellar door was gone. I stopped to feel the empty screw holes and listen. Nothing. Not a sound. I was only seven but I knew the way a child can know without being told, that my great uncle's sojourn in the basement was over.

I turned to enter the kitchen. There were no canaries. No cages. And the cuckoo clock was gone too. By the time we started lunch I knew no one else would be there, and that the women would not be coming to this house again for tea. Lunch was simple mutton pies, a local Irish Paterson delicacy and a favorite of mine. This was followed up with the usual tea and buttered Irish soda biscuits. Without the canaries or the clock there was little to distract me. I just sat there not listening to the two women, day dreaming, looking about the room. On the wall to the right of the large fireplace hung a new large cloth, a sort of tapestry, which reached to the floor. Aunt Tyne looked at me, interrupted her conversation with my mother. "Jerry," she said as she rose and walked toward the wall. "Jerry, come with me."

Startled out of the miasma of boredom, I stood, hesitated, and looked over at my mother. She was as puzzled as I, as if caught off guard, but she didn't speak. As I started toward Aunt Tyne she raised one edge of the cloth and draped it over a nail exposing a large hole, which had been hacked through the rear brick wall of the kitchen and then through an adjoining wall of a wooden house that was tight up against the brick. With a slight air of self-satisfaction, she announced to a large but invisible audience, "My carpenter said it couldn't be done so I did it myself. Now he'll have to come and finish it."

The space beyond the opening was blacker than the front hall ever was. She took my hand and led me down two steps made from an upside down wooden soda case. A good distance into the inkiness, we stopped.

She dropped my hand and left me standing in the impenetrable dark. And then there was the click of a pull chain and a sea of blinding white light erupted as the bare bulbs in the ceiling fixture came on. Every wall, the ceiling and the floor were painted white. The windows in the room and a rear door leading outside door were boarded up and painted white as well. On every wall from floor to ceiling were large, square, birdcages stacked one upon the other to the ceiling, and in every cage were canaries. She had bought the house next door just for her birds.

My aunt was smiling as she focused her twinkling eyes on me and said, "Watch," as she moved from cage to cage opening the doors, releasing the birds. A deafening racket of bird song overwhelmed us as the manically happy swirling birds careened through the air. I followed her from room to room throughout the first floor and the second as she turned on lights and opened cages until there were hundreds and hundreds of birds loosed everywhere. There were bird swings hung from the tops of every doorway that you needed to duck under in order enter a room. Like the day of the cuckoo clock I began running from room to room squealing.

"Don't run. You're frightening the birds. The birds are happy now." My aunt was smiling.

And I stopped of course, not because she was right, but because she seemed so strange. I wanted to ask why had she done all of this. I don't know how long we stayed there. I don't know when we returned to the kitchen. I'm also certain that, oddly, my mother never left the kitchen to join us. The last thing I can recall, I was standing in the first floor hall watching the canaries on a large swing under the staircase. I turned and looked up at my great aunt Tyne and started to ask her "Why?" *Why did she do this? Why so many birds?* But she was staring off into space, smiling, and I never asked the question. It was the very last memory I have of her, for I never saw her again.

It was a cold March morning at the store in West Paterson. My mother, my grandmother Ada, and myself were luxuriating in the warmth of the heat from the floor furnace grate in the doorway between the store and their apartment. We were singing Hoagie Carmichael's

"Gone Fishin'" and the Mills Brother's "Paper Doll" to pass the time, waiting for the Saturday morning rush to start. Ada was teaching me how to sing harmony. I loved how it felt as the sound grew richer from the mix of tones. I could feel it in my mind. It was like seeing into the future, anticipating the melody and plotting the harmony to fit.

In the beginning she told me to "follow the melody, just sing one note away." And it worked. Now we were singing in three-part harmony. Laughing at our weird sounding mistakes, experimenting until we got it right.

My grandfather was out at the meat counter cutting up steaks and singing small fake bits of Italian opera to irritate his wife. My grandmother narrowed her eyes and shook her fist at her husband's back.

"Do you ever visit Great Aunt Tyne when I'm in school?" I asked my mother. "It's been a long time since I've been there."

"No. Not since we went for lunch a couple of summers ago when she showed you all the canaries," said Roselyn.

"My sister's selling the house," said my grandmother.

"I didn't know that. When?" said Roselyn.

"Right now. It's already sold. You know she's been livin' in that house all alone for the last four years," said Ada.

"What about her children? We see Pat once in a while but he never said a thing."

"He wouldn't. He hasn't had anything to do with his mother for a long while. He's never been anything but a disappointment to her. Of course his younger sister died and Barbara got married. She moved to Pennsylvania last spring. That's where Tyne's moving."

"To live with her daughter? They don't get along, do they?"

"I don't know. She just said she's moving there. To Pennsylvania."

I wondered what had happened to all the canaries and then I remembered Great Aunt Tyne's promise to give me Mike's Mayflower model. No one spoke for a while. We had stopped singing so I just sat there next to these two grown-ups, lost in my own recollection. I was just reaching the third floor landing of Aunt Tyne's house, looking into that illuminated glass case at the Mayflower.

"Aunt Tyne said I could have Mike's boat," I blurted out. "You think she'll remember?" I asked.

"I doubt it," Ada said to me.

"Why?"

Her back was to me as she stared out through the screen door into the quiet store. "Because it was Mike's. Because he made it. And because he died in the war."

"He died in the war! I didn't know that. I never even met him."

Both women turned to look at me.

"You're old enough now to understand," said Ada, "He was just out of high school. His father didn't want him to go into the army so he pulled some strings..."

"Pulled some strings?" I didn't know what that meant. She continued.

"...got him out of the draft and into Harvard. He was in his second year when he volunteered, joined the army. He was eighteen, I think. He got sent to France after basic training." She stopped for a moment. "It was awful. He was killed, in his first battle, on his first day in the war. His father never got over it. He just sat there in his office day after day. They had made plans, Mike and his father. They were gonna be lawyers together. Father and son, together."

"What about his daughter, the one in the wheel chair? Did that bother him?"

"She was real talented on the piano. Was going to go to Julliard in New York when she got sick. That did him in completely."

The bell on the shop door rang repeatedly as four customers arrived. The Saturday rush had started up again. I went back into the kitchen. In front of the rear window, in the sunlight, was the canary in a cage that I remembered Aunt Tyne had given to her sister Ada. I stood there attempting my usual twittering sounds at the caged bird. For half of my very young life I had tried repeatedly without success to get a single canary to sing. This bird was not to be an exception.

The customer rush was tapering off, so my mother came back into the kitchen to make a pot of tea. "Don't tap on the cage. You're making the bird nervous," she said to me. "You'll give him a heart attack."

"Have you ever heard this bird sing for anyone?" I asked in frustration.

"That bird only sings when the kettle whistles. Your grandma thinks it's a dud."

"What happened to all the canaries Aunt Tyne kept in the little house?"

Ada came in the kitchen just as my mother was about to answer.

"I'll tell you," said Ada abruptly.

We sat down at the table to have our tea. My grandmother took her time. She lit a Chesterfield and sat there swirling her milky tea. "I asked Tyne what she was gonna do with all the birds when she told me about moving away." Ada paused, she was looking at the canary in its cage. "She said she was thinking of maybe selling them."

"All of them?"

"Yup. All of them."

There was a new customer in the store. I sensed her relief as she got up.

I was married three years when Great Aunt Tyne and the house reemerged from some obscure corner of my mind. I told my wife about my relatives on Ryerson Alley. At that time, we were living thirty-five miles away in Spring Valley, New York.

"Let's go see the house," she said.

"Are you sure? I mean, I'd like to, but you know, no one's there anymore."

"Oh yes! Let's go this weekend. On Sunday. I really have to see the house after that story. We can also stop at Libby's Lunch for some dogs-all-the-way. We haven't been there for a while."

We left mid Sunday afternoon. It was a hot day. The car's air conditioner wasn't working so I kept to tree-covered back roads, which took longer but felt more like the way it was in the 1940s, a time of fewer cars and no super highways. I hadn't been to that part of Paterson for quite a while. I remembered how to get to the house from my childhood home at 99 North Main Street, so I tried to follow that route, but under President Johnson's "Great Society" program to rejuvenate old rust belt cities, whole blocks had been torn down and left vacant. Their house, I recalled, was a couple of blocks from the Passaic River, just off lower Main Street. As we got closer to the area nothing was recognizable. Streets seemed missing. The area I recalled had been a densely crowded maze filled with old frame houses, storefronts, and brick factories. After circling 'round and 'round in a state of increasing confusion, I decided to park the car and continue our search on foot. We pulled into a large parking lot. Being Sunday, the lot was mostly empty so I drove to the far side and stopped in front of a row of older buildings I thought might be closer to Aunt Tyne's house. I remembered that her walled garden was next to a parking lot. We got out of the car. The oppressively hot day made me feel slightly depressed. Why was it that it always seemed to be this sort of summer day when my mother and I went to their darkened house? I put on a hat, locked the car and looked up at the building in front me. It was the building that had stood across the street from their house.

"We don't need to look for the house," I said to Lou, my wife.

"What? Why?"

"We're parked in the exact place the house used to be."

There was no doubt in my mind. We were parked on the spot where my uncle's desk had been, and I thought of him locked forever in his cellar, now paved over with black top.

I had no idea until I was standing there, staring at the building in front of me, how much I really needed to see that house again. I felt apprehensive. The way I felt whenever I entered that mysterious house as a child. I felt like I had misplaced something, something important, but was hesitant to look any further. All the childhood feelings and memories of that house wound around and through me in a continuous loop. The smell of the women, the non-singing canaries, the ship in the glass case, the music room, Bach's "Concerti for Organ," the darkness of the hall, the bright kitchen, my missing great uncle, and my great aunt Tyne standing in the canary house hallway, wearing her house dress and pearls, staring off into space. After all this time had passed I wanted there to be an ending, a tidying up of loose ends. But this was not a Hollywood movie. I was not going to get an ending. Nothing resolved, nothing fully explained, just discontinued. There was no one I could to talk to. No one that could explain. No one who could confirm if what I remembered really happened, really meant what it seemed to mean.

We got back in the car, put thoughts of the house aside, and went to Libby's Lunch for one of Paterson's epicurean delights—Texas Wieners, all the way. A few weeks later my mother called from Florida. She said she and my father were thinking of driving north for a couple of months to visit us, and some friends. Would it be OK if they stayed with us?

"Of course," I said. "That would be fine, but on one condition only. You have to tell me what happened to my uncle and Aunt Tyne and her canaries. I bet you know." I teased.

"Yes. I guess so. I remember some of it. But what made you think of that after all these years?"

I told her about the trip Lou and I had made to see the house.

A few days into their visit I brought up the questions that neither she nor my grandmother would or could answer when I was eight years old. She looked like a person trying to find an exit. I could have waited longer to ask, though I suspect there would never have been a time to my mother's liking, but once I had stirred up those puzzling memories I could not let them go. An important piece of my childhood needed completion.

"There were two of them," she began, "her children…"

She never said their names, as if to protect their reputations, or herself from that specificity, but I knew it had to be the two oldest since the other two were no longer alive at that time.

"They waited for their mother to go out and they set the birds free from their cages," then she stopped.

"That's it?" I asked. Her eyes were wandering around the room and that was it. No fleshing out. No emotional involvement. She looked back at me and continued in the same flat tone, "I don't know what happened to your uncle."

"You don't know?"

She looked away. "No. Not really."

My mother was such an uncomplicated person, not equipped to tell convincing lies. I knew as a boy that my great uncle was the person in the cellar and thought that he had died when I noticed the lock was missing from the cellar door.

"Why did they do it?

"Do what?" She was nervous.

"Set the birds free? Do you mean they let them go? From the house?"

"I don't know."

"Do you have an opinion, a hunch?"

She sidled away from my question, "I never quite understood them."

"Try to guess, Mom. From the house? They let them go from the house?"

"They didn't get along."

They didn't get along? They didn't get along? Not enough. Not nearly enough to say, "they didn't get along." What is it? And then I knew. It had nothing to do with Tyne's children. My mother was just one of those dressed up women at the table pretending not to hear the screams in the cellar.

"Those birds meant everything to her."

"Yes."

I knew from the brevity of the answers that nothing more was coming.

"And Aunt Tyne? What happened to her?"

"She went to live with her daughter in Pennsylvania."

"Are you sure? I mean, they didn't get along, did they?"

"I know she moved there. I figured to live with her daughter. Your grandmother didn't stay in touch."

She was visibly uncomfortable, wouldn't look at me. I didn't care. It wasn't enough. "What really happened? Why did they do it?" I persisted. There wasn't anyone else that could tell me. I knew I was picking at a scab.

After several moments she gave up. "I think it had something to do with the way Tyne treated your great uncle. She ignored him, locked him in the cellar. I think they were getting even," and in the same breath she started describing Florida's superior weather and Early Bird specials at her favorite restaurant and something, else…it didn't matter.

My mind slipped away while my body remained, pretending to listen. I saw myself stepping down from Aunt Tyne's kitchen into the brilliant whiteness of the canary house. I was nine years old, distraught, standing just behind her two remaining adult children watching them waving large terrycloth towels, bleached as white as the sterile white rooms, methodically working their way together through the two story house, driving the hundreds and hundreds of Great Aunt Tyne's precious canaries out of jagged, smashed windows. And I watched as those panicked streaks of yellow, like windblown autumn leaves, arched up and out into the fictitious freedom of a late summer sky.

With little else to do, I spent most of my time at that house watching the grown-ups. Life was completely different there, foreign. Why did everyone do what they did? I have speculated in the years since then. Was it a reality play? Was it a fairy tale about good and evil? It was all of that if you're a child watching from the outside. From the inside it was not a play and not about good or evil. It was my great aunt's creative pretense in the face of a reality that would never become any better, or different or resolved.

5

John and Ada and Rosie
Age 6–8

Dare I speak the obvious? There is no concluding, no summing up to life. Only fiction and religion are expert at such tidiness. Life is just one thing after the other until it stops. It's the wondrous details that matter.

USUALLY ROSELYN, MY MOTHER, and I, her six-year-old son, arrived downtown at the City Hall bus stop by seven o'clock on Saturday mornings, but she had put off going to Posner's wholesale dry goods store during the week. So instead of catching the #22 bus in front of our house on North Main Street, we walked two blocks to Posner's to pick up some cotton shirts, socks and underwear for the dry goods counter at her parents' store. When we finally stepped off the bus behind city hall, it was well after eight o'clock. That meant we couldn't make it to the butcher shop in West Paterson before the morning rush began.

"Shall we?" I asked, expecting a no.

Roselyn looked down at me, smiled and subtly nodded yes. We crossed Ellison Street on the left side of City Hall and entered the open door of The Hamburger Express. The day had started clear and cool. By the time we got to the luncheonette the summer sun was beginning to gnaw at our comfort. The east facing windows caught the morning sun full on, blinding the space with too much light and a promise of unpleasantness to come. Both of us despised summers, I for the punishing heat and short pants and she for her allergies.

"It's gonna be a hot day, hope your father will be alright."

Bill, her husband and my father, liked to ride with the sliding door on the bread truck open in the summer, a habit that terrified his wife in those days before seat belts. The trucks were set up with a high stool rather than a seat. The oversized driver's door opened flush with the floor so the driver could jump in and out quickly for deliveries.

"He'll be fine, Mom. He promised not to do it anymore. Remember?"

"But it's sooo hot!" Her eyes squinted as her lips lingered over the last two words, "and I know the fan on the dash doesn't really do much."

She was a worrier. It was her avocation.

"He's not like us. He likes the heat." But I knew the door next to my father would be open. I had just spent the day with him on his bread delivery route earlier in the week. We pretended the truck was a British Spitfire fighter plane in a dogfight with a German Messerschmitt, with the wind blowing in around us through bullet holes and shattered cockpit canopy as we swooped through the farm roads of Rockland county New York.

It wasn't the cooking at the Hamburg Express but the Lionel train that made the Hamburger Express special. The train set was used to deliver food to the customers at the counter. The track swung in a large oval from behind the griddle, coffee urn, and sandwich table to the back edge of the U shaped counter, and back again. A lone counterman standing inside the oval stirring and spreading a large heap of hash browns across the griddle, turned and walked over to the counter where we sat. He squinted at Roselyn.

"I'd like a cup 'a cauffee and a buttered hard roll please," I said, my shoulders barely above the counter.

The counterman glanced over at me. "It'll stunt your growth kid."

I stared back blankly.

Roselyn ignored the counterman's words, "I'll have the same thing."

The man's deadpan eyes shifted up to Roselyn's face. "That it?"

"Yes," she said. "Thank you.

"No changes?" he pressured.

"Aaaah, yes." Roselyn paused thoughtfully. "Bring me a large glass of milk instead. I'm only four foot ten. It might help me to grow more if I stop drinkin' cauffee."

We nearly feel off our stools trying to stifle our laughter as the counterman walked away shaking his head.

Most people didn't know, didn't understand, we weren't just mother and son, we were best friends. We did things together. Went window shopping every week, then ate lunch at the Deluxe Luncheonette, played Rummy and did jigsaw puzzles. That's when we'd talked about people we knew, relatives mostly, but neighbors too and my friends. Especially how peculiar they were. When I was seven or eight she told me she never wanted to have a baby. It scared her. That she even gave me away to my great uncle Phil. And now, here we were so happy together. It made me seem older than I was.

"Is the train workin' today?" I asked the man's back.

The man turned and looked at me briefly. The man hated the train. It had never worked well, never would work well, and he wished he had never thought of it, wanted to get rid of it but then what could he do about the restaurant's name? "With or without smoke?" he asked.

"With."

"Lou," Roselyn said to the counterman, "guess I'll have cauffee after all."

The train consisted of a Lionel old style engine, like the kind they had once built right there in Paterson, and several flat cars adapted to carry dishes, and cups, and a red caboose.

"You two feeling a bit ornery today?" said Lou as he dropped two smoke tablets down the funnel of the engine and started up the train. Amidst whistles and smoke the train chugged out from behind the sandwich table, clipped the edge of an out of place napkin holder and wobbled up to a stop, at our stools, dripping coffee. After we got our stuff, Lou started up the train again and kept it on until we left the luncheonette. I knew he liked me. He told my mother he only used the train when we were there.

It was a quarter to nine when we walked away from the Hamburger Express. We'd just missed the #4 Signac bus. So we walked down to the Broadway bus garage to get a different bus to West Paterson. The bus was an older, squarish one, the kind that I liked because I could rest my short, six-year-old legs on the arch of the rear wheel well. We took a seat on the right side of the bus. Roselyn began her habitual tuneless humming to sooth herself in anticipation of another nerve-racking day with her parents at their store. I sat by the window and wondered if I would see another long train at my grandparents' store.

The right side of the outbound bus offered the best views of the mill raceway, a canal built of cut stone, old nineteenth century brick mills, the Great Falls, and the Passaic River. A system of raceways had been built to carry water from the top of the falls to the mills below. It had been Alexander Hamilton that first saw the potential of the seventy-seven foot falls for powering mills, and worked to create his vision of a "manufacturing city of the future."

Though it was still early the heat was already oppressive, so I opened the window. The bus rounded the corner by the old Colt Gun factory and came along side one of the still active raceways. This raceway, separated from the sidewalk by an iron picket fence, ran parallel to the street until it reached the Franklyn Mill at the corner. Just at that point, where it turned right uphill, alongside the three-story factory, there was a working wooden water wheel.

Along the flume that led to the twenty-foot wheel were nearly ten boys waiting turns to ride the old water wheel into the raceway canal below, diving off the arc of the rotating wheel at the last possible moment to get free before being sucked back by the currant of the wheel's wake. Some were in bathing suits, some in their underwear, but most wore nothing at all, as if they were protected from the eyes of the adult world by an invisible shield.

"Hey, Mom," I called out, "look, I wanna…" but I stopped myself in time. She continued her humming.

The boys weren't much older than myself, a couple of years at most. *When I'm a little older I'll sneak back over there and ride the wheel too.* But in those next few years the last of the wheels vanished and the raceways began to be filled in.

I was lost in that water wheel fantasy when the bus stopped across from my grandparents' shop. My mother looked pinched. She was chewing her lips. As we crossed the street I could see that something was different. The door to the store at 620 McBride stood open and a new unpainted screen door was hinged to the outside edge of the store's doorjamb.

"I guess my mother got her way," muttered Roselyn to herself as we stepped up from the stoop into the store.

John and Ada Whitehead's mom-and-pop butcher shop was on the corner of McBride and Hillary where they worked twelve hours a day, six days a week. Their marriage stood between them like a brimming pot of boiling water. Scalding innuendoes, scowls, and thick clouds of silence described their mutual dependence. Theirs was a shared life of stifling damage which sucked at the air around them.

The store was a modest size suited to the needs of their local customers in those simpler days before most people owned cars. Their mainstay was the quality meats John Whitehead was mysteriously able to get despite war rationing.

You entered the store from a concrete stoop centered between two plate glass windows. To the right were the store payphone and the meat counter, where my grandfather, John, spent his days behind the long deli case. Opposite the front door was the cash register counter where Ada and my mother waited on customers. Behind them was the door to a three-room apartment. To the left, along the wall and in the center of the floor, were shelves of canned goods, and to the left of the front entry was a long table for dry goods.

My mother stopped just inside the door. I slipped from behind her to the end of the meat case and slid my stomach along the cool white porcelain panel to peer around the corner of the case at my grandfather cutting up sirloin scraps for chop meat. Some flies that had avoided the sticky, unfurled strips hanging from the ceiling were dive-bombing his bald head. He waved his knife at them with irritated boredom and pushed his wire-rim glasses back up his nose with the back of his wrist. My mother dropped her bundles at the dry goods table and, attempting a quick dash, crossed the store to the apartment door.

"Tell him how much better it is with the screen door," Ada chirped. "It's so much cooler."

Ada was four foot eight and already in her mid-forties and looked like a crinkled, ruddy faced figure out of a Frans Hals painting. Her salt-and-pepper hair was bobbed. She too had metal-framed glasses and wore plain white housedresses, a white butchers' apron, rolled-down white socks and penny loafers. She chain-smoked Chesterfield cigarettes but didn't inhale.

"I'm sorry we're so late, Mom. I..." Ada's words caught her daughter's attempt to explain, midsentence.

"Isn't it perfect? Tell him. Soooo much cooler." Ada's words—an effort to enlist her daughter in her pro-screen door campaign—carried past her daughter, over the meat case, and stretched John's ears tightly back against his skull. I backed away from the end of the deli case to stand under the pay phone on the wall. From there I could see all of the grown-ups.

Without lifting his head or a hand from his work, John called out in his phony Irish brogue, "Tell her, 'tis a pain in the arse just like herself, Rosie."

I quietly inched over to the door, and carefully pushed the screen open against the pressure of the closing spring without disturbing the bell and went outside to sit on the stoop.

Still in character, John needled, "Now tell me! Did you not see the struggle of your wee lad, Rosie, pushin' past the great obstacle of that damnable door?" In years past, when they'd first met in the silk mills, my grandfather's mimicking of their Irish straw boss had brought tears of laughter to Ada's eyes.

Rosie, as he called his daughter, still rooted at the dry goods counter, said nothing. The trouble with the screen door was that it swung out over a small concrete stoop making it somewhat awkward to enter and leave the store. The trouble with the store was that there was no other way to escape the stifling buildup of afternoon heat that invaded through the plate glass windows. Awnings were too costly and air conditioning didn't really exist yet. Outside the day's heat was already starting to draw a dull haze into the air. I sat down on the still cool concrete stoop and looked up at the gentle rising hill lined with houses in front of the Erie Railroad Line.

A voice behind me said, "Seen any trains yet?" My grandfather was a creature of painfully predictable habits. He smoked a pipe. He rose at five every morning and had a cup of tea. He never took a break during the day except to nap from 1:00 to 2:00 p.m. when they closed the store for lunch. After six in the afternoon he would go out to deliver orders called in by customers during the day, and stop on his way home to tilt his wrist at the Hillcrest Tavern over in Totowa. On rare occasions he'd take me with him. We'd stop at the Hillcrest. At that hour there were only a few all day men drinking beer at the bar. He'd buy me a Boylan's birch beer and send me off to play games while he tried to catch up on barroom opinions on life with his bar buddies. Like most saloons, the interior was dimly lit. Green glass shaded lights, off when we entered, would be turned on by Timmerman, the owner, so I could entertain myself with all the games. And there were many—shuffleboard, a pool table, darts, bagatelle. Enough to keep me busy for hours until a phone call from my grandmother would put an end to our stay.

It had been many years since my grandmother had gone with him to the Hillcrest. She was bored by him and his barfly friends. By nine o'clock they'd both be in bed, except on the nights when he got back late from deliveries to certain female customers. On Sunday afternoons when the store was closed, he'd go back over to the Hillcrest until evening. Alone. On Monday he'd start all over again. He never spoke of anything but essentials. He rarely came out from behind the meat counter. He seldom jested, except at his wife's expense. He rarely talked to her or anyone, and he never spoke to me. Not knowing what to make of this sudden interest, I turned to look at him through the screen door.

"No." I told him. "No trains."

He came outside and sat down next to me on the stoop. I was dumbfounded. He looked off across the street. "See the house over there?" He was pointing at the old colonial Dutch sandstone house. "The son of General Sickles used to live there. His father fought in the Civil War. He was wounded at Gettysburg, his son told me. Walked with a limp. He used to come in the store. One day he brought over a beautiful cane. Said the King of Siam gave it to his father. He gave it to me. A few weeks later he died. Did I ever show it to you?"

I shook my head no.

"No? I didn't think so." He got up and went back into the store. A few minutes later he came back with the cane. The cane had a very thin but strong tapered ebony shaft. The bottom was tipped with silver. The top had a carved elephant handle attached to the shaft by another embossed ring of silver. Ivory he said it was. He handed it to me. The elephant was loose and fell off in my hand. I looked up to see if he noticed.

"That was a terrible war," he said more to himself than me. He reached into his apron and took out a thin gray paper booklet.

"Here's a picture of him."

General Sickles was in his Union uniform. He wore a funny big mustache. My grandfather started to leaf through the booklet. It was filled with gory pictures of Gettysburg with bodies scattered everywhere, men standing in trenches, others of soldiers with their intestines hanging out, with limbs missing and bloated dead animals with their legs at odd angles in the air.

"Don't let them know I showed this to you. I promised never to..." He cocked his head and nodded back over his shoulder toward the store. "You sit out here most Saturdays lookin' for the trains with the weapons. Those pictures, that's what they do to people, those weapons."

I looked back over my shoulder to see where the women were.

"I hope you never have to fight in a war," he said to me. "They're terrible stupid things. So many of my customers have lost boys in this one. But we're starting to win it. Might be over soon. Do you understand, Jerry? I mean about the War?"

Not quite, but it didn't matter. He was there on the concrete stoop with me. Of course I said yes. I knew about the Germans. That they were doing bad things. I saw them in the newsreels at the movies, marching around. I had learned to mimic their marching. Goose-stepping it was called. I got up to show him right there in front of the store. A six-year-old version, right arm held stiffly up at a forty-five-degree angle, fingers pointing up to the sky, shoulders arched back, left arm swinging from side to center chest, and legs lifted to the horizontal from the hip without bending the knees. Well, sort of.

John let out a large loud roar, "That's great. You've got it down perfect. Has your grandmother seen this? We should put you on the stage at the Majestic Theater downtown!"

"Yes I have," she said.

"He's been doin' it forever," said Roselyn, "even in the store."

Ada and Roselyn were at the screen door. The two of us looked back just in time to see my grandmother walk away.

Rosie looked at her father, "I guess I'll put out the new dry goods."

John got up and went back to work. I followed him over to the meat counter and stood there leaning against the big cool case again, watching his hands move with great skill. We were only a few feet from each other. Neither spoke. He finished cutting and began grinding up the meat for hamburger. He set the filled pan to the side and got out another. When the second pan was almost full he looked around to see where the two women were, took a salt shaker out of his apron, and sprinkled some on two lumps of raw chop meat, one for each of us to eat, then turned and went back to work without speaking.

There were no customers in the store. My mother, arranging new things at the dry goods counter, hadn't noticed the "cannibalism," as she called it. Ada had gone back to the kitchen. I decided to follow her.

"Wanna cup 'a tea and some Saltines?" Ada didn't wait for an answer but set out a second cup. She went out to the meat case in the store where she kept the milk and butter. The kettle whistled and the songless canary that her sister had given her joined in. Why was it that this bird sang for a kettle but never would sing any other time? Though I tried repeatedly to chirp to it the bird ignored me.

Part kitchen, the room was square with a sink in one corner (zink as my grandmother pronounced it, something left over from the Jersey Dutch language of her Vander Vliet family) and a stand-alone four-burner stove on the other side of the room. The largest area was taken up with a dining room set of maple chairs embossed on the back with a wagon wheel design, a pull-out leaf table, glass-fronted china closet and a buffet to match, with still a bit of room left for a daybed that Ada used for her lunchtime naps. We sat at the table and she buttered crackers and sprinkled granulated sugar on them. Depression cupcakes she called them.

"How did you get your grandfather to come outside? To start talkin'?"

"I didn't. He just came out and asked about the trains." We each took a sip of our hot tea. Ada poured hers in her saucer to drink. I sucked noisily at mine to cool it.

"I was watching him work," I said. "He was eating raw chop meat. Can you do that, Grandma?"

"He does." Ada had her chair turned so she could keep an eye on the store through the apartment screen door.

"He gave me some to eat."

"And? Did you?"

"Yeah, with some salt on it. Is it OK?" I asked. It was my first time. She didn't respond but I really didn't care if it was alright. I really liked it and mostly that he gave some to me.

It was an unusually slow Saturday morning. Roselyn helped a lone customer and then went back to fussing with the dry goods table. John was hidden in his cubical.

"I saw some boys swimming at the mill today. Is that allowed?"

At first she didn't respond. Then she asked, "How old are you now?"

"Six and a half." *I know, too young to go swimming in the raceway.*

"I was only a few years older than you," she barely whispered, "when I started work in the mills." Ada had turned again to look out at the store. *Was she speaking to me? Or to herself? I wasn't sure.*

"Really? Which mill, Grandma?"

"The one on the corner of McBride Avenue and Mill Street, the one with a water wheel near the sidewalk. Do you know where I mean?"

"Yeah! That's the place I saw some boys divin' off that wheel this morning from the bus."

"Well that's where I met your Grandfather. Don't you ever try that. You could get killed."

I dropped the water wheel subject. "Weren't you too young to start work?"

"Yeah. I thought so then too. But kids went to work young back then. That's the way it was. There were five of us kids in my family, and we weren't rich. So my father took me down to the mill for a job. He came right into my sixth grade class at school to get me. Told the teacher I'd had enough schooling for a girl. Everybody was staring at me."

The last bit of morning light suddenly left the room as the sun began its daily trip over the roof toward the front of the store. "That was before all the labor strikes, when kids still worked in the mills." Teacup suspended in the air, she was talking to herself. She looked back at me. "I guess you don't know about the strikes. They went on for a long time. Years."

"Was it hard, workin' there?"

"I'll say!" she answered. "I worked twelve hours every day, sometimes more if there was a rush order, six days a week too."

"What did you do?" I asked.

"Well at first, I was a stock boy. All the yarn bobbins and shuttles were made up on the first floor. I had to make sure all the looms in my area were kept supplied with the right yarns and the right colors."

"Did you ever make a mistake?"

"No, not a serious one. But one time something did happen. Each floor had its own boss. They could run things any way they wanted as long as they got the work out. There were two of us stock boys on each floor. One day the other kid, he was a little older than me, brought up the wrong weight yarn and nobody caught it. Our floor boss was a mean Irishman. Usually he'd take away your pay for the day if you made a mistake. Kept it for himself too. Sometimes he'd just swat you a good one. Well this one day he found out a lot of looms were using the wrong yarns. He grabbed the other kid and shoved him hard against one of the looms. The boy's hand got caught in the warp beater and before they could shut the loom down all his fingers were broken."

Ada was leaning against the stove reheating the water. As the kettle began to whistle the recalcitrant canary joined the kettle in a rerun of the wacky shrill duet.

"Shut that kettle off. You wanna kill your damn useless canary?" John called from the store just to pester his wife.

"It's because the canary won't sing for him," she said. "We had to get rid of his cat too, when my sister gave me the canary." She hunched up her shoulders and tittered into her hand. I did too.

"It's not funny," John said from the far corner of the store.

"How can he hear us?" I whispered.

She poured fresh hot water in our cups and buttered some more Saltines. "He can hear when he wants to."

"What happened then?"

"Well, I was a real good worker, so they put me on the looms about a year after I started to work there."

"No. I mean what happened to the boy?"

"Oh. The floor boss fired the boy, sent him home and we all just went back to work."

"Really?"

"Yup. They could get lots of other kids to do his job."

"What happened to the floor boss?'

"Nothing. He was getting the work out."

"Did you like it, working on the looms?"

"At first," she said, "it was more interesting than stock work. They put me to work with someone to show me how to set up the looms. This mill made silk yard goods for men's shirts. By the time I was there two years I was runnin' two looms. I was fourteen. A good weaver could handle three. By the time I was sixteen the floor boss had me doing five looms. But they only paid me for three because I was a girl."

I asked her to describe the inside of the mills, which she told me were boiling hot in the summers and freezing in the winters.

"Never want to be that hot again," she said, "or that cold. Sometimes we'd wear scarves, coats and gloves with the fingers cut out. It was dangerous. The looms were run off' large belts that came down from the ceiling. There wasn't any protection on them and you could get your clothes hung up in them. Some did."

She stopped for a moment and took a couple of sips of tea. "We couldn't take breaks without permission from the floor boss except when the mill shut down for a half hour at lunch and dinner. Because I ran five looms that meant I'd always have to wait 'til there were two stand-ins to cover me, so I could go to the bathroom. And the air was always filled with dust from the weaving which made us cough."

I was trying to form an image of everything she described. It was difficult. I knew what the mills looked like from the outside: long rectangular brick buildings, three and four stories high, with rows of evenly spaced large arched windows. The factories were scattered helter-skelter along the river below the falls.

She got up, went into her bedroom and came back with a book that showed pictures of the mills with workers at their looms. Many were dirty-faced children standing at dimly lit rows of looms. Their eyes dead and haunting. As we look through the book I asked about my grandfather.

"When I met your grandfather there in the mills, I was fifteen. He was running three looms directly behind mine. He had such a good sense of humor. He could imitate the floor boss perfectly. We started eating together at lunch. We became good friends. And we found out that we lived near each other...even had gone to the same school though he was older than me and I never saw him there. We started walkin' back and forth to work together and seeing each other on our days off."

"How did you and grandpa get married?"

"There was lots of trouble in the mills. There were strikes, demonstrations, people got beat up, some got shot and some even killed by the police and goons hired by the mill owners. It went on for years. One day your grandpa told me he and his brother had saved up enough money to put a down payment on a small saloon on North Main Street. It was our way out of the terrible mills so we got married and went in with your grandfather's brother Phil, your great uncle. He'd been working there for a couple a years and the owner wanted to sell. I helped out in the bar until your mother was born." The store bell rang. Ada leaned back to see if there was any need for her to go out into the store.

"How old were you then?" I asked.

"I was seventeen. Your grandfather was twenty." She looked away and smiled some. The outer screen door banged shut several more times.

"I'm gonna need some help out here, Mom," Roselyn called.

"Grandma?" I started to ask. There were so many more questions. Ada got up from the table. I followed her as far as the door to the store.

Ignoring the presence of customers, my grandfather yelled, "I hate that damn screen door. It makes a hell of a racket every time it closes, doesn't it Rosie?"

The two women glanced wearily at each other. The Saturday morning rush had finally begun. I never got to ask my questions.

With the best of intentions John and Ada settle for small pleasures and something predictable in order in make ends meet. John died at age fifty-nine in 1954. Ada ran the store alone for several years, then sold it, moved to Florida with a man that shopped in the store, then died mysteriously a few months later at age sixty-five. He closed her bank account and disappeared within a few weeks. Life is not fiction.

6

Urban Chicken Ranch

Age 7

Is it reality that matters? The problem is everyone has their own perfect version of it and it's seldom discussed, let alone agreed upon. Certainly not in my family. And most assuredly not when it has to do with chickens.

DURING THE SECOND WORLD War, my father had a high-priority job driving a bread truck for the Duggan Brothers out of Clifton, New Jersey. Hard to believe, but really, high priority, and it was also the best job he ever had coming out of the Depression. Yet he went down to the Paterson Draft Board and tried to enlist. He wanted to be an Army pilot, but amazingly the government told him his job was too vital to national security. A year later he tried a second time. Maybe draft exemptions had changed but my mother wouldn't sign off on the papers. If you were married and had children your wife's signature was required. So here it was, two years after the war ended, and he was still driving a bread truck through backcountry roads in Rockland County New York, over an hour from the bakery.

Rockland County was completely rural in the forties, a place of dairy farms and apple orchards with a sprinkling of small towns and villages. His route serviced the rural areas. Many of his customers were farmers. One particular farmer started the whole thing on one warm Friday afternoon. What occurred that day at that farm was to have a dramatic impact on our family but it wasn't until Saturday that I learned what happened up north in Stoney Point, for I found myself in just the right place at the right time, eavesdropping from the next room as my hapless father tried to explain to my mother how it all began.

He was driving around with the sliding door next to him open to stay cool. He pulled into the dirt drive of one of his regular customers. As usual the farmer met my father in the farmyard where they spent a few minutes in friendly talk. In addition to several large apple orchards, the man raised chickens and pigs, traditionally called "mortgage payers." He asked the farmer if he wanted any bread. The man said no, he didn't need any, but he'd take some day-old cupcakes. The man was a penny pincher and seldom bought any fresh baked goods. This proved to be good for my father because the company deducted unsold goods from a driver's pay. Something at half price meant it covered the company's costs and didn't hurt his pay. So the farmer bought a box of day-olds.

"Were you driving with that sliding door open today?" my mother asked. It was a perpetual bone of contention between them. She hadn't saved him from the war to have him fall out of the truck while driving on winding country roads. My father ignored the question, and instead said how much he liked the farmer even though he never bought much. He'd been a customer for a number of years.

"As we got talking, the farmer mentioned that he had too many chickens for the hen house. He said when that happened the chickens stopped laying." He went on to explain just how desperate the farmer was to get rid of some of his poultry and since he liked my father he wanted to give him "first shot" at taking some of the hens off his hands. He appreciated the farmer's thoughtfulness, and the promise of free eggs, made it seem like a good deal. He agreed to take a few and to stop back on the way home to collect them.

"He gave them to me at a good price. Threw in a fifty-pound bag of feed too," he said to my mother.

A little over an hour after he left the farmer he arrived home, late in the afternoon.

We lived then, on the first floor in a two-family house, which meant that the backyard was exclusively ours to use. My parents rented the five-room apartment from my Granma Hazel for twenty-five dollars a month. The house, built for a doctor in the 1890s still had vestigial, though overgrown, evidence of its Victorian era garden: a large French Lilac bush on the left against a tall wooden fence, Forsythia hedging across the middle, a large Syringa bush on the right by our neighbor's shed, with Lilly of the Valley, Morning Blue Bells between the fence, and a slate walk on the left which ran straight out from the kitchen door. There was also a Trumpeter Vine draped over a low trellis near the kitchen door. In the five years we lived there, my mother had invested sporadic money and effort to revitalize the garden. It was now spring and this year's effort was to be the final push to restore the entire backyard. Flower beds had been weeded and edged, shrubbery groomed, the small grass area brought back to life, and new flowering annuals planted.

It was five thirty on that momentous Friday evening. A long row of pansies and petunias, my mother's favorites, had just been lovingly added to the garden. She was in the kitchen preparing supper. I was at the dining room table, with all of its three leaves in place, working on a 1,500-piece jigsaw puzzle of some unidentified mountain in the west that I had been nudging about the table after school for a week. My life was that of a blissfully contented only child. Unlike my friends, I had no siblings to muck up my things, break my model airplanes or steal puzzle pieces. All the pieces were laid out face-up and the border completed. I had sorted everything by color and pattern and was serenely contemplating my next effort. As I reached out to put a piece in place, a cacophony of avian chaos swept by in the three-foot wide alleyway that separated our house from Charlie's Bar and Grill. I got to our back door, just before my mother, in time to see my father propelled from the alleyway by six pair of beating wings. In response to the situation, he did what anyone would who was being battered and feathered. He dropped the squawking chickens and vanished in a flurry of fluff back down the alley to the bread truck. He had a desperate frantic look, which would have alarmed me if it hadn't been for all the feathers stuck to his sweaty face, clothes and hair. He had transported the chickens loose in the truck.

I turned to look at my mother for any trace of comprehension. Her face was ash white, her mouth hanging open. Within moments my father reappeared with six more chickens, which franticly fled his grasp into our fenced in backyard, except for two that tried to dart back down the alley. I leapt off the back stoop to head off the runaways, while my mother took up pursuit of the other overly energized poultry with a grass rake, as my father without a word of explanation, disappeared into the house.

There have, no doubt, been moments in human history when modern scientific developments would have been most welcome— antibiotics during the Bubonic plague, for example, or tranquilizer darts for the chickens in our backyard. My father, fresh out of the Great Depression, ever on the lookout for a good deal, had, I realized, arrived home with one such deal. Unfortunately, it was well in advance of a chicken coop. A few seconds later my father reappeared with a pair of my mother's brand-new mahogany, Chinese Chippendale–inspired, dining room chairs in an effort to construct an elegant but inadequate barricade for the alley.

Tears were running down my mother's face as she turned angrily toward my father, "What are you doing with my new chairs? Take them back!"

He looked dumbfounded. "What's wrong with you? I'm stopping the chickens."

"I don't want chickens!"

But the impatient chickens, unwilling to wait for a coop, my parents, or a better day, headed through, over and under everything. The first line of the garden's defenseless plantings was a row of border plants along the kitchen walk. These variegated broad leaf Hostas, soon to have their delicate lavender bell shaped flowers on long stems, had held the line against children, toys, and household pets since the house was built. They dissolved under the chicken onslaught, as if struck by a tidal wave. Behind the border plants a flowerbed of pansies and petunias also collapsed followed by the adjoining bed of emerging zinnias at the edge of the grass. It was apparent, if one cared, the confinement of these chickens was of paramount importance, and Roselyn, my mother, cared more deeply, at this moment for her garden than her religion, or supper now burning on the stove. For me, the delights of chicken chasing easily won out over the contemplative calm of puzzling. Though our intentions differed, our actions did not. My mother and I ineffectually began chasing chickens.

Even if we had caught them there was nowhere to confine them. However, there were two birds that willingly accommodated our efforts. They voluntarily committed themselves to the Syringa Bush. These two, in their headlong rush to freedom, had collided about two feet above the ground with the only truly neglected tangle of shrubbery still in our garden. This bush was a bafflement of thick woody stems about eight feet tall and six feet across that had defied penetration by one and all of my mother's efforts, regardless of the tools she brought to bear. But not so for these two chickens. One was tangled at a forty-five-degree angle with its wings spread in a frozen Kamikaze dive clucking softly to itself. The other bird, on its back, was compactly folded into a shape that looked like my recently lost football. At the same time another pair had dedicated themselves to aggressively assaulting the height of the back wall of our neighbor's garage which bordered the back edge of our yard. A twenty-by-twenty-foot concrete pad in our yard abutted this garage. On reaching this area, these two birds began running and flapping their wings trying to become airborne, which they succeeded in doing in time to successfully collide with the garage several feet short of its roof, causing them to slide into a befuddled heap at the base of the wall. An endless search throughout all of Paterson could not have produced two finer models of determination and devotion to a task than these two clucking pullets. After their unsuccessful attempt to scale the garage wall, they staggered around the yard until their minds cleared, at which point, like lemmings, they turned and smashed into the wall again….and again…and again. Several other birds, seemingly devoid of imagination, lay motionless on our small patch of grass. They had achieved this state of tranquility by running in diminishing circles causing them to collide repeatedly with each other until they collapsed, exhausted. Except one of the three that was strangely more tranquil than the others with her wings spread out along the ground, her feet in the air and her tongue hanging out, a candidate for the stock pot. Then there were the two off on their own, seriously set on saving the world from grubs by digging up the Morning Blue Bell plants. This left one chicken for each of us. My mother had cornered her chicken in a cowardly stand off to the death. She had pinned down her prey with the grass rake in a corner of the yard. Her chosen chicken proved not to be chicken at all. This chicken had guts. This chicken wriggled out from under the rake, lowered its head, let out a horrific screech, and rushed my mother with its wings flapping wildly. Fearing for her life she staggered backward into my uncle Phil's prizewinning Cana plants. He and his family lived down the street in a house without a yard. He had asked my mother if he could have a small plot for his six plants. So, with only one Cana plant remaining, my mother decided to make a stand. Tapping into a hidden reserve of courage she took a page from her opponent's book, lowered her head, yelled, waved her arms, and counter attacked. The struggle seesawed back and forth ending in a mutual state of exhaustion. I stood mesmerized in the middle of the grass amongst the comatose chickens, watching this barnyard tango, when the last of the frantic chickens crashed into my legs. I was about to dive on this bird when my father reappeared from the back door with another dining room chair in one hand and a chicken under his other arm. Why he was carrying a chicken out of the house was not apparent nor why he had gotten another chair.

Seeing my father so equipped, my mother lost her concentration on her cornered bird.

The chicken darted past her.

"Not my good chairs!" she yelled. "No more chairs." She spread her legs and jammed her fists onto her hips. "Why did you get another one? Was that chicken in the house? Did you carry that chicken in there? Did you? What has happened to you? Just look at my garden! You've ruined everything."

He quickly put the chair down and dropped the chicken as he tried to avoid her eyes. My demure mother, terminally fearful of chickens, having found a hidden well of courage and inner strength, switched her battle from chickens to her husband. This was certainly an aspect of my mother I had never seen before. My father, at a loss as to what to do, looked more like a mortified younger brother than my father. He had gone into the house for another chair to fortify the barricade in the alleyway, and found the chicken in the house leaving an unpleasant deposit on the dining room chair. Not something he wanted to mention to her as the chicken landed on the soiled upholstered seat again. As he reached down to push the bird off the chair he looked over at me, the witness of this bit of urban theater. I had never been so excitingly and unrepentantly and euphorically entertained. Wide-eyed and giggling, I reached down to pick up the last chicken that was now pecking at my shoes.

"Jerry! Stop!" he yelled, "Don't pick up that bird. She'll peck your eyes out. There's already been enough henpecking for one afternoon," he added belligerently looking back at his wife.

Surely, these words of warning came just in time to save me for I had no desire to be henpecked. They also struck a deeper note of budding comprehension that drew me into the timeless ritual of boneheaded male bonding, a moment of collective enlightenment and wisdom that many fathers pass down to their sons about the henpecking proclivities of the gentler sex.

My chicken, my mother's chicken, and my father's, now completely exhausted, had found safety huddling under the tangle of the Syringa bush. The battle was over. His mental faculties revived, Bill, the family provider, went to get a roll of chicken wire and wood stakes out of the Dugan truck, which haphazardly came together as a chicken pen in the back corner of the yard. When he had all the chickens sequestered, proving his revived resistance to henpecking, and while we all stood there looking down at the huddled heap of quivering feathers my mother muttered, "Why do we have these chickens in our garden?"

"For the eggs."

She turned her moist eyes on her husband. She knew a bit about chickens. "They're all roosters," she said.

At the age of seven I thought that life was like a community sing with everybody on the same page. In reality most of us aren't even using the same songbook. After the eleven surviving chickens were penned up, we, and all our loudly protesting neighbors were wakened each morning by a crowing rooster at the crack of dawn, which was 4:00 a.m. that time of year. My father literally got up with the chickens and went outside to kill the offending bird. Then the next morning and every morning after that, the next chicken in the pecking order took over. What I learned at the age of seven was that after you cut off a chicken's head it runs around for nearly two minutes.

7

The Snow Fort War
Age 8, Fourth Grade

A few words about the world, the weather, my city, my parents, neighbors, grandparents, school, friends, follies, foes, euphoria, my uncle's car, and spontaneous repercussions.

DESPITE THE BRITISH GRANTING independence to Pakistan and India, the Truman Doctrine, intended to stop Communist advances in the world, the passage of the Taft Act, blacklisting in Hollywood, the House Un-American Activities Committee, the discovery of the dead sea scrolls, and the invention of the microwave oven...oh, and the discovery of radiocarbon dating, nothing eventful took place in the first eleven and three quarter months of 1947, when I was eight years old. Except, my mother had started to work as a waitress to supplement my father's income as he struggled to get his new floor sanding business going. She also intimated that she needed something else in her life beyond caring for her husband, their only child, and the house. The only complication, who would keep an eye on me until they got home from work? Next door, to the left of our house, was Charles Bar & Grill, the local gathering place. Charlie and his wife, Molly, the owners, were Jewish. They lived upstairs over the bar. Schwartz was their last name, and in retrospect it seemed out of character for a Jewish couple to be in the bar business then. Intolerance of Jews was vigorous and rampant in America in the forties. Yet the bar flourished. It opened at 7:00 a.m. and closed at midnight on week days, and much later on Friday and Saturday. My father opened for them in the morning before he set off on his own day at nine. When Molly found out that my mother had started to work, she offered to take care of me when I came home from school, and also included lunches.

The Schwartz's were not religious Jews, rather they were pragmatic and philosophical, especially Molly. She not only made me great deli sandwiches and homemade soups, she also seasoned the time with provocative Yiddish insights.

Every lunch ended with a half grapefruit, a digestive she told me, to help the meaty sandwiches go down. If I complained, I got this strange response, "There's a lot more juice in grapefruit than meets the eye." That one lodged in my eight-year-old brain, along with, "Nothing should never be a total loss." It took me years to understand the humor of the first. The irony of the second was to occur in the weeks ahead. In the meantime, Molly's "Nothing should never…" caused me considerable mental confusion. I had just learned that double negatives make a positive. Was that a double negative, I wondered? It sounded so strange to my ear that I couldn't even remember what I might have said to prompt that response from her.

The unmemorable Christmas of 1947 had come and gone except for the new sled I had asked Santa for down at Quackenbush's Department store, and Meyer Brothers' and Sears, and the fight I had with a kid in my class who told me there was no Santa Claus. It was creeping up on the New Year with no reprieve in sight for the unavoidable return to school. But then, the day before New Year's Eve, it began to snow, a lot, for three whole days, and when it stopped, several feet of snow lay on the ground and joyously school was closed because the city was shut down. Wind whipped snow into six and seven-foot-high drifts. The buses couldn't run, the street venders weren't able to sell their wares and the city garbage trucks stopped collecting. They were converted to snow plows. My parents and I, and the whole city, were stuck at home and my school would not open again for more days than I could ever have believed possible.

During the last day of the storm, my father said he was going to walk up Haledon Avenue to his parents' house on Carbon Street to see if they were alright. Would I like to go too? The phones weren't working. In those days the phones didn't work well even when they were working. Most people shared a party line with six other people, which meant there was always someone you didn't know on the phone when you wanted to make a call. You'd have to wait for them to get off the line before you could make your own call. But the phones weren't working at all after the storm, so we set off midmorning to hike ten blocks up the hill to my grandparents' house through the unshoveled, unplowed snow. My father went ahead, breaking the way through the three-foot deep snow, skirting the drifts. Like all children, I loved the snow, the way it transformed the mundane world into a foreign land. The snow was thigh-high on my father. For two blocks I managed to keep up even though it was up to my chest. After three blocks, I was completely done in. I collapsed out of breath. We had come too far to turn back he said. The only alternative was for him to carry me. It took us nearly two hours to travel the ten blocks up hill. My grandparents were fine, but cold. They needed some help with their cranky furnace. I sat in their dining room looking out the window. *There's just too darn much snow. If I can't walk in it how can I play in it?*

When we got back to our house it was dusk. The next day the city started to dig out. Our street, a main access to downtown Paterson from the north side of town, had not been touched by a plow. In those days plowing only started when the snowstorm ended. The buildings on my street were built right up to the sidewalks, and vehicles lined both curbs on this one way street, so the only place to put shoveled snow was in-between and on top of the parked cars. Every car become an amorphous lump of snow. My uncle Phil couldn't find his car for weeks. Of course it didn't help that he forgot where he had parked it. Not that it mattered. There was no way he or anyone could drive. The first snowplow that came near our street, flipped over on its side while rounding the corner from Haledon Avenue and lay there for three weeks, partially blocking the street. The weather turned bitter cold, nothing melted. The snow banks along the curbs were so high that tunnels had to be dug through them so you could cross the badly rutted streets. Only large trucks with full chains could handle these conditions and even they got stuck.

A week passed. My new sled and I were still stranded in the house. The snowstorm of a lifetime was turning out to be the bore of a lifetime. Then another week passed before P.S. 12 was reopened. It was four blocks from my house. A single file trail snaked through snow-drifted sidewalks to school. As I clumped along in my galoshes, I hoped that the school playground would be cleared. As I reached the top of the twelve steps that led up to the playground from the street, my hopes vanished. Snow, untouched by human hands, had been whipped into gigantic ridges that lay spread across the space like an ocean of peaked meringue.

The same thin track that had led all of us here from our homes crept on over this dismal waste land toward the school entrance where multi-colored, penguin shaped children stood passively in shivering clumps waiting for the doors to open. No one had even tried to clear the schoolyard of snow. So what was an unrealistic boy of eight to do? Halfway across the yard I slumped against one of the disgusting, warty, snow peaks, forcing a seat into the snow. I sat there in a self-indulgent sulk ignoring the calls of my friends. Supposedly responsible adults had let us down. They hadn't cleared the streets, hadn't cleaned the sidewalks and no one even tried to shovel a path across the playground.

The bell rang. My friends gave up on me and went into the warm building.

"What's your problem?"

I was staring at my hated galoshes and hadn't noticed Mrs. Vander Cleek, my teacher, walking toward me.

"I'm sick of this! You can't do anything." I knew I sounded whiney, something Molly Schwartz had admonished me about, but I didn't care.

My teacher made a sort of resigned grunt of agreement and put her hand on my shoulder.

"Why," I asked, "didn't they shovel off the playground?" In those days, before Toro snow blowers and 4x4 pickups with snowplows it would have been a nearly insurmountable task.

"Sounds like you've got cabin fever," she said.

It was even worse than that. "I got a new sled for Christmas and I can't even use it," I said.

"Maybe we can do something about this situation."

I looked up. "What?"

"You'll have to wait and see."

When we reached the door to the school she sent me on ahead. "I have to stop by the office for a minute. I'd like you to be room monitor until I get there."

I wound my way up to the top floor. Both my parents had gone to this school, which had been built in the early twenties. All the floors were wooden, the metal ceilings very high, and the desks bolted down in straight rows and equipped with inkwells. In front of each classroom were two doors on either side of the blackboards, which led into a cloakroom about six feet by thirty feet. Dim lighting fixtures were suspended from the ceiling, the walls were covered with dark varnished vertical matchboard and there was a double row of coat hooks down the wall opposite the doors.

Before Mrs. Vander Cleek entered the classroom, some of us were still struggling with our galoshes, rubber boots, snow pants, coats, scarves, mittens, gloves and each other. The galoshes worn exclusively by boys were the worst. Even after you managed to undo all the metal clips they would not come unstuck from your shoes. At that moment there were several boys rolling about on the floor in a semi-fetal position trying to rid themselves of these inquisitional contraptions. Others, in their frustration, were hanging from the coat hooks trying to kick the rubbery horrors from the ends of their feet. Other boys, having managed to pull, kick or shake themselves free, found that their shoes were still firmly trapped inside the galoshes. Of all these approaches, I preferred the rolling-around-on-the-floor method. It was not the one that really worked the best but it put you in the best position for watching the girls. For some reason known only to the mothers of America, girls wore their snowsuit leggings underneath their skirts. I imagine it was to prevent the skirt from getting wrinkled but the point

- 74 -

of a snowsuit is to keep you and your clothes warm, and above all dry. Yet this was the accepted and only way for girls to dress for winter. Now, in order for a girl to remove her leggings she had to hold her skirt up and tuck it under her chin. Yes! Unbelievably. Yes! And upon occasion, an impatient girl, trying to wriggle out of her snow pants without undoing all the snaps, buckles or zippers, would inadvertently pull her underpants down along with the snow-pants. Or at least that is what my friends and I theorized. There is of course, a grown-up name for this, which men with unflagging little boy interests are willing to pay for, but after all we were young and on the correct side of youthful innocence. So then, in reality, what we were doing was rolling around on the floor for educational reasons. We, all of us, bright studious boys, were thirsty for this knowledge. So, there we were, me and four other boys, sisterless, even lacking anecdotal access to any information about, or even any possible idea, of how girls might differ from boys. We were pretending to take off our galoshes. We were still down there— according to plan—on the floor when Barbara Liddell came through the cloakroom door.

Exotic, rumored to be from Quebec, Canadian Barbara Liddell. I thought she was the most beautiful, the most feminine snowsuit-wearing girl conceivable. I was in love with Barbara Liddell, although, until then, from a distance. I did buy a box of chocolates for her on Valentine's Day, a month later. It took me a week to muster the courage to go to her apartment to give her the heart shaped box. I climbed unlit stairs to her family's apartment and knocked. Her mother opened the door and snarled, "What do you want?" Her dark outline filled the doorway.

I removed my cap and said, "C-c-could I see Barbara, please?"

She scowled at me. "What's that you have there?"

I showed her the box of chocolates. She grabbed it out of my hands and said, "Go away," stepped back into the apartment, slammed the door, and left me standing on the stairwell landing. I could hear Barbara and her mother talking in their front room. Then she walked back toward me and said, "Go away," through the closed door and locked it.

I murmured not a word to my fellow cloakroom rowdies. I knew that being pierced through my eight-year-old heart by love was difficult enough to bear without adding the arrows of my friends.

Yes, Barbara was wearing a snowsuit. And yes, she was wearing it with her skirt on the outside. She pulled off her rubber boots with ease. Then she lifted her skirt and tucked it under her chin. In any other place or circumstance no girl would ever have considered such a thing, but somehow in the inner sanctum of the cloakroom, normal conventions and inhibitions seemed suspended. Her hands moved to her sides and she began to pull at her snowsuit leggings, in haste, without undoing any of the snaps, buttons, zippers or whatever. A silky, smooth sliver of skin, framing her navel, appeared. Barbara was often late to school and our teacher had told her, just the day before that she would have to stay after any time she was not in her seat when attendance was taken. The sliver of vanilla skin expanded as she tugged harder on her pants. We reduced our rolling about just enough to look sincerely engaged in galoshes removal but free enough for discreet perusal. In amazing slow motion, that thin band of skin grew to reveal her curved hips. And now for the educational, scientific payoff. The edge of Barbara Liddell's underwear was fractionally away from the confluence of shapes at the top of her legs.

"What are you boys doing?"

The words passed through the right side of my head and ricocheted around the inside of my skull. With pathos and too much volume I said, "Oh no." *Is this really happening? Is it?*

The impact of Mrs. Vander Cleek's voice caused Barbara to turn away from us and drop her skirt.

"You boys finish removing your things in the classroom," said Mrs. Vander Cleek as she maneuvered her matronly body to block our view.

Man talk erupted in frantic whispers as we filed out of the cloakroom.

"What did you see? You were closest Jerry," John Van Koppen asked.

"Everything, everything!" I said.

"Everything?" Buddy's eyes were bulging.

"Yup. Everything."

"Yeah. Me too," said Buddy. "What was it like?"

"Aw, you know, jus' like we thought," was my vague answer.

Mrs. Vander Cleek emerged from the cloakroom. "From this time on boys, you will remove their snow clothes in the classroom and hang them up after the girls are finished in the cloak room. And you, Jerry, will no longer be class monitor."

Well, I hated being class monitor anyway.

Sheepishly we went to our seats. When recess came most of the girls opted to stay inside while the boys struggled back into their clothes and went out to make the best of the snow. My friends and I trudged off toward the side of the yard to continue our discussion of what we thought we saw. None of us were willing to admit that we were still ignorant. As a result, none of us noticed our teacher coming toward us until she spoke. I couldn't tell from her face what was coming. I just knew it was going to be terrible. Maybe we'd have to stay after school for a week and wash blackboards. I'd never get a chance to use my new sled, but at least I might get a chance to see Barbara since she usually had to stay after school once a week for being late. Or, what if we had to see the Principal? I'd already been to see him several times for fighting with Henry. He told me he never wanted to see me in his office again. Or worse yet, what if I had to bring my parents to school and explain that I was trying to look at Barbara Liddell's naked crotch?

"I've just talked to the Principal…" *Here it comes. Oh no! Oh no! Just as I thought.* "…and he said to bring a note from home."

My chattering mind had blanked out the middle part of what she had said.

"What note?" I looked at my friends. John was jumping up and down. Doug kept saying, "Oh! Oh! Alright! OK! Great!"

"WHAT'S GREAT?!?" I asked. "Are we in trouble? Was it about the cloakroom?"

"Nah," John said. "If we bring a note from home sayin' it's OK, we can play in the sandlot across the street at recess and lunch. Didn't you listen?"

We turned and looked through the iron picket fence at the place where we played baseball in the summer. It was bounded on two sides by streets. On the other sides, by the backyards of wood framed houses. Sometime in the morning snowplows had made a feeble attempt to clear the streets around the school. All of the snow had been pushed up to the right side of the lot leaving a large cleared area directly across from the schoolyard. Off to the side of the cleared area was a truly enormous heap of plowed snow filled with room size voids. It stood nearly two stories high in some places and looked like a castellated fortress positioned against the open sandlot. On the far side the snow heap ended against a steep bank that flowed down to North First Street.

At lunch most of the boys from our class came back from home with permission. At last, after being trapped for weeks, there was room to run, to enjoy the snow.

Within a few minutes we divided up into sides and started a battle for control of the snow fort.

It had been more than three weeks since Christmas. Trash and discarded Christmas trees were starting to pile up everywhere. Many of the local houses took advantage of the open space at the back of the lot to shed their unwanted holiday debris. It was taking time, but the city was getting the streets cleared of snow by carting it away to the Passaic River.

At lunchtime the next day another fourth grade class—just the boys, this was a different time entirely—challenged us. It now became an epic battle of capture the flag, a classic struggle between two foes with no quarter given. My class kept the fort. But we were nearly overrun. While there were many nooks to hide in they weren't connected. We weren't able to move about or get away from the barrage of snowballs that were lobbed at us over the top of the fort. We went back to class badly battered, sopping wet, and demoralized. We needed a plan. We needed to change the fort. During afternoon break we decided to connect the spaces and roof over some areas.

"Let's do it after school today," said Pudgy. Pudgy was about eight inches taller than me and thin as a pole.

"That's not gonna work," said Dougie. "The other kids'll come back after school. They'll murder us."

Dougie was right. We'd have to act fast. We wouldn't go home. We'd stay and fix the fort. We thought we might have twenty minutes.

When class ended Pudgy ran home for a couple of shovels. Buddy stayed, even though he thought he'd get in bad trouble.

We connected the spaces, made a stockpile of snowballs from the shoveled snow. The roofed areas were more difficult. A bunch of us collected discarded Christmas trees from the neighborhood for that job, but the trees were too skimpy to hold snow. "At least they might break up the snow balls," said John. We laid some over the top as a shield, others we propped up along the edge of the fort.

A cry went up, "Here they come!"

The other class had come up with a plan too. They were carrying metal garbage can lids to use as shields. They split into several groups and came at us from different directions, most from the sandlot side. Some made it to the top. It was hand-to-hand combat. But our work paid off. The connected spaces made it easy to repel all their attacks. It was dark when we left for home.

The next day the battle continued where it had left off, with each side taking up its former positions. The battle wavered back and forth with wild giddy intensity and heroics. The fort changed hands repeatedly. Some were forced to eat snow. Others had their clothes torn open and their underpants stuffed with snow. There were some bloody noses. No one complained. By sundown we had recaptured the flag and were back in control of the fort.

Once a week, on Wednesday mornings we had assembly. Announcements were made by the principal, then someone might give a little talk or there might be a guest visitor who would perform something, tell funny stories, play an instrument, or the music teacher would have the whole school sing old Stephen Foster songs. Once in a while one of the grades, from third to eighth, would put on a musical themed performance. During this particular assembly the principal told us no one was allowed to go across the street any longer. Traffic was once again flowing through the snow cleared streets and the town was sending a crew over to shovel off the playground that afternoon so we could have a place to play. At recess we stayed inside and at lunch they let us back into the building early. Men arrived and began removing the snow. By the next morning half the playground had been cleared.

Well, that was that.

"He can't keep us away when school's out," said John.

School let out at 3:20 p.m. Within a short time, every fourth grade boy was back at the snow fort ready to take up battle where it had left off the afternoon before. Each day the number of boys increased and the fort size grew as new areas were reworked. On Friday almost forty boys were on the battlefield. Kids I didn't know, and had never seen. It was a Kipling story come to life, a pageant of romantic struggle, of nobility and purpose, for a fortress on a cliff in the Himalayas.

The battle resumed Saturday morning. Men from the neighborhood began to gather in the sand lot. Some even brought kitchen chairs to sit in comfort, smoke cigarettes, drink beer and cheer the mad spectacle. There were also toddlers with their parents building snowmen, mothers with babies in carriages, gossiping, indifferent to the war raging nearby. And some young children, also indifferent to the war, sliding down the bank to North First Street on pieces of cardboard they found in the uncollected trash.

Sunday was quiet, at least for me. A parentally imposed day of rest that I spent in the usual way, from nine in the morning until nearly nine at night, at the Methodist church. I seem to remember it was damp, cloudy, and a threatening snow kind of day and the same again on Monday, which turned out to be perfectly suited to the malevolent events of that afternoon.

At Monday recess, confined to the playground, my friends and I stood about listlessly in a clump like gossipy girls, complaining amongst ourselves. The cleared playground offered no appeal. Not even the whispering, giggling girls watching us, pointing at us, tempted us into our usual hair pulling attacks. When the school day ended we rushed home to change into battle clothing.

Twenty minutes later Dougie, John, and I reached the fort. We were the first to arrive. We had brought peach baskets with us to help move and store snowballs. Good packing snow was getting hard to find so we went off to the far edge of the lot to make snowballs. As we worked we heard a lot of yelling behind us. We could see Pudgy, Jeff, his brother Jonathan, and Buddy struggling with some large boys at the top of the fort and not doing well. We dropped the baskets and ran to help them. When we reached the fort all four boys landed in a heap at the bottom of the fortress.

"Hey! That's our fort," all seven of us yelled.

"Yeah? Nobody was here so we took it." There were four eighth graders sitting on the highest blocks of snow. The one that spoke stood with his hands on his hips.

"We made it. It's not yours," I said.

"It is now. Besides, you didn't make it the snowplows did," said the standing boy. "What do you think guys? Am I right?"

At this point our side numbered over twenty fourth graders standing there with us, with more coming.

"No. Give it back you shitheads!" Dougie added.

There were now about thirty boys from both third and fourth grade armies, united in one intention—take back the fort.

"Go to hell, sissies," standing boy motioned with his arm. "Come 'n' try."

Eighth graders that had hidden out of sight began to stand up all over the fort. There were twenty, maybe more. Too much for the thirty of us, but up the slope we went in an angry surge of adrenaline under an avalanche of our own stored snowballs, and just as quickly we were discarded like crumbled pieces of paper. Repeated efforts accomplished nothing. We tried all sides with the same results. At one point the usurpers came out of the fort and pushed most of us down the bank toward North First Street. When we tried to get back up the bank they pummeled us with more of our snowballs and pushed us back down again. During that half hour battle more fourth and fifth grade boys joined us on the bank, making the count close to forty-five. It didn't matter. Just charging willy-nilly up the bank wasn't gaining us anything. Pudgy and I took a break. We were off to the side at the bottom of the bank by the small church on the corner watching nothing being accomplished, when I got an idea. "Pudgy, you got that lighter with you?"

"Yup." Pudgy's father had given him his Zippo lighter that he brought home after the war. "Why?" he wanted to know. I described an Errol Flynn movie I had just seen at the Fabian Theater, and how it would help us get our fort back. He liked the idea but wasn't sure it would work. Nor was I. The eighth graders were now throwing kids down the bank by the church. Some had been hurt. We looked at each other and then he went to get some kids to help us.

The little church was getting a new roof. I started picking up some old shingles, tarpaper and pieces of wood. Pudgy came back with two boys from the fifth grade class. We told them what we had in mind. They agreed to help. We organized every one into two groups. Most of the boys kept up an attack at the bank, while the rest of the boys went to hide on the other side of the church. I took a rope from one of the roofer's ladders. We tied two small birch tree saplings together and bent them down. I fastened a flat piece of wood to the trees, added some burning shingles and tarpaper, cut the tether and catapulted the flaming bomb up in an unbelievably perfect ark toward the fort. Some of the flaming tar actually landed on the dozens of tinder dry Christmas trees we had used for roofing. Flames exploded high into the sky. At that same moment Pudgy gave a signal to the boys behind the church sending them up around the building to the other side of the fort. Eighth graders, fleeing in panic from the burning trees, were trapped between the boys coming up the bank and those from behind the church. We gave no mercy, stuffing snow down their clothes, stealing their shoes. The bully invaders fled in all directions. The fort was ours. Then, I heard the sirens.

You might call it cowardice. You might. But I thought it prudent to slip off home. I turned around, thoughtfully and deliberately, and walked down North First Street in an artfully contrived air of innocence. I could tell from the sounds behind me that the fire trucks had arrived. At a safe distance I turned around and saw a large plume of gray smoke rising high above the houses, and kids scattering everywhere. Just a few minutes before I had felt euphoric. Now, came an epiphany. It was too easy to get a bunch of crazed kids to do something really dumb.

The next day there was a special assembly. Since it wasn't Wednesday I had a good idea what was coming—a long stay in reform school. Of course we were told by the principal how stupid and dangerous yesterday's events in the sandlot had been, and it was fortunate no one was hurt. The police were now going to patrol the lot. If anyone knew anything about the fire, they were to come to the office. No one ever did.

That day the city came and removed all the plowed snow and started on the weeks of trash in the sandlot, especially the Christmas trees.

On the day of the snow fort debacle, as I escaped down North First Street, in an effort to calm myself, I fell into my habit of guessing the number of steps it would take to reach the next corner. I took in a deep breath of relief knowing I had gotten safely away. And as I puckered up my lips and blew out all the air in one single rush, I noticed a familiar lump peeking out from under its mantle of snow—my uncle Phil's Buick. I couldn't wait to see his face when I told him. *Well the afternoon wasn't a total loss. Thanks Molly Schwartz.*

You could tell the naivety of that era. My friends and I were innocently in need of sex education and glorious Hollywood style war. What I found out from this mad affair—if you want to be a leader, just act like one and most everybody else will fall into line. Also, serious introspection and leadership are not a good fit. This stood me in good stead in my future life as an artist. Art's a much better fit with introspection.

8

Sleigh Rides

Age 8–9, Fourth Grade

My sleigh ride began several weeks after the 1947 New Year's Eve blizzard and ended sixty-five years later.

WE STARED INTENTLY AT each other. No one spoke. I felt like this might be the last chance to find out about his childhood and his family. His ability to remember was diminishing. His family never talked about their past. They behaved as if it required too much effort, that it was none of anyone's business, certainly not mine. Now they were nearly all dead.

"I can't remember," he said dismissively. I think I'm getting old," as if his age was, for him, a surprising realization.

I ignored his standard brusqueness, his brisling reluctance to talk about the past. "Once when I was really little you told me about a farm your parents had."

But then he went on, "Yes! They did have a farm. A dairy farm." He seemed surprised by the memory. "They lost it when the Depression started."

"Where was it?"

"In Clifton."

"Clifton? There are no farms there now. It's all houses and factories."

Ignoring me he went on. "One winter day me and my brother went sleigh ridin' down the hill at the farm." An inward smile flickered across his lips.

"Which brother?" I felt pleased with myself for getting him started.

"Pete. He went down the hill before me. There was a turn at the bottom of the hill next to the barn. He didn't make the turn and went into the manure pile. It was a steep hill. He was goin' really fast. Went all the way in. What a mess. My mother took him into the house, took all his clothes off and stood him in a large washtub on the kitchen table to clean him up. He was mad at me because he didn't want me to see him without any clothes on being washed like a baby. I kept staring anyway. It was too funny. By the end everybody in the family was in the kitchen staring at him."

"How old were you then?" I asked.

"Oh I don't remember that. We were young. Little kids. I was born in 1916 a year after Pete, so it might have been in the early twenties—maybe he was eight or nine. So I was probably seven." He was still staring at the TV. "I'm too old now I can't remember anymore. What am I, ninety-four now?"

"You're ninety-seven."

"Really?" My father said. "That's old. I'm really getting old. I miss Roselyn. Why'd she have to die?"

"She had colon cancer, Dad. She wasn't in pain at all. She had an easy passing."

"When's my daughter coming over?" He always changed the subject when he didn't like its direction.

"Jenny?"

"Yeah."

"She's your granddaughter, Dad."

"Oh? Why'd she have to die? What's wrong with God anyway?"

It was a recurring theme. His life had run the gamut from a child musical protégé, to a near death episode from alcohol poisoning, to becoming a Christian fundamentalist, to becoming a Baptist minister, to not believing in a caring god. He continued on, repeating over and over to himself, about the good mother and wife that Roselyn was—she was—but my mind drifted away.

I guess it couldn't have been more than two weeks after the Snow Fort Debacle. I was sledding on Jefferson Street on the new sled I had gotten for Christmas. It was the first time since the blizzard that I could use it. Like everyone else that had been snowbound, I was bug-eyed crazy to be out of the house sleigh riding.

Jefferson Street was the best sledding hill in that part of town, but too dangerous to use above the bottom block because of the cross streets. But this year, due to the extraordinary snowfall, there still weren't many cars on the road. Because of this some of the older boys were using the entire hill, though most kids stayed on the bottom block. This short block was so steep it had stairs instead of sidewalks. It finished with a flat stretch long before the next cross street, leaving plenty of room to stop.

It was nine o'clock in the morning before I got to the hill. It already had far too many riders on it. Every kid on the north side of town seemed to be there that Saturday, cheerfully careening into one other. I immediately threw myself into this crazy quilt, and for the first half hour just the thrill of using my new sled was enough to keep me happy. But too many kids are too many kids. It started to feel like I was on a conveyor belt. An itch developed in some feverish part of my brain telling me I should sled the entire hill. Start all the way at the top, many blocks away, with the older boys. But I couldn't. Not because I was afraid of the hill, which foolishly I wasn't. It was because the older boys wouldn't let me be there with them. The half dozen boys were like an exclusive club. They began every run clumped together, yelling and whooping as they launched themselves in a pack, running half a block toward Seventh Street, where the hill started, before belly flopping down on their sleds across the width of the roadway. Several times that day I had dragged my sled up to the top of the hill with the intention of joining in the exciting madness. Just a few subtle glares kept me away. Maybe it wasn't the boys that stopped me. At least I'd like to think so. Maybe for once it was common sense. It could have been the cross streets. There were several of them, which flattened out the hill as they cut across its slope at the end of each block. And while cars weren't able to maneuver the hill, they did randomly pass along the cross streets making sledding from the top a gamble. Occasionally there would be volunteer lookouts at the corners. If not, the boys just took their chances.

Now, late in the afternoon, the bottom block where I had spent the major chunk of the day was still swarming with frenetic, screaming kids spread out across the width of the street. As the boys from the top of the hill reached the flat of each cross street they became slightly air born, and at each successive cross street, with increasing speed, that distance grew until at the last steepest stair bracketed block, the six-pack of boys, in a thrilling, uncontrollable blur, were launched in an arc that didn't reach earth until they were half way down that slope. It was a mad scene with sledders on that last block scrambling for safety.

I knew I was on the verge of asking my father to remember too much, but I had to push him past the mental fog of age. There was this impression I had of my father's family as remote, of encapsulated units trapped in silent proximity to each other.

"No. You're ninety-seven," I had to tell him once more. "What about your brothers and sisters? You told me once that Neil and Joe didn't get along."

"Did I? Oh yeah! They fought all the time. Real fighting, to hurt each other. My mother kept a cut off broom handle behind the kitchen door that she used to hit them with to stop their fighting. They wrecked the kitchen one time. She hit them as hard as she could. It was the only thing that ever worked."

"Did they ever get along?"

"I don't remember. I don't think so. No."

"What about the other kids in your family?"

"Other kids?" He looked unsure.

I had been sleigh riding all day by myself, not taking any breaks except to eat a mangled peanut butter and jelly sandwich I had brought from home. I was tired, unwilling to stop, and trying not to pee in my pants. Just one more run and I'll quit, I thought. The weather had turned damp and colder with the threat of another snowstorm. It must have been a bit before four o'clock, and though it was starting to get dark the hill was still crowded. I decided on just a quick ride on the bottom block. I was waiting for an opening to get a running start. All day I had been looking over the whole hill hoping to see one of my friends. We had agreed to meet up if any of us could make it. None did. The only one I knew was a new kid that had just transferred into my fourth grade class before Thanksgiving. His name was Gerry like mine, although he spelled it with a G. He wore glasses that made him very strange looking and the butt of endless name calling by the school bullies. He must have had a serious eye condition because his glasses were extremely thick making his irises look like two distant dark dots. He was all alone that day. He was always alone. No one ever talked to him. No one ever walked to school with him or went over to his house to play. He was nervous and twitchy like a rabbit. I remember that he had a brand new sled, probably got it for Christmas too. I felt sorry for his loneliness that day, and though I thought I should go over and say hello and do a few runs with him it was late and I just knew he would latch on to me forever. It seemed I attracted kids like this. Henry was the first, a boy in my class with mood swings from neediness to cruelty. Then there was Myron, the overweight Jewish boy who played chess and was always getting hurt, and shy Eugene Boucher, the French-Canadian who talked with a funny accent, and even my best friend Mary Robinson because she was a girl and a Catholic to boot. I glanced quickly at Gerry. He hadn't seen me. I was relieved. A second later the hill opened up and he launched himself a fraction before I did, just as someone called out "Jerry! Hey, Jerry!"

"Beside your three brothers there's Eva and Bessie," I reminded him. "Tell me about them."

"Eva. Yes, Eva." He had the vague look of someone thinking to himself, but spoke too loudly against the annoying background sound of the television set perpetually tuned to channel seven out of New York. He was sitting in his favorite blue wingchair that we brought back north from Florida when my mother died. Her matching chair sat unused at the other end of his room.

I walked over to the television and turned it off.

"Eva was my mother's favorite," said my father, still looking intently at the television. "Everyone loved Eva. She was the happy one in the family."

"The happy one in the family," I repeated softly to myself.

The one who yelled, "Jerry," sounded like my friend Douglas. The other Gerry, hoping someone was calling him, tried to turn and look over his shoulder. A strange sinking feeling came over me. He twisted further about, looking back up the hill, as he picked up speed. How could so much happen in just a few seconds? I called out, "Gerry! Turn around. He's calling me not you. Turn around!"

But he didn't turn around. He kept looking for the voice that called his name. All his twisting had subtly altered his path causing him to drift to the far left side of the street. In his path, where the hill flattened out stood a parked Model-T Ford. We were three quarters of the way down the hill when he gave up and faced foreword. Our eyes met in recognition as he turned his head. A second later he crashed into the only car parked on the block. I rolled off my sled in an effort to stop so I could go to him. Just then the screaming boys from the top of the hill came cascading through the air above us. Everyone on the slope scattered while I lay there, immobile, hoping I wouldn't be crushed. I watched as the silvery metal runners of six sleds landed all about me.

My father realizing that I must have just said something asked, "What did you say?"

"I just repeated what you said, that Eva was the happy one. Why did you say that? Was no one else happy?"

"When are you going to get me a new TV remote?"

I ignored his obvious attempt to change the subject. I knew I had pushed too hard into a forbidden area, but I was anxious for him to continue. I knew very little about Eva, only that she had died some years before I was born.

Just when I had thought his mind had shut down he began to speak again. "She was engaged to be married. In the spring. She was nineteen years old." He paused. "It was that winter. It had snowed a lot. She and her fiancé decided to go sleigh riding. 'It will be the last time I can do this,' she said. 'After I'm married I'll have to behave like a grown up.' But she didn't have a sled so I loaned her mine."

"Where did they go sleigh riding?" I knew the family had rented a house on North Main at that time, near Haledon Avenue. "Was it on Haledon Avenue?" I prodded.

"How you doing, Jerry? You got plenty of work? You know I got money if you need it. Anytime. I don't need it anymore."

"Thank you, Dad. We're okay. What about Eva?"

"Eva? What about Eva?"

"You said you loaned her your sled?"

"Oh yes. Did I tell you? They wanted to go sleigh riding for one last time before they got married. Did you ever meet her? She's really nice."

I got up, dragged my sled over to where Gerry was laying on his side in the snow in front of the car. His legs were jutting out into the roadway and he wasn't moving. His glasses were out in the street. I called his name. He didn't respond. I knelt down and rolled him on to his back to see how he was. There were two small trickles of blood coming from his nose. His eyes were almost closed, his head shoved down into his coat. On his forehead was a deep diamond shaped depression running from the bridge of his nose to his hairline that mirrored the bumper bolt on the Model T. His mouth was open and his top lip curled back. I rocked back on to my heels and froze. A few feet away the flying boys' club were goofing on each other, throwing snowballs, while the rest on the hill had gone back to sleigh riding. I looked around to see if anyone had seen what happened, to see if anyone was coming to help. I turned back to stare down at Gerry. I wanted so much to talk to him now, but he was so still.

A large hand came to rest on my shoulder. "How you doing, son?" said a gentle male voice. "My wife and I saw the whole thing from our living room across the street." He bent down to look at Gerry. "You can't stay here."

"I can't just leave him. I know him. He's in my class."

"There's not much you can do. You nearly got killed by those boys. Why'd you roll off your sled?"

I looked up. I couldn't tell him. Wouldn't let him know what my part had been in this thing that had happened. I hoped he couldn't guess. "I wanted to help him." I turned away to stare at Gerry again. Kids were still just whizzing by inches away. "We can't leave him like this," I said. "Someone might run into him."

"Oh yes. Did I tell you? They wanted to go sleigh riding for one last time before they got married."

"Yes, you did. What happened then?"

"They went down Jefferson Street from the top for their last run. Too fast. She lost control. Couldn't stop. She slid into the middle of Garfield Avenue in front of a car. That car stopped but there was another car behind that one. He was too close to stop so he went around the first car. He didn't know she was there." He stopped and looked up at me.

The man asked, "You alright? My wife's called for an ambulance. Why don't we move him out of the road so no one hits him. You need to help me. Can you do it?"

The man grabbed Gerry by the back of his coat collar supporting his head on his forearms and I got his feet so we could put him on his sled. I picked up his mangled glasses and laid them on his chest. Then we pulled him across the street onto the sidewalk in front of the man's porch. "Let me walk you home now."

I couldn't leave I told him. I needed to know. I just couldn't move. His wife brought out a blanket to cover Gerry.

"Do you know his last name?"

"No, just Gerry. He's in my class at Twelveses."

"Why don't you come into the house while we wait for the ambulance," said the woman. "You're shivering. I'll make you a cup of hot chocolate. Can I call your parents for you?"

"We don't have a phone," I lied. I sat in their living room looking out the window. The ambulance arrived. The man went out and talked to the attendants as the reckless flying club reappeared from the top of the hill. He pointed at the car and then at me in the window. The attendants handed the man's blanket back to him. They moved Gerry to a stretcher and covered him with a sheet. The attendants said something to the man. He shook his head no, turned and walked back toward his house as the men put Gerry in the ambulance and drove slowly away.

The strangest thing, I could never understand why no one else noticed anything unusual had happened, not even when the ambulance was there. I never saw Gerry again.

"It sounds like you were right there, Dad. Did you see it happen?" he didn't respond. He turned away from the TV screen to look at me. I repeated the question, but I already knew the answer.

"I was standing right on the corner just a few feet from her when she got crushed." His voice had turned impersonal, informational. He didn't leave a particle of space between sentences. "She was laid out in our living room. That's how they did it then. It was bad for my mother. Too hard on her. Eva was her favorite. She spent most nights until the funeral sitting by the coffin. She didn't cry. She didn't talk. The day of the funeral crowds of people turned out. The local policeman gave her an escort to the cemetery. Everybody knew her and loved her. She was the happy one."

"Let me walk you home," said the man.

"No thank you." I didn't want my parents to know. I sat silently in their living room finishing my hot chocolate, trying to understand what had happened. They walked me out on to the front porch. "You sure you're OK?" they asked.

I said yes and thanked them again without looking up. Gerry's new sled was leaning against the porch railing now. I crossed the street and walked to the corner of Jefferson and Garfield. I remember turning to look back up the hill, probably from the same place my father stood watching his sister come down the hill six years before I was born. It was nearly dark. There were still some kids sleigh riding. I walked down to North First Street, turned left and started for home. I never went back to Jefferson Street or anywhere else that winter to sleigh ride and I never said a word to anyone about Gerry.

Is it real when something really feels unreal? Always.

9

The Movies

Age 7–8

The theaters in the 1940s were more, the atmosphere was more, the movies were more, the glamour was more, the music was more, the magic was more, and it only cost a quarter.

JUST AFTER MY EIGHTH birthday in February 1947, I convinced my mother that I could cross North Main Street, something I had already been doing. I was allowed to cross side streets to see my friends, and my street occasionally to go to the store. But the really busy streets were off limits. Of course, I had been crossing them already. I just wanted to make it legal before her radar figured it out. The problem with my big street sneakiness was getting back home on time so my mother wouldn't get worried, or more likely, suspicious. Often she would add errands to my outings. If I got sloppy and lost track of the time, something I excelled at, and needed to get something from the store to bring home for supper, well I was afraid she'd call Dougie's house on our new six party telephone line and find out I wasn't there. That would be a big problem.

Besides, I had plans. The main reason I wanted to get permission—I wanted to go downtown to the movies by myself.

I loved the movies, the magical movies, on a screen so big you could get lost in stories of another world in an even more magical theater. It was a year since my last upgrade for street crossing around the neighborhood and I felt it was time for me to move on. As I was walking home from baseball one day I conjured up a subtle strategy.

"Mom, *Miracle on 34th Street* is playing downtown at the Fabian. I'd really like to see it. It's really supposed to be a good picture, with Margret O'Brian."

"Yes, I've heard that. Maybe. I'll talk to your father. See if we can afford a matinee."

I'd better start over. She doesn't get it.

"I think it's gonna be gone by this Sunday. Mary saw it and she said it was great. I could go by myself. It'd be cheaper that way." I said this really, really quickly, so she would say OK before she realized what was up.

Wrong. I could see from her face that the alarm bells were going off. My blitzkrieg tactic had failed. But I was prepared for this likely outcome so I switched to my second strategy, cool reasoning, to deal with her predictable classic "mother" response which went about like this—you're too young to go by yourself, you don't know how to cross big, busy streets downtown, it will cost too much, you'll get lost, and the finale, someone might kidnap you. And what, hold me for a big ransom?

No problem here. I said coolly and most reasonably, "I'm almost nine (in eight months I'd be nine), all my friends can go (a small fabrication—actually only Benny who was ten could go downtown by himself), I've been crossing all the big streets by myself since I was little," I confessed. I thought revealing some of my illicit behavior wasn't clever. But it was too late.

"I'll use my allowance. It won't cost you anything. I won't get lost because I only want to go to the Fabian theater. For now. It's near the last bus stop. I can outrun anyone that's trying to kidnap me." (I had just gotten a new pair of Keds.)

She had stopped ironing, and patiently waited me out, then simply said, "Mmmm, no," and went back to her ironing. Then she added, "And no more crossing Haledon Ave." *What? She just took away something I'm already now allowed to do! This is going backward!*

My father had gotten home from work early and was quietly standing behind me in the back hallway. He had been listening to the whole exchange. "Tell me, if we let you go to the Fabian how would you get there?" As he said this as he went to stand next to my mother. He smiled knowingly at her.

It was a test and I was prepared. "I'll get the number twenty-two bus at the bus stop down the street, or the number fourteen, ride it to the back of city hall and get out there. The Fabian is only a block away, so I'd cross Colt Street, walk one block down Ellison to Church and cross over to the other side. They're both quiet side streets. The Fabian is only a half block up Church toward Market. It only costs a quarter in the afternoon. That's when I'll be going. I can use my allowance to buy the ticket. It won't cost you anything." All this I said in one long dwindling breath. I had rehearsed this speech a number of times that afternoon and felt pretty cocky that I had nailed it.

"I don't know, your mother thinks someone might try to steal you."

"It's only a block away from the bus, Mom!"

"I'm very impressed," he said. "You covered everything. I think it would be alright with me. How 'bout you Roselyn?" She wrinkled up her face, shrugged her shoulders. "There's only one major thing that doesn't work. Do you know what it is?"

I had no idea what he was suggesting, so I just stared back at him.

"You forgot the money you need for the bus. Five cents each way. You're ten cents short. Where you gonna get the extra money? When you figure that out, you can go to the Fabian on your own, but just the Fabian. The other streets are too dangerous for you to cross by yourself."

Ten cents wasn't so much, but I didn't want to do extra chores. I had a busy social life, and of course homework to do. The solution proved to be simple, though it took me several days to think it up. If I only went to the movies once or twice a month I could save my weekly allowance without the need to scale back on my other activities, except the occasional ice cream cone or my peculiar passion for kosher dill pickles that I bought at Joosten's deli on the way home from school. And so, at the end of June in 1947, it came to pass that I started to go downtown on my own to the Fabian theater.

I missed *Miracle on 34th Street* which had been released in May. (I didn't see it until the late fifties on TV. Instead I saw a western,

Cheyenne with Dennis Morgan and Jane Wymann. I also saw *Key Largo* and *The African Queen* at the Fabian.

The Fabian was one of those fabled old theaters that transported you into a world of elegance and drama unimaginable in today's multiplex rabbit hutches. I had been there many times with my parents, but had never actually looked at the theater until I went there by myself. And what an extraordinary experience that was.

It was a weekday matinee, not very crowded. Shows started at 1:00 p.m. Most theaters then showed two feature films—an A film and a B film—also a newsreel, a cartoon, coming attractions and sometimes a short. These programs ran in a continuous loop so you could go in at any time and stay on to see anything you might have missed. I hated being late. The thrill of the Fabian for me was the total experience. Getting there well before the first movie of the day started. This I always did solo. I think it was when I started on this movie odyssey that I realized that I needed to go by myself. You might speculate that it had something to do with being an only child, which means spoiled, but of course I don't think so. I found that going to this fragile, fantasy universe was easily destroyed by being with someone that might be a fidgeter, a compulsive foot swinger kicking the seat in front of them, a chronic talker, or loud chewer that needed to have a copious supply of popcorn and candy to rummage around in throughout the entire show. Even when I went alone I sometimes sat in the last row to reduce the chances of anyone bothering me, breaking my concentration. I had stopped going to the Friday afternoon movies at my school because the other kids were too noisy.

Once I was persuaded by my friend Eugene to go to the State Theater, originally the Orpheum, a vaudeville house, but at the time I went it was a down and nearly out movie house that showed a special kids show on Saturday afternoons, usually two B movies, ten cartoons, two or three shorts like *The Cisco Kid* or *Buck Rogers*, and coming attractions. The show started at 1:00 p.m. and got out at six—five hours of screaming, and thrashing, magic destroying bedlam. I never went back.

As soon as I passed the ticket booth at the Fabian I became a different being. I had no choice nor did I want one. The Fabian was meant to take everyone out of their everyday, everyman life. It was a palace, a cathedral, and a time machine. The first space you entered was the barrel vaulted, gilt molded, intricate terrazzo floored lobby. Large paintings hung on flocked wallpaper. Crystal chandeliers lit the space. Wide marble steps led up to the loggia and balcony and box seats. When you entered the theater itself, a white gloved usherette in a daring Roxy Theater pantsuit greeted you and asked you where you would like to sit, then led you down a plush carpeted isle by flashlight. If you arrived early, and I always did, the theater was brightly lit by enormous crystal chandeliers, in a 3,500 seat space, even more richly decorated than the lobby. About a half hour before the first movie began the lights would dim to spotlight a large organ in front of the stage. There were no crass hair salon ads or auto sales pitches. No requests to shut off cell phones, or prompts to hurry up and get your thirty-two ounce soda and stale popcorn before the show. No loud, third rate, recorded music. Just live music on the large organ, played by a real person.

There was a full size stage capable of theatrical productions and vaudeville, which had once been a part of this venue when the theater opened in 1925. At the start of the show a heavy curtain would be drawn up into a series of scalloped swags beneath the arched shape of the proscenium. Then as the organ music faded a second gossamer curtain would part to reveal the screen and so the show would begin. It was a totally irresistible fantasy and I loved every bit of it.

For the next three years I finagled the money for as many matinees as possible, a process that nearly took over my life. Eventually I got my parents to raise my allowance in exchange for more help around the house, which meant I could go to the movies more often. And I did. Sometimes two times a weekend, but only if I could finagle my way out of the extra help. By now my finagling had become a fine art form.

In all there were eight theaters in Paterson in the forties, all large, not as elegant, nor quite as big as the Fabian, but thriving. The Garden, down near the train station on Market Street, is where I saw my first horror movie, a rerun of the 1931 *Dracula*, starring Bella Lugosi. One of the few times I wished I had gone with someone. I spent most of the movie on my knees between two rows peering fearfully between seat backs at the horror on the screen.

Eventually I did go to all the other theaters. At the US Theater on upper Main Street, I saw Danny Kaye in *A Connecticut Yankee in King Arthur's Court*. I think I saw *Abbot and Costello Meet Frankenstein* at the Fabian. I don't think I went to the Rivoli on the corner of Main and Broadway often, but I saw the comic movie *The Great Rupert* with Jimmy Durante there. Why I remember those two silly films of Danny Kay and Jimmy Durante doesn't seem sensible. Danny Kaye was always Danny Kaye and Durante was always The Schnoz, but there they are stuck in my brain. There was another film that's forever and to a degree, embarrassingly stuck there—*The Wizard of Oz*. It played at the Regent Theater. I can't recall what the Reagent looked like. It was on an alley between Hamilton and Veteran Streets. There was a long lobby entry, not as elegant as the Fabian but I liked it. In August 1939, six months after I was born, Oz was released, with Judy Garland, Ray Bolger, Jack Haley, and Bert Lahr. It was just a modest box office winner when first released. In 1949, when it was rereleased I thought it was just another kids' movie. I got there halfway through the one o'clock show, which I never would have done had it been a film I was really excited about seeing. Then I sat through two more full showings, not leaving the theater until six o'clock, got home too late for supper and was grounded the next day. During the next three weeks I saw *Oz* (can I admit this?) sixteen times. I did whatever it took short of theft to get the money. I'm not even sure how I managed it time wise. It was summer, so there was no school to contend with. And what I told my parents is also lost to time, but by then they were used to me disappearing all day. This was my very own, cult, *Rocky Horror Picture Show*, though going in character was not an option at that time. But I was partial to the scarecrow.

Directly across the street from the US Theater was the Majestic, originally a large vaudeville theater. In the forties its shows consisted of a movie followed by five vaudeville acts. I had no idea what vaudeville was, but a Roy Rogers western drew me there. It was a winter afternoon. Only a few people were in the audience, maybe five in all including myself. After Roy, his horse Trigger, and Dale Evans, in that order of importance, left the screen the house lights came up. I thought the show must be over. Since there were so few people in the theater I had moved down near the front to be closer to the screen. As I stood to leave a curtain descended to conceal the stage. No one else in the theater moved. Then a man walked out in front of the curtain and said something. The other patrons applauded. I sat down. This was to be my very first live theater experience. I had no idea what to expect but was charged with excitement. The curtain drew back and a man, perhaps in his fifties, walked out on the stage with an arm full of hoops and bowling pins and began to juggle them. He dropped a few. No one seemed to mind. Then he finished, and left the stage without a sound or response from anyone. That seemed strange. Was it like church, irreverent to applaud? The man in the suit reappeared, told us how good the juggler was then introduced the next act. Something with dogs and a monkey. Then a couple came out carrying suit cases and performed magic tricks. He had on a three-piece suit, a tie, a top hat and spats, she wore a skimpy bathing suit and a tiara.

Again no one applauded. I looked back at the house to see if I was alone, to see how I was supposed to respond. My first live theater did not feel exciting or captivating. I was feeling deadly earnest, or restless, or perhaps apprehensive. It felt like I was halfway through a church service. All I could think about was getting outside to take a deep, clean breath of cold, crisp air. The fourth act was a standup comic. He too had on a three-piece suit with a rumpled fedora hat. The suit was badly stained, all the cuffs frayed. He was the featured act so we were told. The man stood absolutely still, told one liner jokes, pausing after each one, waiting, a bit too long, then told another. Silence. And another… Not one sound, one laugh or even a snicker emerged from out of the far-flung few that sat immobilized throughout the bright cavernous theater. I again turned, hoping to see if anyone could give me a clue, some indication of how to respond. There was a man about ten seats away several rows back. His elbows rested on the arms of his seat, his hands templed in front of him. He briefly looked at me then back to the stage. Another joke ended. Silence. And again…dead silence. Someone toward the back coughed.

It was not earnestness, nor restlessness or apprehension I felt. It was a terrible empathetic sadness for the humiliation of the person onstage. This wasn't live theater, this was some kind of awful reality. I couldn't watch any longer, and I didn't have the nerve to leave. So for the second time in my movie going life I sank down between two rows of seats and hid myself from this, a very live horror show. There was another act but I couldn't watch. I stayed where I was until I was sure everyone had started to leave. I promised myself never to go back to the Majestic again.

Certain thrills can only come once in your life. For me, my first pair of long pants met that level of delight, first time boy adventures, learning to sing harmony, and then the first time I made love—and I was in love too. That was much later. But nothing, nothing else in my childhood ever came close to that special magic I felt, on my own, at the movies.

10

Guardian Angel
Age 8

I have worried this guardian angel thing like a dog with a bone. What did it mean? I'd been told everything happens for a good reason. Right?

BEING OF LOW RESOLVE or absent minded, I did go to the Majestic again and broke every one of my movie rules. First of all, I went with Billy Vanderbrink, a new boy in the neighborhood that I had an off and on friendship with because my best friend, Mary, didn't like him. He lived on the other side of her house. He was a fidgeter and a talker. We sat near the front of the theater. We shared a bag of popcorn. I had a Coke, and several boxes of Raisinets. Just before the vaudeville acts began I became ill and ran outside. A half-hour later Billy joined me. Asked how I was. He went back inside and got me a drink of water from the fountain. I asked how he liked the acts.

"I should have left when you did. That Vaudeville stuff is weird."

Mary was wrong about him. He was nice and the only one I went to the movies with. The last time was at the US Theater on Main Street to see *Captain From Castile*, a seventeenth century swashbuckler staring Tyrone Power, fleeing the Spanish Inquisition to Mexico during the destruction of the Aztec Culture. Plenty of action including an erupting volcano. After the show was over we decided to walk home instead of taking the bus. As we moved down lower Main Street reliving the movie, we realized that a large boy was following us. We sped up. He sped up. We went down Water Street instead of turning down North Main—at that time both streets terminated at the Main Street Bridge—thinking we might throw him off. It seemed to work. So we turned up a cross street to bring us back to North Main. He was waiting for us, jumped out in front of us waving his fists in our faces. Neither Billy nor I knew who he was yet he knew our names. Completely caught off guard the two of us froze. He wanted to fight us. Why? We didn't know. Who was he? We just stood there befuddled as he started to swing at us. The most we could manage was to duck under his windmill swings.

"I wouldn't do that," said a strange voice off to the right.

The three of us turned to see an even larger, older teenage boy standing about ten feet away. I'd no idea who this second boy was either. I studied his face hoping to find something, anything, familiar. Nothing. He returned my look then turned toward the stalker. "I don't want you to ever threaten or bother Jerry again."

He knew my name! Didn't use Billy's name or seem to include him in his remarks. Who was this person?

"Go home now Jerry." Gesturing at the stalker he said, "I'll hold him here for a while to make sure he doesn't follow you." Turning back to the other boy, "If you ever bother him again I'll come after you."

Billy and I turned and walked away. We were completely mystified.

"What was that all about?" asked Billy.

"I don't know. I have no idea. NO idea."

"Did you know those boys?"

"Never saw them before!" I said. "You?"

"Nah."

And we never saw them again.

It would be less disturbing if everything happened for a good reason. Boring, but less disturbing.

11

The First Television Set

Age 9

"All God does is watch us and kill us when we get boring.
We must never, ever be boring."
—*Chuck Palahniuk,* Invisible Monsters

YOU CAN'T BEGIN TO imagine what it was like. The madness. We were like chimpanzees looking in a mirror for the first time. We even watched channel 11 out of New York telecast a Yule log fire for hours on Christmas Eve.

In the forties, if you wanted to watch television you had to go to a saloon. No one, well no one I knew, had a television set in their home. Our first television arrived sometime in 1948. My father had quit Dugan's Bakery and had started a floor finishing business. One of his customers owed him a large final payment so he settled up by giving my father what was dubiously described as a brand new, latest, just out of the box, push button Halicrafters television set. The set, 2' high x 3' long x 2' deep, with a seven-inch screen, required two men to carry it.

My father and the set arrived home without warning one afternoon as my mother was preparing supper. Where to put it immediately became a problem. The living room was out. We only used that room when we had company. The dining room was also out for the same reason. The kitchen, where we spent most of our time, was deemed the only suitable place, if rearranged. Disregarding supper preparations, my father and his partner nudged Roselyn aside, pushed the white

Formica table, set with dishes, against the wall and piled the chrome chairs up against the front of the icebox, carried in the buffet from the dining room and placed the TV set on it amid my mother's toppled collection of ceramic elves from Ireland.

"I'll bet we're the first people in this neighborhood to have a TV set in their house," my father announced.

"I'll say!" said his wife in a pejorative tone, just like her mother and father did when being sarcastic. She was struggling to free herself from the furniture logjam on the far side of the kitchen.

The set got plugged in and the rabbit ears antenna attached. My mother rushed to the rescue of her elves, which thwarted the two men, impatient to see if we could receive the five channels out of New York City. "You're acting like two little boys," she said to them. Actually she should have included me since I was just as eager as the two men. She was taking her time gathering the little ceramic creatures. Before she could step away an arm reached around her and switched the set on. Everything worked but with a fair amount of off and on snow. It was chaos. One person kept moving the antenna about in an attempt to reduce the snow. Another person's hand was changing channels. My mother, back from rescuing her elves, joined in the mayhem, turning random knobs in an attempt to adjust the picture contrast while the volume deafened us all. A short while before the afternoon had been progressing calmly toward dinner. Now all the adults were crazed and the simmering supper sat forgotten on the stove. Squeezed out of the way I left the room for the more peaceful environment of my jigsaw puzzle on the dining room table, while listening for sounds of success.

At first, it was just a few neighbors and ourselves, mesmerized in front of this box each night after supper. The small screen required the kind of intimacy usually associated with two lovers in a darkened theater. Not an appealing situation for a nine-year-old. It was the beginning of TV frenzy.

Every night saw an increase in curious neighbors and seldom seen relatives eager to add to the human heap in front of the postage stamp screen. We were now eating earlier so we could get the table out of the way and set up chairs in time for the big evening crush. Every straight-back chair we had plus several others that people brought with them were arranged in two rows. Someone suggested that it would be nice if we had popcorn. And soda, someone else added. So my mother obligingly made popcorn after super while my father rearranged the room.

The seven-inch screen was literally that. Anyone farther away than three feet couldn't see anything more than a vague, quivering, black and white glow, which forced everyone to crowd up against the front row. This, on hot summer nights. was like a group orgy in an airless closet.

What we needed, someone suggested, was one of those new magnifying lenses that mounted in front of the picture tube. There were now regular viewers we'd never seen before, in our kitchen, every night. The lens my father bought cost about $20.00, a lot when you realize that the monthly rent for our five-room apartment was twenty-five dollars.

The lens was ten inches by ten inches, a state-of-the-art plastic magnifying glass designed to mount in front of any television set, which meant there was no easy way to install it on any set. Everyone was delighted with the addition except my father who was still working on the installation one night, when everyone began to arrive. He stood there in front of the TV with an assortment of tools scattered on the buffet and protruding from his pockets, rummaging through a jumble of mounting parts, while casting franticly through several pages of installation instructions. It was Tuesday night. Everyone was there to see the new Milton Berle Show, which came on at eight o'clock. The show was a phenomenon. Mundane life vanished for that hour-long, magical odyssey. There were now fifteen chairs needed.

The show opened each week with three men dressed as gas station attendants (a now extinct practice—no uniforms and absolutely no attendants exist anywhere today, except in New Jersey, but no uniforms) singing the Texaco theme song—"We are the men from Texaco. We work from Maine to Mexico to bring you…." which finished just as my father completed the installation and stepped aside. We all gasped.

The magnifying glass had democratized the screen. Now the people in the back row could see Uncle Miltie's facial expressions, only slightly distorted by the wacky plastic lens, as well as anyone sitting in the front row. However, the outer inch of the lens elongated and compressed all images passing along the edge of the screen. If your seat was far to the right or left you saw only half of the picture. It meant that if you wanted a good undistorted view you had to come earlier than anyone else. Thus, people started to arrive as we cleared the supper table. They were polite enough to stand to the side while we set up the chairs. Thank you.

Color television was far off in the distant future, but this didn't stop anyone longing for that day's arrival, and it did arrive one day with the help of one of our mystery watchers. The funhouse quality of our magnified screen was about to undergo a radical transformation with the latest technological development available, the application of a triple colored transparent film made to fit the magnifying lens perfectly, with the top third colored sky blue, the middle third red, and the bottom portion acid green. Who could say no to a total stranger's, no-strings generosity? As evening guests began to arrive a soft murmur of concern evolved into an almost universal agreement of great intensity. The color improvement had to go. It made Uncle Miltie look ill, his head blue, his body red and his legs bilious green. Truth be told, the lens too was useless unless you were, as I said, directly in front of the set. This meant a person, had to come earlier than anyone else to get a good seat. Really earlier. Now people were showing up before supper. That was the limit for my mother.

"Take the magnifying lens off," she said as my father walked through the kitchen door after work one night.

"The lens works perfectly," my father insisted, "when you're directly in front of the set and I like the color." He was trying to protect his investment and not hurt the feelings of the color giver.

"Before anyone gets here tonight?" my father asked.

"Before anyone gets here before supper."

Within a few days the audience dwindled to a handful and a short while later the push button channel changer broke, leaving the set stuck on black and white snowy static. Too heavy to remove by himself, my father shoved the set to one end of the buffet where it sat as a useless, lone bookend. I was relieved. I preferred life without TV to hordes of disgruntled presumptuous strangers in our house every night.

It just so happened that Charlie's Bar and Grill right next store had just gotten a new ten-inch TV set. I really liked the owners, Charlie and Molly Schwartz, and their two sons. The boys were in their late teens. We occasionally played shuffleboard together in the bar. I suppose, technically, because of my age, I shouldn't have been there, but this was our neighborhood bar, not a sleazy dive. It seemed more like a grown-up version of an ice cream parlor than a saloon. It was a place where everyone knew one another. Afternoons were always slow. In the summer the door would stand open, inviting a splotch of afternoon sunlight into the unlit, wood-paneled interior. The only other light was from the hanging lamps over the shuffleboard table, that took up the whole right side of the room. The bar ran the full length of the left wall, starting just a few feet in from the entry door. When your eyes grew accustomed to the duskiness you could see there were also dim lights behind the bar. There was a large front window admitting little daylight because it was filled with neon beer signs and made opaque by decades of cigarette smoke. There were two tables under the window, with middle of the room was left open for dancing. On the back wall were two doors and the jukebox. I truly loved this jukebox.

Not many places that I knew of then had one. We had a small radio in our living room, but no record player. Whenever I was at the bar I would put a nickel in the machine and ask to hear the Mills Brothers' record, and you did have to ask. There were no records in this jukebox. It looked like one but it was actually a kind of telephone. You deposited your money in the machine. Then an operator would come on and ask what song you wanted to hear. "I wanna hear 'Paper Doll' by the Mills Brothers," I would say. "Thank-que sir. Here's your seeelection," and the song would be played. I liked that she called me sir.

One warm summer day my father got home early from work and suggested we go next door to play shuffleboard. There were only a few regular customers present—barflies, my mother called them—so no one in the bar objected to my presence. My father got a beer and we played a few games then we took a break. He went to the bar for another beer and I stayed at the table practicing my aim with the weights. As usual in the afternoon, Molly was on the bar.

"You want a birch beer?" Molly called out to me.

"Sure," I said. I loved Boylan's Birch Beer, and they had it on tap.

She beckoned for me to come over to the bar. "Sit up here." She pointed to a stool at the far end of the bar. "Let's see what's on TV for you."

I looked around in amazement. I had never sat at the bar. It was something kids weren't allowed to do. I wasn't supposed to be in a bar at all. I looked over at my father for approval, and then the three all day regulars on the stools. It seemed OK with them too. Molly switched on the TV as I climbed onto the stool where I sat sipping a soda, eating free pretzels and watched *Uncle Fred's* show that was mostly old *Farmer Gray* cartoons, made in the twenties. In the glory days of the seven inch Halicrafters I hadn't known about afternoon kids' shows. Our set never got turned on until after supper. I thanked Molly.

"You can come back any time you want," she said. And so I did. I became a regular—fourth afternoon barfly.

I liked my special privilege, but being of a somewhat gregarious nature I discovered that drinking alone at a bar wasn't to my liking. So I asked Molly if I could bring Mary with me the next time. My best friend Mary lived on the other side of Charlie's.

"Sure," said Molly, "bring her along."

Mary was delighted with my invitation and seized upon this opportunity to display her talent for drama.

"I'll see you there at four o'clock," I said.

"Oh no! Come and call for me about three forty-five. That's what boys are supposed to do for a date."

God. She was always instructing me on etiquette, and besides, who said this was a formal date? I just wanted some company at the bar.

"And no play clothes Jerry," she yelled after me.

Ugh. I hated it when she switched into her mature-woman-in-control persona. The next day, after school, I came home and changed into pressed, gray corduroy pants and my new maroon argyle patterned pull over shirt with its elastic waist and my polished school shoes. At 3:45 p.m., I was at Mary's house. Normally I would have gone around back to the kitchen door, but moving in the spirit of Mary's commanding vision I rang the front doorbell. Nellie, Mary's aunt, answered the door.

"Come in. Mary's almost ready for your date. Wait here on the porch." She had that the-children-are-being-so-cute-look on her face.

Date! Who said anything about a date? She told her aunt Nellie we had a date? Maybe drinking alone wasn't so bad. Her bedroom was just off the glassed in front porch where I sat waiting. I could hear her banging around in her room for fifteen minutes.

At 4:05 p.m., twenty minutes late, she appeared, "I'm ready to go," she said as she slipped her hand inside my arm and indicated that I should open the door. This was really, really too much. She was presumptuous, bossy and dressed in her Sunday church clothes, complete with white pump shoes, a small pill box hat and white cloth gloves. When we entered the bar Molly's face lit up with the same quirky expression Nellie's face had worn.

We were so cute. I *hated* being cute. It made me feel like an insect pinned to a mounting board. We walked to the TV at the end of the bar and climbed onto the stools. Molly poured out two Birch beers, switched the channel to the cartoons and settled back to watch us be cute. When we left the bar, Mary told me to get her tomorrow at the same time. Mary assumed that the date arrangement was permanent.

Something had to change. After several onerous days of dates and considerable thought, I came upon a perfect solution. I asked Molly if I could bring someone else to watch cartoons too. I felt that I was asking too much of Molly, but to my relief, she agreed happily. Of course I asked another boy, the boy Mary loved to hate, Billy Vanderbrink. Why she hated him I never knew for sure, something he said was all I ever got out of her. But it was a deep-seated hate. It's what made Billy the perfect choice. I explained to Billy what was up with Mary.

He was thrilled for the chance to help me out and maybe get back at her. I really didn't want to hurt Mary but I wasn't ready for white gloves, fancy hats and being cute.

We needed a plan. One that would let me off the hook. Billy thought he should be at the bar watching TV when Mary and I got there—not say or do anything weird, just be there. I held the door open for Mary. We walked to the end of the bar. Mary stopped dead when she saw who was seated there. Two sodas were waiting for us on the bar. I climbed up onto the stool next to Billy and said hi. She was standing a few feet away. I asked her if she was going to watch cartoons with us. She took the next seat down the bar, and drank her soda. Billy said hi. She didn't say a word. After two days Mary stopped coming. She also stopped talking to me. For a long time. Oh well. At least I wasn't cute anymore.

During the next month the half hour of *Farmer Gray* cartoons got extended to more cartoon shows: *Felix the Cat*, *Betty Boop* and *Captain Video and His Video Rangers*. With Molly's permission there were now four boys seated at the bar knocking back sodas and eating pretzels. The three afternoon regulars got pushed farther down the bar toward the front door as the room took on the atmosphere of a party for a bunch of nine-year-olds pretending to be grown-up.

It must have been contagious, for the all-day barflies got caught up in the buzz as well, and came to life, laughing at and goofing on the cartoons with us, in this possibly first ever in the world Happy Hour at a bar for kids. And, for anyone else as long as they liked *Farmer Gray* cartoons and drinking only soda. Molly wouldn't serve any alcohol while we were there. This only lasted a few weeks. The cartoons were old, scratchy, films with repetitive stories and garbled sound. The novelty wore off, and the spring weather was too nice to keep us sitting in a darkened room. Eventually, I was the only kid there, though only intermittently. Molly never said no to me. I'd walk through the front door like a regular customer, except I never had to pay. By the time I got to the back end of the bar a birch beer soda and pretzels would be waiting, and the TV switched to cartoons. It wasn't the TV that kept me coming back. It was the calm and peacefulness in the bar and

Molly's smiling face. If she wasn't busy she'd turn down the sound and we'd talk a bit, about school, the neighborhood, events in the news. I ignored the TV. I liked my time with Molly better.

With the arrival of TV we no longer sat on the front porch on warm evenings visiting with our neighbors as they passed by on their way to the ice cream parlor.

12

Mrs. Levy's Class

Age 9–10, Fifth Grade

There comes a time in childhood when you must acknowledge the adult world's intrusive existence. When you must helplessly look it straight in the eye and are compelled to ask, why me? And the answer seems to be? It's your turn.

I F PATERSON, NEW JERSEY, were dropped into any state west of the Mississippi River it would be the second largest city in that state." This was Mrs. Levy's dramatic tactic for teaching geography to her fifth grade class. She seemed to enjoy creating curious comparisons and unusual images, which she believed would stick in the easily distracted minds of her students. But in my case, this technique proved to be too stimulating. I sat there picturing her words as literal events.

The Enola Gay, the bomber of Hiroshima fame, had just taken off from a secret airfield in Caldwell, New Jersey. It circled the field several times trying to gain altitude. The payload it was carrying was unique and more enormous than any in the history of aviation. It was the entire city of Paterson, including the Passaic River and the Great Falls.

Mrs. Levy's lesson and I parted company somewhere in the skies over New Jersey. She went on about Paterson being number three in size in New Jersey while I flew on toward a mysterious destination in the west.

We were only a few miles from our target but still had not reached a high enough altitude from which to escape safely when the payload was released. The super-fortress strained against the wind and all odds. The drag from the huge payload was terrible, causing the airplane to shutter. I wondered if the silk cords tethered to the bomber would outlast the strain. Then the plane suddenly lurched upward as the city of Paterson slipped away toward its final destination.

I sat there at my desk picturing the entire city falling, spinning at an odd angle from the sky, landing like a bolt out of the blue upon some prairie cornfield, like Dorothy and Toto's house in the Wizard of Oz. My mind was always set loose by Mrs. Levy's lessons in geography. What if Paterson were to land in Kansas, I wondered? Would it still keep its spectacular waterfall? Would the silk mills then weave with corn silk?

There was always a deep red smudge on Mrs. Levy's coffee cup. It came from the fashionably unnatural, dark red lipstick, that coated her mouth, from which also came a dark, booming voice. It was a voice that could liquefy your internal organs from across the school playground.

On the first day she said, "You may sit anywhere you wish.'" With that voice it seemed like a command, not a choice.

"Wow!" I thought. "This was unheard of freedom!"

It was an age when desks were bolted to the floor in straight rows. I chose to sit in the back of the room with the rest of my friends.

"If you don't behave though," she added, "you will have your seat changed."

She had set aside three seats in the front of the room for this purpose. The one directly in front of her desk was reserved for the most disruptive among us. We all looked about trying to guess which one would be moved first. It was Sammy Voss. With great exasperation, Mrs. Levy changed his seat to the left of her desk. This came as no surprise to anyone. Whatever was in Sammy's mind was soon out of his mouth. Next was Henry Vigliano, for fighting. He got the seat to the right of her desk. After this, life in our classroom settled down and the last seat in front of the teacher's desk went empty.

Though the threat was still clear and present, no one seemed destined to sit there. The desk got covered with books and school supplies.

Mrs. Levy was a short, energetic woman. She wore her crinkly hair in a manner that made her look like the Egyptian Sphinx. But unlike the Sphinx, she had her nose. A rather large one, which supported a pair of yellowish brown, heavy, horn-rimmed glasses. Her shoulders were made large, humped and square by the shoulder pads in her dresses, which in turn made her look neckless. The shape of her fabulous deep red lipstick had little to do with the actual shape of her mouth. When you were close you could see how she had drawn two tall points on her upper lip with lip liner just under her magnificent nose. This, coupled with her kluge horn voice, was formidable. She would have been a force to reckon with except for one small detail—a small abnormality, but one that could not be ignored. Mrs. Levy spit continuously whenever she spoke.

"Chil (spit) dren! This (spit) year the (spit) fifth (spit) grade classes (spit) have been select (spit) ed to (spit) present (spit) a musical play about Columbus (spit) Day for the rest (spit) of the school (spit)."

I never could understand why every sentence always ended with a terminal spray regardless of the final consonant sound. It was just another of life's mysteries. She went on to explain that our class had to provide a student to sing some solo pieces. Mrs. Levy's classes were known for their musical abilities. Every day she would have us sing old-fashioned standards like "The Old Mill Stream," or the "Ash Grove." It just so happened that along with Scrabble, street skating, and sleeping in church, I loved singing. I had an ear for music and a clear, high-boy's soprano voice. My mother too loved to sing and also had a beautiful soprano voice. Her mother, Ada, sang alto, and between the two of them they taught me how to sing harmony. It was a delicious feeling to sense the shape of the sound in your mind and hear how it could fit into the space around the other voices. When the harmony was true you heard an over tone as if another person had joined the singing. I liked singing more than anything else really, but I'd rather have died than let my friends in the back of the room know this.

Spitting all the way, Mrs. Levy continued, "We're going to select the singer for the performance by having every one of you sing the first few lines of "God Bless America" by yourself. She began at the row nearest the door. I was six kids back. The first two children were too nervous to sing at all. After a few whispered notes she thanked them and told them it was fine but too timid. All my friends were snickering.

"This is girl stuff," whispered Douglas, "boys don't do that."

I was snickering along with the best of them. What was I to do? She was getting closer. I had slouched down behind the huge hulk of Rodger Parks, who sat at the desk in front of mine, in the hope that she would not notice me. *No! I can't sing, not with all my friends here! They'll murder me.* I was panicked. *OK, I'll sing off key. I'll pretend I don't know the words... I'LL REFUSE.* I sank down further in my seat and made believe I didn't hear her. *If I don't make eye contact with her she'll skip over me.*

I lapsed into my days spent in Rose of Sharon Tree, doing bird imitations, pretending I was invisible. I tried to slouch through the bottom of my seat.

"Do you know the words?"

Anyone who had listened to the radio then knew the song that had made Kate Smith so famous. I nodded yes. That was my first mistake.

"Well, begin then," she demanded.

My next mistake was fatal. I opened my mouth with every intention of failing miserably. What came out was my clear, high, boy soprano voice. The song took me over. The feeling of threading the melody and words together was irresistible. I sang as I always sang, for the total pleasure of it. Without my being aware Mrs. Levy had stealthily moved down the aisle. It would have shown some consideration for me if she had cleared her throat or taken a deep breath before taking action. Instead she threw her head back, pointed her faux ruby red lips at the ceiling and boomed, "He's a bird! A bird! He sings like a bird!"

WHAT HAD I DONE? I glanced quickly around the room. All my friends looked stricken.

"Did you hear class (spit)? He sings like a bird. High up in a tree!" The words and saliva rained down on me like a withering storm.

Oh! Damn that tree, and those bird impersonations too. Where had Mrs. Levy been all those many years ago when I was sitting in the Rose of Sharon tree in front of my house pretending to be a bird? I needed her approval then when I was four years old. Not now! Having her approval now was like getting a bad case of poison ivy.

"Do you know 'April Showers?' That's my favorite song," she said.

How ridiculously appropriate—a spitting teacher that liked "April Showers." *Was this a joke? Why had the universe suddenly chosen this moment to focus all of its attention on ME?* I opened my mouth and the word "yes," fell out. It was a song that Al Jolson sang. My grandmother had taught it to me. My tormentor grabbed me by the arm and dragged me to the front of the room.

"Sing 'April Showers' (spit) for the class, please. Sing it now."

I stood there, helpless, my glasses speckled with saliva, and sang the song, "Though April showers, may come your way, they bring the flowers that bloom in May..." And on and on, through every verse and chorus.

"That's wonderful," she shrieked. "Now come with me. Henry, you monitor the class."

Henry lovingly picked up Mrs. Levy's black board pointer. It was an opportunity for him to transfer the tyranny of his home life onto someone else.

Down the hall we went to Mrs. Saunders classroom. I waited outside the door while Mrs. Levy spoke to her. I was relieved to be away from the startled faces in my own room.

Mrs. Levy motioned for me to come into the room.

What is she up to? I was so naive.

"I want you to sing 'April Showers' for this class Jerry."

If ever there was a time I needed to be invisible, that time had come.

The bewildered class sat there with the same amazed, goofy, dumbstruck looks on their faces that my own class had shown me. I finished the song by looking at the clock over their heads on the back wall. In another forty minutes school would be over. The two teachers "Oooohed" and "Ahhhed," delightedly and applauded when I finished. I had never, in all my nine years, conceived of a torture to equal this. *Why? Why is this happening?* My life was in shambles. We continued the tour for several more classes so they too could hear that song come out of my mouth. I wished never to look anyone in the eye again. As it turned out my wish was partially granted. When we returned to our classroom Mrs. Levy explained to the class that I would be sitting in the front of the room at the desk she had always reserved for that very special student amongst us.

Yeah, I thought, where she would, no doubt, shower more blessings upon me throughout the rest of the year.

People ooohed and ahhhed over my cuteness, and good behavior, and then my singing from the time I was a toddler until I was in high school. In retaliation, I have created a mental list of exquisite tortures for each adult that accosted me with their kvelling. Even though I must wait until the afterlife, I'm coming for you Mrs. Levy.

13

Henry

Age 9

The difference between a real war and a personal one is...

THE SPIRITUAL HAVEN OF my young consumer's soul was Max Specter's store down the street. One side of the store was a ho-hum sandwich shop. The other half was devoted to everything a boy could wish for, a large selection of comic books, an area of board games, picture puzzles, model boat and airplane kits, cap pistols and BB guns. Most of the store's depth was divided by a tall row of magazine racks, greeting card, and stationary cabinets so placed, that a boy, in particular this boy, could sit on the floor behind those cabinets covertly reading comic books. Only if certain precautions were taken. If you stood outside on the sidewalk by the showcase window to the left of the entry you could watch to see if Mr. Specter was at the cash register in the front of the store. If he wasn't, you stood a good chance of sneaking in behind the card cases without being seen. I wasn't the only kid to do this. It wasn't something I did often, just enough so I could hold my head up with the other kids. Besides, it was uncomfortable sitting cross-legged on the floor, plus the fear of getting caught cut into that reading experience.

I really loved all of Specter's. It had a classic soda fountain, a white marble counter, mahogany wood paneling to the ceiling, chrome and red leather stools, six tall very private booths, and lots of chrome and stainless steel gizmos to make every imaginable combination of ice cream and sundae toppings.

My preference was to sit at the far end of the counter and order either a hot fudge sundae with chocolate ice cream, dry walnuts, malt dust and whipped cream (no cherry) or a chocolate malt with a double deep of ice cream at thirty-five cents each. I could only afford this once in a while if I did extra jobs for my grandparents, or was careful with my allowance, which wasn't easy considering my two main passions—the movies and building Strombecker solid wood models of WWII fighter planes and bombers.

I had just checked out the new model kits Specter had gotten in and was eating my usual hot fudge sundae while lusting after my next model. I had completed the B-17 Flying Fortress and the B-25 Liberator bomber models, which were hanging from my bedroom ceiling below day glow stars, and was now scheming to find a way to finagle the money from my mother to get the B-29 Super Fortress kit. And then Max Specter cut my legs from under me. Each day I passed his store going to and from school. The store was on the same side of the street as my house, which made it impossible to avoid the large plate glass display windows. On one particular day, prominently displayed in the front of the left hand window, was a double, real white leather, holster set with fringe, leg ties for a quick draw, silver star reinforcing studs and two chrome plated six shooter cap pistols with fake white ivory handle grips. I absolutely had to have them. But how was I going to get then?

It took me several days to devise a plan. I was savvy enough to realize that asking my parents outright for the money would result in a definite "no." My plan had to be subtle. I would become helpful.

When I got home from school, instead of changing into my play clothes I went directly into the kitchen to put my scheme to work. "Do you want me to help you with anything before I go out to play?" I asked my mother.

"What do you want?" was the response.

"There's…what do you mean what do I want?"

"How much does it cost?"

'What cost? What?"

"At Specter's."

"At Specter's?"

"I know he just set up a new window display. Is it the double holster with silver six guns?" She nailed it.

Were all grownups like this or just my mother? It was pointless to continue my charade. I blurted out, "They're only eight dollars."

"Eight dollars is a lot...your father works all week for twenty-five dollars."

I launched into a passionate explanation of how much happiness would be mine if only I could...blah, blah, blah.

My mother assured me that anything that could bring that much satisfaction to one's life was worth working for. She made me an offer, in addition to keeping my room orderly, I could sweep the front porch and front side walk each day, take out the garbage, set the table for supper and whatever else needed doing. She would pay me a nickel an hour if I didn't dawdle at the tasks. Slave wages. At that rate I calculated it would take me eight weeks to earn enough if I worked for two hours after school and put in an additional eight hours on the weekend and I'd have to stop seeing my friends outside of class. "It's a deal." I said. I already had a great pair of white-tooled leather cowboy boots from my great aunt Tyne and a white cowboy hat that had been her son Billy's. The white holster would be perfect with them.

"Maybe you should ask Mr. Specter if he'll do a layaway plan before we make it a deal."

A layaway plan? I had no idea what that was! But Max Specter knew, and agreed to start a layaway for me without any thing down. But, he would only give me four weeks to come up with all the money. After that he would put the set back in the window. I knew four weeks weren't enough, but that was all he would agree to.

I stopped seeing my friends and did everything possible to earn as much as I could. At the end of four weeks I had $3.75. Mr. Specter took my money but told me he had to put the guns back in the window. Each day I stopped on the way home—they were still there. During the sixth week I gave him another $1.75. In the middle of the seventh week

I was staring through the window at my future happiness when I sensed someone standing beside me.

"Whatcha lookin' at?"

"Nothing," I said. It was Henry from my fifth grade class. Henry had hired two eighth graders, two weeks before, to hold me while he punched me in the stomach. Several times. Hard.

"Stay away from Joanie. She's my girlfriend." He had said.

Joan Courtier had told him she liked me, not him. I had no idea that Joan liked me. I liked Barbara Liddell. But then Barbara's mother had given me the brush-off when I tried to deliver that box of chocolates to her house on Valentine's Day. I found out later, she liked Henry.

"I bet it's that double holster?" Henry was right but I couldn't admit it.

"No it's not. It's that bicycle."

"Yeah? I heard you telling Douglas about the guns. It's the guns all right."

"Maybe, maybe not! I changed my mind! My old bicycle's too broke to fix. I need a new one. That one's a beauty."

It was a sky-blue, twenty-four inch bicycle with whitewall balloon tires, coaster brakes, full fenders, and a coil-spring shock absorber suspension system on the front wheel, with streamers on the ends of the chrome handlebar, plus a bell.

We stood side by side silently looking at the window display.

"Why did you do that...hit me like that? That was rotten. You never even asked me about Joanie!"

"Aw, that didn't mean nothin'. I don't like Joanie no more. Let's be friends again. C'mon, come over to my house to play." This was a pattern of Henry's I had grown to expect, a fluctuation between aggression and friendliness.

"I don't know. Maybe." I didn't want to tell him about the extra work I was doing to make money. He might figure things out so I avoided him in school all that week and the next.

Two weeks later I went down to the store to give Mr. Specter another dollar and a half. He was just inside the door arranging comic books. I didn't see the holster set. "Did you sell it?"

"Yes. Yesterday. I'm sorry Jerry. I couldn't wait any longer. Come over to the soda fountain, I'll give you your money back. Would you like a hot fudge sundae? Free? On me."

"Who bought it?"

"I'm sorry Jerry, I can't tell you that."

When I was four years old I couldn't see over the wooden picket fence that separated our front yard from the street. It was a narrow rectangular area between our house and the bar next door. A small portion jutted out beyond the house to meet the sidewalk. In the left hand corner of the yard, next to the gate, grew a Rose of Sharon Tree. It was the summer before I started kindergarten, and the tree was filled with raucous pink blossoms the size of teacups. Both the bees and I were irrepressibly drawn to this tree, they for the nectar, I for the aerial perch two feet above the ground where the tree forked providing a place for me to stand and see over the fence into the world beyond. I felt invisible in the tree, like a bird hidden among its branches. Both the bees above and the people on the sidewalk passed within a few feet of me without notice. I began making up bird calls to enhance what I imagined as my invisibility. It was actually a kind of singing. I didn't know how to whistle yet. It only resulted in unwanted double takes from people passing by. Not what I wanted at all. The day I stopped my brown sparrow impersonations a gentleman, strolling by, came over to the picket fence, and asked, "Aren't you the boy that sings bird songs?"

"Yes."

"Well they're quite lovely. But you're not singing today."

"I stopped."

"Why"

"People looked at me funny."

"Don't mind them. You really do sound like a bird. You should change your mind."

I didn't respond.

"They made my walk down the street so pleasant."

But I didn't change my mind. Instead I began to seriously watch the world beyond the fence, which was the reason I had climbed the tree in the first place. My view was boxed in by the buildings that flanked my house and by the narrowness of the street. North Main was a one-way thoroughfare headed southwest toward the center of the city, busiest during the morning rush hour with buses and people walking to work. The rest of the day the street pace slowed to local shoppers, street peddlers and visiting neighbors.

In the late nineteenth century the street was a neighborhood of modest Victorian homes and the first street to be electrified in Paterson. Now most of the houses had had storefronts added to them, which brought them right up to the sidewalk. My house was just as it had been originally built, with its small front yard still intact. I was learning how to watch and listen and anticipate what would enter my narrow window on the world. I also got some help in this quiet art of observing.

Harry Tribuker and his wife owned the hardware and paint store across the street from my tree perch. There never seemed to be a lot of customers in their store, a situation that didn't seem to trouble Harry. On warm sunny days he would spend much of his time standing outside his door looking up and down the street. Observing Harry taught me how to watch discretely, which was vitally important to a child pretending to be an unobtrusive bird in a tree. Harry was silent. He seldom interacted with anyone that passed by. However, if something or someone of special interest caught his attention he would step out from the store front, crane his neck to look down the street, then step back into the open door to secret himself, to look them up and down without notice. This procedure was, of course, reserved for the most interesting passersby. When I felt the urge to climb up into my tree I would check to see if Harry, my lookout, was on watch.

Mr. T. never brought out a chair to sit on. I wondered why until one day I saw his wife, Mrs. Tribuker, display total disrespect for his skilled observational technique. I never saw her work in the store. It seemed her self-appointed function was to swoop silently down on her husband, scold him back into the store to shuffle paint cans about or dust stock on the shelves. I could see them through the plate glass windows. He at his appointed task, she standing rigid in the center of the store watching every move he made.

Harry did have a few tricks that he used to justify his time in the sun. He would feign washing the windows or sweeping the sidewalk.

While Mr. T. was my early warning system for approaching pedestrians, I was on my own for street sounds emanating from unseen sources moving toward me on the street. Most were uninteresting traffic sounds, but some I grew to understand brought with them another world entirely, of horse drawn wagons and peddlers hawking their wares and services. Each one had a distinctive look. The knife sharpener's rig was a neat forest green, arch roofed wagon, like the ones the Gypsies used. The Gypsies came to town every fall, rented empty stores on Arch Street by the river, lived in them until spring, then disappeared.

The knife sharpener had a shop set up inside the wagon. He could handle any job on the spot. He would stop every few houses and wait for a response to his singsong call, "KNIIIVES SHARPENED! SCIIISSORS!" Every vender had a distinctive call, meant to summon you from your house. They were gregarious, good listeners, cheerful— except for the junkman—and oblivious to backed-up traffic.

There was the greengrocer's wagon, open sided, with tiers of fruits and vegetables, a fishmonger with his catch displayed in ice filled milk cases. And a roofless ice wagon layered with straw and loose canvass to protect the ice from the warmth of the day. In the winter he sold coal by the pail.

It was a time when everything you needed passed by the front of your house. If you could reach the curb you could do all of your basic shopping and spend time socializing with your neighbors, while haggling over prices and have it all delivered to your kitchen for a few pennies more. There were peddlers for dry goods, work clothes, yard goods, bake goods, dairy, cleaning products, even recycling too. The ragman and junk man came 'round regularly all year long. They had the worst wagons and the mangiest horses. The junk man's gelding was an old bony sway backed gray. The horse's stride was funereal except when the junk man raked the air above his head with his whip and scolded. Instead of picking up the pace, this equine disaster would creak to a sagging halt, lurch his head around and snap at the whip. The junk man, enraged by the horse would leap to his feet in response, ranting and cursing. The horse ignored him. It was obvious that the horse always won this argument for the driver had no intention of hurting him. It was just the bickering of an old married couple. I had seen the man tenderly stroke the horse, whisper in his ear, and feed him an apple. I saw this little vignette play out from snug in my secret seat, and understood that the horse would out-wait the man. And when the horse was sure he'd made his point and regained his dignity, he would resume his weary pace and tug the battered wagon out of sight while the silvery bells, strung between two poles, jangled sweetly over the junkman's head. "METAL! JUNK! OLD FURNITURE PLEASE!" he would call out above the impatient motor noises behind him.

It was a quiet spring morning. Mr. Tribuker was leaning on his broom in the sun. The traffic was light and the street almost silent. Mr. T., with his ever-present broom in hand, moved to the curb and craned his neck to look down the street toward town. At the same instant I heard a small child crying off to my right, very faint. As the sound drew nearer, Mr. T. moved back inside his doorway and peered around the edge of the doorjamb as a small women and a young boy, about my own age, came into view on the far side of the street. The woman was screeching and the boy squalling. Mr. Tribuker closed the door to the store and sank back out of sight into the dim interior.

The boy's mother, for that is what I assumed she was, was dressed in a cotton housedress that peaked out from under a long unbuttoned black coat. She wore white bobby socks and black low heeled shoes. Her dark hair, piled absurdly high upon her head, seemed to press her down. Her face was plain, pinched and ashen. She stopped in front of Tribuker's and began slapping the little boy about his head. I heard the snap of each stroke from the safety of my airy perch. She attempted to move again abruptly, except the little boy, in childlike defense, pulled away and raised his left arm against any new blows. This only infuriated the woman further. She grabbed the boy by his right ear and set off at a pace too fast for his legs. When he stumbled she dragged him to his feet and began to shriek at him and beat him all the harder as he collapsed upon the sidewalk.

I couldn't watch. I couldn't listen. I couldn't move. I covered my eyes with my hands but felt compelled to peer between my fingers and listen in confusion to sounds I never heard before. This was an adult deed beyond my comprehension.

There was no one to step forward on the boy's behalf. Mr. T. had fled. No one else was on the street. The boy gave up defending himself and was dragged whimpering out of sight. Mr. T. reemerged from the store and watched until they disappeared, then turned to look at me for one frozen moment. We both knew he had done nothing. Then he turned and disappeared again into the unlit store.

The next time I saw the boy was in first grade at PS 12. I was drawn to him within the first couple of days because he seemed familiar. I had no specific memory of him at first that tied him to that terrible scene. His name was Henry. He seemed eager to be my friend and invited me to his house after school. Within twenty minutes he proved to be a better bully than ever a friend, and a continual torment for the next six years of my life as he seesawed back and forth between those two extremes.

It was his ninth birthday. He invited me to his party. It was sometime in the winter. There were several other kids there. I didn't know them. His mother served us birthday cake and ice cream, then left the room.

"I want that piece," Henry said as I scooped the icing rose off the top of my slice of cake. "That's the best piece. It's my birthday and it should be mine."

He lunged at me, knocking both the cake and me to the floor. I jumped up and shoved him back. He fell onto the hot coal stove and was burned. His mother, hearing our struggle, rushed into the room, started violently shaking me and yelling, "Leave my sweet Henry alone." As she was shoving me about I noticed she had left the door to the other room open. It must have been Henry's bedroom, for hanging on the bedpost was the double six-gun holster from Specter's.

She abruptly turned from me to her son, "Are you hurt, my darling boy?"

She frantically hugged and smothered him with kisses, over and over, stroked his hair, placed her hand every so tenderly under his chin and stared deeply into his eyes while the rest of us sat immobile and silent.

She sighed, "My wonderful Henry. My love. My baby boy." Henry was squeezing the flesh around an angry red welt that had appeared on his arm from the hot stove.

Beginning with my view over our picket fence at the age of four, I had seen Henry's mother beat and badger her son with the same devotion and boundless energy as she administered kisses that afternoon. More times than I wished to recall. Whatever else I knew had happened in the past, at that moment, at his party, I heard her say she loved him. Love him. Him. She never noticed the exchanged glances of embarrassment between Henry and myself. Nor did she notice that the face he turned back toward hers was a composite of fear and longing. This was a morsel of maternal love in a banquette of continual high pitched, nagging, suffocation that never paused for air, never ever stopped. Ever.

"She really loves me," Henry said, still squeezing his burned arm as she turned to leave the room.

I sensed this was a practiced pretense, this lie he told for my benefit.

I wanted to run. To escape that house. I did nothing. I said nothing. Instead I moved next to Henry. I looked in his face, then away at the room, then his mother's back as she walked away from his birthday debris. And I understood, right then, what it all meant. How curious— what a distant word, curious, like coming upon a fatal accident, unable to turn away—that the innocence of his childhood was turned against him. This thing that was his life was all that Henry would ever know. "SHE REALLY LOVES ME," he had lied.

And in that same moment I knew Henry in a way I never knew anyone before. Not as a child. But as a human being. He needed to trust in his life, for there was nothing else. He needed to trust, with or without genuine love. And he needed me to believe with him. Not because it was me, but because I was there. I watched a desperate sadness fill his eyes before I turned away, for I could not return the lie. I realized this life was driving him slowly and totally mad. It was arresting him and distorting his soul. This was my last memory of Henry. To this day a piece of me weeps for him.

Life is not smooth. And now I know that we lucky ones whose childhoods were closer to perfection, eventually too, in a more abstract way, often live lives arrested at some more distant, and less personal moment. One day we find we need to let go of our childhood dreams, work at jobs that suffocate our souls, or worst of all believe the lie that we need weapons of mass destruction to create lasting world peace. But such disillusionments would never be within Henry's reach. I never knew or understood the reasons for his mother's phlegmatic fits of anger and love. On his ninth birthday I stood in his living room and watched his childhood vanish, replaced by stagnant isolation. I too contributed to his isolation. I avoided him from then on.

Many years later, when I was married, I received a phone call.

"Have you heard about Henry?" Said the voice from my childhood. It was Joan Courter.

"Henry? No. No, what?" I said. 'Where is he? Is he still in Paterson?"

"Yes, at the same house," she said. "When was the last time you heard from him?"

"Well the last time I saw him was in seventh grade. That would be, oh, twelve, thirteen years ago. I heard from John Van Koppen, a couple of years back, that he was still living with his mother. I think his father died. He's still there? With her?"

"He never moved out," said Joan.

"How did you find me? I'm not in Jersey anymore."

"Mary Robinson. She thought you were up in Rockland County, New York."

"I haven't seen Mary since I got married. What are you up to? Are you married?" As we made small talk I wondered if I wanted to find out the reason for this call. She had been married, was divorced, her parents had moved away, she was living outside Paterson and finishing up a degree.

Bromides kept bubbling up intrusively in my mind as she spoke—*no news is good news, out of sight, out of mind, the die is cast, not my cup of tea*—diverting me from my single thought, *why had she called?*

Sensing that, after years of silence, this wasn't going to be a good news call, I cut her off, "Why did you call? You started to tell me about Henry."

"OK. After he graduated from high school he tried collage but dropped out. He's been workin' at different things since but nothing steady."

"How'd you find out all this stuff?"

"It was in the Paterson Evening News, well some of it."

"The newspaper? Why was it in the newspaper? "

"I also got in touch with Diane. You remember Diane? She lived over on East Main. She's still in Paterson."

"Yeah, Diane Van Houten."

"Yes. Diane told me that Henry heard the Paterson police force was hiring so he went down and applied for a job. He had to be evaluated and interviewed but after a week or so they turned him down. But he didn't quit. He kept going back. I'm sure he thought it would be a perfect job for him. You know how he always got to be class monitor, how he liked to bully people, so he kept at it, and at it, and eventually they made him an auxiliary policeman."

"What's the difference?"

"Oh I think they're used if there's a big fire or a parade, for crowd control. According to the paper he passed all his background checks and took the oath to uphold the law and all that." She paused. Then said, "The day he was sworn in and got his badge and gun he went home and put a bullet in his mother's head over each eye."

I knew, even when I was sitting in the Rose of Sharon tree at the age of four, that things would never go well for him. I do think of him from time to time and have often thought I should tell him how sorry I am. But it is, after all, too presumptuous, even condescending. And far too late. Useless. Far, far too late.

He was found guilty of first degree murder committed in 1968.
There is nothing more.

14

Kodak Brownie Box Camera

or Where Do I Go From Here?

Ages 8–9

*In the middle years of my childhood—in some males, that could possibly
occur in their mid-forties—I came face to face with an amazing concept:
responsibility for a commitment.*

IT WAS HOT AND muggy. Must have been late July or early August,
before I mustered the temerity to use my first camera. My preceding
birthday my parents had given me a No. 2 Kodak Brownie Box
Camera. The little black box measured 2 ¼" x 4 ¼" x maybe 6" with
a small carrying strap, a twist knob to advance the film, and a fixed
focus lens. It took 120 roll film, which produced squarish, black-and-
white pictures. The camera rested in a revered spot among the clutter
on top of my chest of drawers, where it remained unused until that
summer. I had film but the camera was so tantalizing for me, like an
icon for a marvelous world to come, that I couldn't take pictures of
just anything. Most of the time it sat there, ignored. Occasionally
I would pick it up and speculate about a possible first picture—my cat
Percival, my favorite tree, my uncle's Buick, my parents, me, but I was
not sufficiently inspired to actually use it. Until that day my uncle Joe
Cerroni, with a knowing smirk on his face and without preamble, asked
me what I wanted to do when I grew up. It was a serious question for
an eight-year-old, one that I had never considered before. I'd seen him
do this at other times, take delight in catching people off guard for his

own amusement. I didn't like him, or trust him, not since the night he got me drunk.

I guess I should explain. My uncle and aunt lived a few blocks away. My aunt used to babysit me occasionally at their house. Her husband often worked at night. One night he was there and he was drinking Sidecars, a strong drink made with Cognac, Cointreau, lemon juice, sugar and orange peel. I asked for a sip.

"How you like it?" he said. My aunt was out in the kitchen. It was sweetish, but strong. I said I it was alright. He made another one. Said I was old enough to start learning how to drink. He slid the glass over to me. I was flattered. If he thought I was old enough, I must be.

It took me about fifteen minutes but I finished the drink. When my parents came to pick me up I was drunk. There was an enormous scene. I got sick. My mother started to cry. And my aunt never came out of the kitchen. Uncle Joe had given her a black eye when she tried to stop him.

"I want to be an astronomer," I said instantly in answer to his question. This came as a surprise to me but I gladly accepted the idea wherever it had come from.

"Really! Astronomer?"

It gave me a moment of satisfaction to see that I had caught him off guard.

"You have to be really good at math. Are you good at math?"

I had no idea. "Really good," I answered. I was just learning fractions. There couldn't be anything more difficult than that.

Well of course I wanted to be an astronomer. I had recently been to the Hayden Planetarium in New York City, and had come home with a star chart for the northern hemisphere and a package of self-adhesive, glow-in-the-dark stars, some of which were now carefully stuck to my bedroom ceiling in the form of constellations. Had I been to the circus instead, I'd have wanted to be a trapeze artist or a lion tamer. But I must confess there was something to this astronomy idea that overtook me.

For the next few days my firm decision to become an astronomer was greeted with a dismissive, "that's nice son," from my parents. I got out our stepladder and pressed more of the day-glow stars on my ceiling. It was incredible. I had a purpose in life, my very first, even if it was inadvertent. A surprising new landscape had opened in my mind. I had taken an important step toward adulthood, aside from learning how to hold my liquor, that I recognized required immediate action.

So, the very next day I went to our local library to find books on my intended new career. The library was a converted bank. The outside was a formal symmetrical design in white limestone with Greek columns. Inside was a square space with a high ceiling and terrazzo floor. Straight ahead in the middle of the room was the librarian's desk. To the left were the book stacks, which wrapped around behind the desk. To the right were reading tables with green glass shaded lamps. On the right of the entry were newspapers and magazines.

This was my second trip there. We had recently learned about the Dewey Decimal system in class and been required to go to the library get a book and do a report on it.

When I entered the library I skirted the checkout desk, and with Flash Gordon-like determination headed to the 500 shelves for science. After some time, I selected three books and headed back to the desk. The librarian recognized me.

"Aren't you the boy who tried to check out fifteen Zane Gray Westerns?"

Reluctantly I said yes. When I had arrived at her desk the last time, she gasped and told me to put them all back on the shelf, in their proper order, except for the three I was allowed to take out. With certain subtleties of Dewey's system missing from my brain, I had no recollection of how they were arranged so I went back into the stacks and put the books on the floor, and waited a while so she would think I had done what she asked of me.

"How many books do you have this time?"

I placed the three books on the desk.

"Astronomy huh? These are too grown up for you. Put them back and go to the children's section. You'll find something better for you there."

"But I like this one." It had lots of pictures. Besides, it had taken me a long time to find it.

"Put-them-back-and-start-over-I-said," she said.

After a fruitless check of the children's section I returned to the Science area, reexamined the three books and put back the one with the least pictures. I returned to the desk and placed one of the original three books on the desk and put my library card on top.

She gave me a stern look, then hesitantly and begrudgingly began to check me out.

As she started to stamp the date on the take out card, I placed the second book on the desk and slid it toward her. "And this one too," I said. It was about the origin of the universe.

"Only one. You're on probation."

"Huh? My teacher said we could take out three books at a time."

"That is correct. But not if you are seven years old and returning library books late.

"Eight and a quarter I corrected her." I was small for my age.

Ignoring my important correction, she continued, "I see you owe fifteen cents late charges. Do you have the money?"

I had dropped the late books in the outside book slot a while back so I wouldn't have to see her. She had made it clear during my Zane Gray debacle that I was not ready for the library, and I'd better "improve significantly" (humph!) if I wanted to take out more books in the future. I placed a fist full of coins along with pocket lint, a broken lead soldier, a stick of Bazooka bubble gum, and whatever else was in my pants pocket, on the desk. Before I could sort out the correct amount she reached across the desk grabbed the whole mess and counted out the amount due, mostly pennies, and pushed the rest back to me, along with one book and my card. It was obvious to me that she didn't have any confidence in my superior math skills. Not a good sign for a wannabe astronomer.

"Can't I have the other book too?"

"Probation means PROBATION. One book!"

"How long am I on probation for?" I asked in my most imploring little boy soprano voice.

"Until you prove to me that you are responsible," she said coldly.

I left the library feeling lucky to have the one book and my life in tact though diminished.

She was right of course. The book about the formation of the solar system was too difficult for me, but I stayed with it long enough to learn of Galileo's struggle with the Catholic Church concerning the Earth orbiting the sun. I felt an immediate bond through my own struggle with the high-and-mighty librarian. I was really very irritated with her. I was a very responsible person. How did she expect me to proceed with my planned career if I couldn't take out the books I needed? And why did she grab my money? I had good math skills. It kept me awake that night. Well. Maybe.

I'd never been fond of sleeping, never required more than five or six hours as an adult. It occurred to me at that time, having just acquired fractional math skills, that sleeping eight hours a day was equivalent to sleeping one third of your life away. Any promise by the grown-ups, of a life after death, I considered faint compensation for going to bed early as a child.

My mother's philosophy on sleep differed greatly from mine. Regardless of the sun's position in the sky bedtime was 7:00 p.m. until I was nine years old. So every night, when the coast was clear of parental scrutiny, I would sneak out some toys or a comic book. On this occasion it was the library book that I attempted to read by the dying light of the day.

I had been in bed for nearly two hours listening to the rhythmic beating of the ribbon factory looms behind my house. Summer sunlight was still seeping into my room, diminishing the drama of my stars, when my father opened the door to my homegrown planetarium and asked, "Are you still awake? You shouldn't be reading. Your mother wouldn't like it." Thinking quickly, I responded, "It's so hot. I can't get to sleep."

"Come on. Let's go outside on the concrete."

The concrete was the twenty-by-twenty square foot floor of the long since vanished nineteenth century carriage house and witness to our chicken fiasco. We spread out blankets and deposited pillows there. Buddy and Tommy, the Hemingway boys were asleep in the screened in sleeping porch upstairs, an advantage that came with renting the second floor of the original one family house.

"We need to be quiet," said my father. "I think the boys are asleep upstairs."

I had never slept outside before, but that's not why my father had brought me to our backyard. I lay there in the hot night air looking up into the sky. It was my first real night sky. Living in a city, I took the sky for granted and the night sky on blind faith. All you need to know is that it's staying where it belongs. But it didn't that night. As the sun set the sky seemed to fall down about us and hover inches above our heads. The stars so intense, looked like pin pricks in a dark green shade, like sparks spreading out from a bonfire to settle over the world.

"Do you know where the Big Dipper is?" I asked.

"Yes," he answered, and he showed me how to find Polaris, the North Star, the Little Dipper, Cassiopeia, the Pleiades, Orion, and Sirius the Dog Star. He showed me some of the signs of the Zodiac and told me about the ancient Greek legends. It made the space above magical, to know that we were lying there together connected to the people who saw the same sky so long ago, and their constellations whose names we still used. It amazed me that the information seemed to flow from a hidden compartment in my father's mind. Could this person be the same person who had brought home twelve hysterical roosters in his Dugan bread truck?

"It's too bad we really can't see the Milky Way very well. We should go out in the country some night where there are no city lights."

"How do you know all this?" I asked.

"I was an Eagle Scout," he said. "It was one of my Merit Badges."

Amazing. Once more, I thought, another hidden compartment. I had joined a scout troop. I lasted two weeks. It was too much like going to school. Was I wrong? What was I missing?

"Have you ever used the camera that you got for your birthday?"

"No."

"Why don't you go get it?"

I went to my room, got the camera and film, which had to be loaded in a darkened place. He taught me how to do it. "Are we going to take a picture of the sky?" I asked.

"Yup. It takes a long time though. We have to set the camera in a still place and set it to stay open for a long time so the film will get enough light."

What a great idea, the perfect idea for my very first picture and the launching of my astronomy career. "What will I get? Won't that ruin the film?"

"No. We have to close it before morning. You'll have to wait and see. What do you think you'll get?"

"A picture of the stars!" *OF COURSE* was in my voice but I didn't say it.

"Not quite. What else? What will the stars do?"

I tried to visualize what was going to happen. "I'll get a picture of the stars moving?" I said.

"Close, but not quite."

I sat there in the dark puzzling out the question.

"You read about Galileo in the book you got out of the library. What did he discover?"

"That the earth moves around the sun. So, I'm taking a picture of the earth moving, right? Not the stars."

"Right. Now let's go into the house. It's getting too late. I'll come out in a while to get the camera. You go on to bed now."

Over the next few weeks I took more pictures of the night sky, until I used up all the pictures on my first role of film. It was the best, the best first reason to use the camera and better yet I got to stay up after dark. I taped the pictures on the wall in my room, inky dark squares with whitish streaks of star tracks, which reminded me of some of the pictures in the library book. I had lost track of the book. It took me a considerable amount of time to find it in my room and when I did, I realized that the pictures of stars in the book weren't white streaks but dots of light. How did they do that I wondered. There were star charts, diagrams of our solar system, how it worked, and who had figured these things out, and I realized that I was in over my head. It was humiliating to admit it but the lady watchdog at the library was right. The book was too difficult for me. I never finished it. I did stay with it long enough to learn about how Galileo proved that the earth was not the center of the universe. But the book was twenty days overdue. I cleaned off the residue of dust bunnies it had collected while under the bed and decided that I had better return the book as soon as possible, and not through the book slot either. If I ever wanted to extract more Zane Gray Westerns, which now I understood was my preference, I would need to go into the library and face down the scowling book warden. I fantasized that I would throw the door open, sweep into the library, march straight up to the desk, look the librarian in the eye and forcefully place the overdue book in front of her and place the money for the late fine on top, showing her I was not afraid to confront her.

However, when I arrived at the library, a very overweight woman was breaching the entry just before me. My bravado evaporated. I seized the opportunity of that girth to sneak unobserved behind her through the closing door and into the book stacks. I found my way to the Zane Gray Westerns, and with great deliberation and restraint restricted my selection to only four books. I then eased my way to the checkout desk. It was a Saturday morning and the library was quite busy. There were, not one, but two librarians at the desk, the unsmiling book warden and a younger cheerful woman. I waited for the right moment, when the book warden lady was checking someone out. I sidled up to the desk and placed my Zane Grays in front of the cheerful librarian along with my card. As she began to process the books she asked about the late book. I slipped the book on to the desk and placed four nickels on top to cover the late fine.

"You're not old enough to take out more than three books at a time. Which Zane Gray would you like me to keep?" she said.

At that moment the other librarian finished with her checkout. At the sound of Zane Gray her eyes came up and shifted to my face. "Four books huh? He knows better than that. Let me handle this."

The sweet librarian slid the books over to her.

"Is that a late book? Is he returning a late book? Let me see that too." She picked up the book and checked the due date. "Twenty days late. I'm not surprised."

At the end of a long reprimand she sneeringly asked if I read the book. Some I told her. Mostly about Galileo. At this point she thumbed through the book, even picked it up and sniffed it. She took the Westerns back and said, "You have failed your probation," and she informed me there were other mitigating factors that would restrict my library usage for an indeterminate period. This did give me a momentary hiccup of distress, but in the next moment, to my great relief, I realized that my budding career as an astronomer was at an end. I did feel a certain remorse however about my loss of face in the library. But on the way home, while feeling sorry for myself, I realized that Galileo and I shared a similar fate. He was forced to live his life under house restraint by the authoritarian. And I had been banished from the library forever by the book warden. I should confess though, that there was also some serious concern expressed about one particular factor, peanut butter stains throughout the book.

Some people care about the right way to do things, some care about people.

15

Clear Sailing

Age 9

Why are the grown-ups in your life so mysterious? Why is it so difficult to see them as dimensional beings? They seem to hold themselves so aloof. It takes years, at least it did in my family, to piece together dimensional pictures from faltering memories and faded snapshots. I met my seventy-two-year-old grandmother's older brother for the first time at her funeral. He tried to avoid me, so I let him.

W HEN I REALIZED I could never be the owner of the splendid, double, white leather holster with chrome-plated, fake, ivory-handled cap pistols, I switched my heart's desire to the blue bicycle that was still in Max Specter's store window. Instead of taking back the money in the layaway plan for the guns I asked Mr. Specter if I could do the same layaway plan for the bike. I had outgrown my first bike, a small twenty-incher, it was totally broken as well. The money I had given Mr. Specter was just shy of a quarter of the bike's $24.00 cost. So, I was back doing extra errands and being extraordinarily helpful around the house. But after several weeks of lackluster effort, I realized I would be in high school before the bike would be mine. I asked for a raise.

"A raise, huh. Why do you think you should get a raise?"

I realized I was looking around the room too long. No response, nothing was forming up in my brain. Nothing believable. Nothing convincing.

"Alright. What's going' on?" my mother asked.

Was I so blatantly obvious, so inept? "Specter sold the holster set to Henry," I blurted.

"So why do you need a raise then? And it's Mister Specter to you," said my mother.

"Well my bike is broken. He's got a really neat bike in the window."

"How much?"

"It's really special. It's got white wall tires and it's much bigger and better than my old one and there's a coil spring thing on the front wheel to make it ride smooth." And in my best clear-eyed, innocent, most endearing, sweetest, contrived voice that every ham actor child uses when they know they haven't got a chance, I said, "It's only twenty-four dollars and it's much better than the old one."

"You said that twice. It must really, really be a better bike."

I may have been transparent but I was sincerely transparent.

"How much of a raise do you want?"

"Five cents."

"A week?" she smirked.

Why was she making it so hard? "No. An hour."

"You want to double your pay? I'll have to think about this, and I want to see this bicycle.

I took her down to Specter's. "Isn't it a beauty?"

"It's a nice color blue." She said.

"And I could put a basket on the handle bars so I could do bigger errands."

My mother didn't agree to a raise but offered to loan me the money.

"You're really sure that you want this bike? If I loan you the money you have to pay me back fifty cents a week."

"Oh! Yeah. I do." And I knew I did because I had that feeling of excitement that every good red-blooded American consumer gets when they willingly mortgage their future for something so significant in their lives, as a house, or a car, or a dustpan.

However, when you buy a car you get to take it for a test drive. If you buy a house you at least get to walk through it first, even get to check it out. But when you buy a dustpan or a bicycle, nothing.

The day I got the bike I took it out for a ride to show it off to Dougie up on North Third Street.

"Remember," said my mother, "Stay on the sidewalk and walk across streets."

I took off from my house in a flurry of excitement, peddling as fast as I could. I rumbled over the irregular slate sidewalks heading east on North Main. The coil-shock absorber smoothing the way. Then, turned up Haledon Ave toward North First, flew off the curb with total disregard for traffic or my promise to walk the bike at street crossings and lost control of the bike. The whole front end wobbled and vibrated so violently it spilled me on the pavement with the bike landing on top of me. *Well that's interesting.* I said to myself. I looked the bike over. Nothing seemed wrong. *Let's do that again.* I peddled back down the block to North Main and set off again, peddling as fast as possible, flew off the curb and wobbled into a heap again against the far side of the street. I picked myself up and stood there staring at my sky blue bicycle with the dawning realization that I was now the owner of a scratched, sky blue, "lemon" bicycle.

It was that stupid shook absorber. Made the wheel wobble. What could I do?

I still owed sixteen dollars on it. That came to 160 hours of errands. I didn't want to use it ever again and I couldn't complain to anyone. I looked at the bike to see if I could change something, maybe fix it. There was nothing. So I parked it under the back porch and didn't go near it again.

My friends wanted to know when I was going to get my new bike. I didn't know what to tell them so I stayed away. And after several weeks of doing errands for my mother on foot she asked why I wasn't using my bike? I made up a lame excuse that I didn't want to get it scratched up. "That's not a good enough reason. What's goin' on?" she said. So I told her what had happened.

"Maybe Mr. Specter will take it back?" she offered. "We should talk to him."

But we didn't. Several more weeks passed. During that time, Max Specter sold his business to the Popewynie brothers and that was that.

Except my mother started to waitress for them. I thought maybe she could work something out. But they were changing the store—no more kids' things. And absolutely no bicycles. Besides, why would they want a scratched up bike?

By the time summer vacation started I was used to not having a bike, until one day, while walking down the street, I saw a kid on a strange looking bike. He stopped at Popewynie's, leaned the bike against the window and went inside. I was looking it over when he came back out holding an ice cream cone.

"What is it?" I asked.

Pretty neat, huh?" he said.

"Yeah. But what's all this stuff on the handle bars?" It was a three-speed English racer, he explained. "It's the latest thing." There was a three-speed shifter and two hand brakes for the wheels. The tires were black and skinny and the bike was as light as a feather compared to my bike, which I couldn't even lift off the ground.

"How fast is it?" I wanted to know.

"I got it up to forty one day."

"How'd you know that?"

"Got a speedometer on it."

This seemed like the answer to my prayers, had it ever occurred for me to pray for such a thing. I had to have this bike. I was blissfully, eagerly willing to rush back into the arms of red blooded American consumerism with the first bike's debt still hanging over me. How could I go about this? The new bike cost the equivalent two weeks of my father's pay. There was no chance, I knew, of getting a raise or a new loan out of my mother. I could sell my bike though, or trade it in on the new one. I could also work for other people besides my mother.

The first and easiest thing to do was to get the sky blue beast out from under the porch to check out the damage. Not so bad. It was dirty and there were a few scratches on the rear fender. I cleaned it up. Went down to the store and got some blue model airplane dope for the scratches. I put a for sale sign on the bike and began to use it.

Next step, get more work. My mother washed our windows once a month. "Could I do that?" I asked. She liked the idea and she said she would pay me ten cents an hour if I did a really good job, which meant inside and out and perfect corners and edges too. The first week she didn't pay me because I didn't do a good job on the outside. The next time I got it right and got paid.

When my mother and I went to her parents' butcher shop I heard my grandmother pestering her husband to cut the grass in their backyard. He disliked this job and always put it off until it was impossible to do. It wasn't a large yard but this was before power mowers existed. They had an old push mower and the yard was sloped which made it an exhausting job.

"You want me to do it?"

My grandmother looked at me doubtfully. "Maybe." Then she looked at my mother. I was small for my age. No one spoke.

"Sure. I'll give you a chance. If you do a good job, I'll pay you seventy-five cents."

"OK. How often do you want me to cut it?" Every day would have been fine with me.

"Every other week if there's a lotta rain."

"Is there anything else to do?"

"You could restock the shelves in the store."

"How much...."

She looked at my mother again. "He's trying to pay off the money I loaned him to buy his bicycle."

"I'll give you ten cents an hour but you have to do it right, clean the shelf, move the old stock to the front and make sure that all the labels face out. Can you do that?" Then she added, "Is it a nice bike? Do you like it"?

"Ah, yeah. Sure. It's a great color blue too."

A few days later I went into Popewynie's to buy an Uncle Scrooge comic book. It was a deluxe edition that cost twenty-five cents. I was feeling flushed with all the money I was making.

"I hear you got a bike?" The older Popewynie asked.

"Sure."

"I need somebody to do errands. Pick up stuff for the store. I'll give you twenty-five cents for each trip. That sound OK to you?"

"Yes. I'll have to ask my mother."

"I already did. She said it was OK with her.

"Will I have to cross streets? Is that OK with her?" What I really needed to do was stay in the street so the bike wouldn't wobble going up and down curbs.

"Yeah, she knows. There's other jobs around here too if you're interested."

"What?"

"Putting out magazines, washing the windows. Ten cents an hour."

"I guess so. Sure. How often?"

"Few times a week for everything. I'll let your mother know when we need you." Things were definitely looking up.

A few weeks passed. I sold the bike. There were no lemon laws then though I did caution about curb jumping. I had saved about six dollars from my new jobs but without a bike I had put myself out of work with the Popewynie's.

It was Saturday morning and my mother and I were on the bus to West Paterson. We got off across the street from my grandparents' butcher shop. Leaning against the front of the store was a red, three speed, English Racer. We went inside. There weren't any customers in the store. My grandmother said, "Hi." My grandfather was behind the meat counter and didn't speak.

"Whose bike is that out there?" I said.

"Bike?" said my grandfather. "Somebody left a bike? Ada, do you know anything about a bike?" He was looking over the top of the meat display case, which meant he was standing on his toes since he was only five-foot-four-inches tall.

"I don't know. Let me see." She came out from behind the register and walked to the screen door. We both peeked out. "There's a tag on it, Jerry. Go out and see if there's some body's name on it."

I walked over to the bike and fumbled with the tag. "It says Jerry on it." I looked up at my grandmother. "Do you know who that is?"

There's something really sweet and innocent about little boys, so open and naïve, maybe in contrast to what they become when they grow up, or in my case just plain thick headed.

"You're the only Jerry I know," she said. "Must be yours."

"How did it get here?" I asked, still not able to put it together.

"It's an early Christmas present from your grandparents," said my mother.

"But you still have to cut the grass," yelled John, over the deli case.

There are times in life when everything is so perfect. Not often as it turns out. But that day, that bicycle and everybody I knew was just so perfect. I went whooping and skipping around the sidewalk in front of the store. "Can I...?"

"Of course. Just be careful. Go check out the carnival. It's setting up down by the river."

I took off down Hillary Street. My friend Eugene Boucher was standing in front of his house around the corner from the carnival.

"Hey, Eugene," I yelled, "I'm gonna check out the carnival. You wanna go with me?"

I squeezed the brake on the handle bar to stop and while the front wheel locked, the rest of the bicycle spun sideways and dumped me over onto the gravel walk in front of him. Ten minutes later I was back at the store limping, all skinned up. I had forgotten that there are two hand brakes, one for each wheel.

Naturally they asked, "What happened?" And while my grandmother iodined and bandaged me up, I told them, with great pathos and tears, and painful complaints about the painful care I was getting, how I had flown through the air for many, many yards to land in the only patch of giant sharp gravel with short pants on—I hated little-boy short pants—and maybe there was something wrong with this bike too.

"I...I don't think (sniffle) I can cut the grass (sniffle, sniffle) this week."

Not one to show any emotion, I heard my grandfather mutter impatiently under his breath, "Oh God," then, "I don't want you to cut the grass this week. I want you to go into the living room."

"Why?"

He took me aside, "I want you to look at the book. It might do you some good." He made it sound like an educational punishment, which he and I knew it wasn't.

The book was a set of folios published by *The Paterson Morning Call* of grim grizzly Civil War pictures taken by Matthew Brady. He had shown me a few pages about General Sickles once before until we got yelled at. The folios left nothing to your imagination: disemboweled dead, dismembered corpses, bloated upside down horses and devastated landscapes filled every page. Not fit for a young boy according to my mother and grandmother, unless as my grandfather sensed, said young boy might be feeling too sorry for himself and needed to be educated by events far worse than falling off one's new bike because he forgot how the brakes worked.

I liked the book, and at the same time felt really cheated by the cruel day that had venomously schemed to bring me the bike I longed for and then made it impossible to use. *It wasn't my fault.*

I was so eyebrow deep in self-pity I did not notice my mother enter the living room.

"Are you looking at those gory pictures? You're too young. Give that to me," was the general tone for the next fifteen minutes. My response. Silence.

At the same time my grandmother, in the next room, was acidly berating my grandfather. "You know we don't want him to look at those gory pictures. He's too young. Why did you give them to him?" His response. Silence.

I gave up the folios and my grandfather put them away. I was sort of stuck. Unable to stir, when my grandfather came back into the room.

"Why don't you go back down to the river? See what's going on with the carnival. They're getting ready to open." he said.

Still in the throes of self-pity I sighed dismally, "I guess so."

"Better not ride your bike. Those skinned knees'll start bleedin' again."

Neither Eugene nor my friend Tippy were around. Everything was ready to go, all the rides set up, the sideshow tent pitched. A few carnie men were loafing on wooden boxes in the shade of the mangled willow by Tippy's house that had resprouted a hundred thousand branches. Set up work done, they were waiting for the afternoon opening. I walked down along the riverbank looking at all the rides that I knew I wouldn't go on because they made me nauseous. The same carnival came every year for the last weekend of summer. A seedy, rusty collection of rides—the Whip, Tilt-a-Whirl, Merry-go-Round, and a Ferris wheel—were spread along the river for a few hundred feet, followed by a half dozen travel weary trailers. It seemed desperately sad. Starved for air.

Not much to do, I started back to my grandparents' store. As I arrived back at the front of the carnival, the ice cream truck opened for business. It was parked next to the shady place where the men were sitting. I needed something to cheer me up. An ice cream would certainly do that. I had just enough change for a double dip chocolate cone. I walked over to the river to enjoy my ice cream in the shade of another willow. The same handful of men were still sitting, on the other side of the lane smoking. One man seemed to be pointing in my direction.

If there's anything that could make me forget feeling sorry for myself, it's ice cream. I was in ice cream nirvana when two tiny black hands reached down out of the tree. They latched onto to my double-dip cone and tried to rip it out of my hand. At the other end of those two thieving hands were two monkey arms and a monkey body dressed in a funny looking uniform. Outmatched in strength, I still managed to pull the cone away only to see tiny fingers leave jet black dirt streaks up the sides of my double tall chocolate happiness. I jumped away and ran, ignoring my bicycle debacle injuries, with the South American demon close behind, shrieking and waving his arms at me, while the men watched and laughed themselves silly.

"Give him the ice cream," shouted one. "Share. He won't eat so much," said one man hysterical, gasping for breath.

"What happened?" Ada, my grandmother, was waiting on a customer when I burst into the store half crying, half yelling what must have sounded like madness.

"Fix it. Wipe it off."

"What happened?"

"There was a monkey, then some men laughed at me, then my ice cream got dirty, then he chased me all the way home! Can you clean it Grandma?" I was standing in the middle of the store. It took some doing but my grandmother got me to slow down so I could explain what had happened.

By now the ice cream was running down my arm and dripping on to the floor. "I wanna get the dirt off."

Everyone agreed, "You can't eat that. You'll get some sort of monkey madness."

My mother took the cone and disappeared. I was nine-year-old miserable again.

"What you need is another ice cream," said my grandfather. He moved out from behind his butcher counter to the center of the store and squeezed through the women clustered about me.

"Give me your hand." He reached into his pocket and brought out a silver half dollar. "Go get another ice cream. And keep an eye out for the monkey."

Feeling somewhat better, I took the money and cautiously left the store, expecting the monkey to leap out at me. When I reached the ice cream truck. I asked for another chocolate cone.

"Back for more ice cream to feed the monkey?"

"Where'd he come from? I mean where is he now?"

"He belongs to the Hurdy-Gurdy man. He's tied up now. Under that tree. He's got a good memory so don't go near him."

I got my cone and immediately headed to the tree, which was set back from the end of the truck. It was where the men had been sitting, waiting to see what would happen to me. Everyone was gone except the monkey. He was tethered by a long rope to a stake in the ground. As soon as he saw me he started making faces and grunting. In that moment I knew what to do. I moved closer. Just within the rope's radius and began eating the ice cream pretending not to notice him. He jumped to his feet and charged me. At the last second I stepped out of the rope's length. I knew he knew who I was. But he didn't remember how long his rope was until he reached its end and was knocked flat. He lay there thrashing and thrusting his arms out at me.

The ice cream man stuck his head out the back window of the truck, "Hey, leave that monkey alone."

I ignored him. It was time to get even. I sat down on the ground just out of the monkey's reach, by inches, to eat the best ice cream I would ever have and savor the best ten minutes in the entire day. I sensed someone behind me.

"What's goin' on here?"

I pretended I didn't hear.

"Stop that you nasty kid. You're making him crazy."

I ignored the man, even though part of me said, Better get out of here, but another part that hadn't had its fill, said, *NO. TEN MINUTES ISN'T ENOUGH.* So I stayed. Until the last bite.

When the Hurdy-Gurdy man reached me, he grabbed me under the arm and yanked me to my feet. "You son of a bitch. Why'd you do that?"

"'Cause, he tried to get my ice cream. He messed it up so I couldn't eat it.

"He's just a monkey. You came back to do this?"

I hadn't planned it, but I was glad I'd thought of it. "You all thought it was funny when your monkey tried to get my ice cream before."

"Get out of here or I'll turn the monkey loose."

It was nearly noon when I got back to the store.

"How'd it go?" My grandfather was grinding up chop meat. He took a pinch, put salt on it and gave it to me.

"OK. I got my ice cream." I took the thirty-five cents change out of my pocket to give back to him.

"No. You keep it. Use it for some rides this afternoon at the carnival."

"It doesn't look like fun. I don't think I'll go back."

"What about the monkey?"

"I got even."

"With a monkey? How do you get even with a monkey?"

So I told him. He didn't say anything. He just frowned.

He made up two more pinches of raw chop meat for both of us. "We sure got in trouble this morning over those Civil War picture books. I'll let you see them some other time." He whispered. "I put them away so your grandmother can't find them. I found something else though that I think you should see. How are all your scrapes?"

"They don't hurt much. Are you gonna show me now?"

"Later when we close for lunch at one."

I went back into the kitchen, looked out the back window toward the river. I could see the top half of the Ferris wheel over my friend Tippy's house. My mother and grandmother came into the kitchen with cold cuts for lunch.

My grandfather came in from the store and motioned for me to follow him. We went down to the basement. Laid out on a table were some pictures. Paintings actually. Most were postcard size. Paintings of old fashioned sailboats. Some showed people on a boat. One painting was the size of a newspaper. It was of a young man climbing aloft in the rigging of a sailing ship.

"That's my grandfather. Your great-great grandfather."

"Who did these paintings?"

"I did, years ago, before I got married."

"Did you know him? Your grandfather?"

"No. But I heard about him from my father. He told me he was very brave."

I was completely surprised by the beautiful paintings my grandfather, the butcher, had done. "How do you mean 'brave'?"

"Sometime in the 1850s your great-great-granddad was a sailor in England. He was very poor, working all the time for almost nothing. His life was terrible. He decided to come to America. Somehow he got a small sailboat."

"To America. In a small boat? How big was it?"

"Not big. Maybe big enough for two. There was another man. A friend. They decided to sail across the Atlantic together in that boat. They ran out of food. There were storms and they almost sank." He stopped talking.

In all my nine years I had never spent time like this with my grandfather, talking about a past I'd never known about, looking at his paintings, staring into the eyes of my great-great-grandfather.

"What happened to him, Grandpa?"

"Oh, they made it here. It didn't work out. He got married, had a son but he died before his son was born.

"That's a real sad story."

"Yes, it is. A lot sadder than skinned knees and lost ice cream cones don't you think?" He stopped again.

"Yeah," I said sheepishly. I wanted him to go on. So we could stay there, together, in the musty cellar, but he was already on his way to the door.

It was several days before I could even begin to think about riding my new bike. If I moved too much, one or another of my skinned spots opened up and bled. I longed for that perfect bike ride. I wanted it to be something special. Something I'd never done before. A great adventure. It had to be important, like my great-great-grandfather's sailboat trip. I needed time to imagine such a trip, but there was a loan to repay. Now that I had a bike again, I'd be able to work for the Popewynie brothers. There were chores around the house to do, and school work. The perfect ride would have to wait.

I felt sorry for myself when I fell off my new bike, when I was yelled at for looking at the Civil War pictures, when the monkey grabbed my ice cream and I then behaved so badly by getting even with him. I knew what I was doing then and I didn't care, and I don't care now, because I got to have my grandfather, all to myself, for the best of all time.

16

Under the Porch

Age 9, Fourth Grade

Memories are like skipping stones on water with your eyes shut, trying to guess the number of hits before the ripples in your mind vanish.

My friends and I had an ongoing, years-long challenge of stone skipping on the Passaic River. I held the highest count for the most times, twenty-two skips. So before my memory fails me I feel I must pass along this knowledge of stone skipping, that will be my contribution to the pool of meaningful human accomplishments and perhaps my modest fifteen seconds of fame.

There are five things you need to be aware of in order to be really good at this stone skipping. The riverbank must be flat and low to the water. There must be a supply of thin flat stones of the right weight that fit perfectly with in the circle of your thumb and first finger. The water must be smooth and slow moving. There must not be any wind. You must lean over in such a way so that your arm can release the stone as close and as flat as possible to the water's surface with a snapping sling shot action. Follow these steps carefully and let me know if you best my record.

We also did two skip challenges for distance—two skips with the longest space between hits. For this you need choppy water and intuitively perfect timing. I never mastered that one, until I remembered what happened under the porch and what happened a decade later.

I WAS STARING AT the Felix-the-Cat wall clock over the buffet in Hendrik and Clara Vis's dining room, watching its tail swing and its eyes move in time to the ticking. It was a hot summer Sunday and there was nothing to do. We were at my father's parents' house at 89 Carbon Street for the weekly clan gathering.

"You wanna see something? I found a really good hiding place where the grownups can't find us," said my cousin Ann. She lived upstairs from my Dutch grandparents with her mother, Ella, her older brother Bobby, and her older sister, Barbara. My cousins would come downstairs on Sundays, at their mother's insistence, to visit, but seldom for dinner, except Ann. I sensed something wasn't quite right about their visits. They avoided all the grown-ups except for Hendrik and Clara.

Ann and I were the same age, and though we only saw each other at these family gatherings, we were very best friends.

We had just finished dinner. The adults were about to have coffee when I asked. "May Ann and I go outside to play?"

Dinner rules at my Dutch grandparents' house were quite strict for children. We needed permission to leave the table, but were not allowed to ask, only one cookie for dessert—the adults were permitted two—never speak unless spoken to, and never make a disturbance.

My mother, trying to head off a generational disaster, smiling benevolently at Ann and I, asked, "Wouldn't you like to have your coffee-milk and a cookie first?"

The cookies were my grandmother's own homemade Dutch butter cookies with bits of almond. A divine treat, but still I pressed on, "Can't we wait until later?"

"You know that once dessert is over your grandmother will put away her cookies and that will be that."

Annie, sitting next to me, ever reticent to speak aloud in the company of adults, leaned over, and whispered in my ear, "Let's have our cookie."

I really wanted to get outside to see this secret place but relented. "OK." I whispered sarcastically, "Our cooookie!"

Staying for coffee-milk and a cookie meant we might not be able to leave the table until all the adults were finished, not only with their coffee but with all the endless boring words they needed to say. There was only one possible way to escape. I waited for them to start smoking. I coughed lightly several times and asked again. Within a few minutes we were outside. I asked Ann why she had wanted to stay for dessert.

"You know, Grandma. She'd get mad. She'd want to know why we were asking to leave the table. Dinner's not over until after dessert."

I hadn't thought about that. I knew in a remote way she was very strict, that she could cut you in two with her eyes, but she seldom said anything to us kids. And as an only child I wasn't troubled by such things. With a touch of belligerence, I said, "Yeah. So what!"

"She's really nice to me, and Bobby and Barbara."

During this exchange, Ann and I had been wandering aimlessly about the lawn.

"Hey, where's this here place you told me about?"

Ann walked slowly around to the front yard, stopped along the sidewalk hedging and looked back at the house. There was a deep porch that ran the full width of the house about three feet off the ground. It was closed in with green latticework trimmed in white.

"It's there. Under the porch."

It looked dark and forbidding and perfect. "How do we get in?"

She led me to the right hand end of the porch. There was a lattice panel that was hinged by its top to the porch floor framing.

"You ever been under there?"

"I can't lift it up enough. It's stuck." The hinges were rusted in place but with both of us working at it we got it open. We propped it up with a stick and crawled in. There wasn't room to sit up until we reached the middle of the porch, right up against the latticework. "Hey this is great." I said. It was the only place I had been for days that was a bit cool. I took off my polo shirt, which was sweaty and sticking to me.

"That's a lot better," I said. We sat there looking at each other. After a few more minutes of looking Annie said, "I'll show you mine if you show me yours?"

She didn't wait for me to respond. She took off her blouse and then her skirt.

– 154 –

"You ever seen a girl down there before?" She tilted her head and looked down at her lap then raised her eyes to mine. We were kneeling in the dirt inches apart just under the porch floorboards.

"No. Never… How 'bout you? Ever seen a boy there?" This was becoming biblical. I was being seduced with the fruit from the Tree of Knowledge by the classic female temptress and realized suddenly I wanted a bite.

"Uh, no. Now you take something off," Ann said.

Feeling sort of—not nervous—pleasantly feathery inside, I took off my short pants. It was going to be my very first time naked in front of a girl. She took off her half-slip next, which exposed her silky white panties.

"Now it's your turn. Socks and shoes don't count."

I wasn't wearing an undershirt. The only thing left was my underpants. "Listen, listen, I hear something,"

"Come on. There's no one coming."

The cramped space under the porch forced me into an awkward position again as I pulled my underwear down around my ankles and knelt back down. I watched her looking at me. She glanced up, didn't say anything and then she reached out and touched me.

"Is this where you pee?"

I nodded. She reached out again and squeezed me, scrunched up her nose and said, "Euww." and let go.

"You go now," I said, "and no socks and shoes either."

She performed the same maneuver with her underpants. At last I would find out. She knelt back down. There was nothing there. Nothing at all!

"There's nothing there!" I blurted out. I looked up into her face, "It's empty." It was more a question than a statement. I was confused. She looked hurt. Didn't say anything. And it was, empty. I didn't know what to expect but it was just smooth. pink…skin…that disappeared in a vee between her legs? I reach out to touch her.

"Quiet. Someone's coming," she whispered.

"No there isn't. You're just chicken."

"Shhhh!"

"Remember when you were working at Tarradash's grocery downtown on Washington Street?" said Grandpa Hendrik to my father. They were standing directly above us having a smoke, while Ann and I knelt naked in the dirt facing each other inches below. "I thought you'd get robbed on the way home that day," said Hendrik.

"Yeah, I remember. I was so surprised when I saw you outside the store the Saturday I got that raise," said my father.

"You were such a skinny kid."

"I was nearly twenty then. And I was strong. I was used to carrying one hundred pound sacks around in the store."

"Well, your mother and I thought we better not take a chance. That seemed like so much money then. We felt like it was our chance for a big turnaround."

Neither of us moved, though my fingers, twitched with thwarted curiosity.

"If it hadn't been for Roosevelt...he made things happen," said my father. "When was it, when he signed the minimum wage act?"

"I think it was thirty-seven or thirty-eight," said Bill. "No, it was thirty-eight. I remember because I got married that year."

"That saved our lives. It almost doubled your pay didn't it?"

"More than doubled it. I went from twelve cents to twenty-five cents an hour.

While great issues of survival stretched out above, the cramped legs beneath Ann and I were growing numb. We were trying not to squirm. Even though our bare legs were touching, Ann and I had grown modest during this explorus interruptus. All we could do was wait for the voices above to depart.

"And when you married Roselyn you still gave us half your pay until Jerry was born."

I could smell the pungent smoke from my grandfather's Dutch cigar.

"It made things hard again for a while," Hendrik said.

"I know," said my father. "That's when you gave the second floor to Ella and Joe's kids so you could help them, but we needed the money. There were all those hospital and doctor bills to pay."

"We understood. But someone had to help Ella after she and your brother got divorced."

I looked at Ann. Did they mean Uncle Joe, my father's older brother, was Ann's father?" Ann had reached the end of her sitting still endurance. Until then she had sat as demure as a first time naked in front of a boy, girl could. Now, with her squirming it seemed… promising, I thought…that I might…possibly…(If she didn't make too much noise)…see…if there really was something there.

"I need another cup. Let's go in."

They threw their smoked stubs off the porch and went back into the house. We were safe.

We should have stayed where we were. I certainly hadn't finished my learning experience, but instead, we behaved like children. We got dressed and got the hell out of there as fast as we could.

In the midst of our flight from Eden, we began to play tag. Well, a sort of tag. She ran and I chased her. There was a large open lawn area that sloped south, away from the side of the house to a grove of scrubby trees. I caught up to her there.

"I didn't get my turn."

"Yes you did," she said in a novice's I-have-a-headache-tonight-don't-bother-me kind of voice.

"I didn't get to see good. I didn't get to touch you."

"Oh. All right. But you have to take off your clothes too. Everything."

"Alright. Everything," I said. "You too."

"No socks or shoes, again."

I nodded agreement. We both undressed. She lay down in the luxuriant flora and looked up into my face. I knelt beside her. This time I would see. I reached out to nudge her legs apart, slowly, to touch the unknown as if there were some irresistible danger involved, and there was.

"Ann. Jerry. Where are you?"

"That's my mother," squeaked Ann.

I could see my aunt through the tangle of trees looking for us, slowly walking in our general direction.

"Are you kids down here in this smoke? Get out of there," said her mother.

I was alarmed. She knows where we are! We hadn't noticed that the air was filled with smoke. The neighbor to the south was burning brush. "Do you think she knows what we're doing?"

We jumped up, got dressed and ran out of the trees just as Ella reached us. Ann started coughing from the thickening smoke.

"What were you kids doing down here?"

"Ahhhhhh. We were watching an ant war." I lied. It was one of those nine-year-old boy preoccupations that I thought she would believe.

A few days later I was covered with poison ivy. I mean completely.

"Your aunt just called," said my mother. "Your cousin is in the hospital. They don't know if she's gonna live."

I wasn't in great shape either, though not life-threatening. My hands were so swollen and oozing that my fingers were painfully glued together as well as other recently exposed parts of me. Ann too had poison ivy everywhere, especially in her lungs, which kept filling with fluids, suffocating her. This information stopped me dead on my way through our kitchen. I could feel the blood draining out of my face as I stared into the vivid memory of that thwarted afternoon's experience.

"What's wrong?" asked my mother. "And stop scratching you'll make it worse."

"She's in the hospital?" I repeated. I was standing with my back to her feeling the hair on the nape of my neck stand up.

"Tell me. How did you kids get poison ivy so bad? It's everywhere! Even under your clothes."

I was trapped. The misdirecting (lying?) part of my brain shut down. I wasn't going to get out of it with an ant war excuse this time.

"Maybe the neighbor was burning poison ivy. Maybe it was in the smoke." My mother offered.

I wasted no time in agreeing. "Yeah. I'll bet that's it!" I said as I turned to face her. I felt my shoulders relax. Once more we hadn't been caught.

But we had been caught. We sampled the fruit from the tree of good and evil. Sort of. I mean, I hadn't daydreamed through all my

Sunday school lessons. Ann and I had been cast out from the Garden of Eden (under the porch) right into a punishing bed of poison ivy. And the lesson I learned? You shouldn't ignore Sunday school lessons even if you don't get your turn. Even if you are doin'-what-comes-natcherly for you will live to regret it.

I literally oozed my way through the next several weeks in bed, or at least at home, until the poison ivy subsided and I was able to reenter my place in the outside world.

It was several months before we were back at the house on Carbon Street. During this hiatus my grandmother, having contracted pneumonia for the third time in two years, died. The whole family was there to help Hendrik Vis put his life and the house in order.

I was eager to see my cousin again. There had been no further word about her condition. When we arrived I immediately walked across the lawn to find the poison ivy. I had since learned what it looked like. There was a massive carpet of the stuff under all the trees at the edge of the lawn that spread down into the neighbor's yard where the burning took place. I returned to the house. Everyone was seated around the dining room table speaking in reverential hushed tones. I didn't see Ann. "Where's Ann," I asked. They stopped talking and looked up at me. No one responded. I turned and ran down the front hall to the stairs calling her name as I climbed the steps two at a time. The door to their apartment stood open. Everything was gone. They were gone, as if they had evaporated.

It was ten years later. I was going to college part-time and living in North Haledon.

"Phone call Jerry."

I motioned to my mother—who is it?

"I don't know. It's a woman."

"Hello?" I said.

"Jerry? This is your aunt Ella."

"Yes? Oh! Yes. How are you?" I felt as if a ghostly miasma had surged out of the telephone into my body.

"Fine," abruptly dispensing with small talk she said, "Ann and I want to see you. Can you come by our house sometime soon?"

"I guess so. Sure. I'm off from school this Friday afternoon, is that all right?"

"That would be good. Is two o'clock OK?" I agreed and she gave me their address. It was only a half-mile from our own place on Belmont Avenue. We hadn't seen them in years.

"Who was it?"

"Aunt Ella. She wants to see me."

"That's strange. We haven't heard anything from her in years! What about?"

"I don't know. Annie too."

All that week I tried to guess what had prompted her call. I asked some of my cousins if Ella had called them. "Not at all" was the response.

When I arrived at their house, the door opened as I was reaching for the doorbell. No greetings were exchanged. My aunt led me into their dimly lit living room where Ann was seated on a straight back chair, her elbows resting on the wooden arms, her hands folded in her lap. My aunt told me to sit in a similar chair facing Ann. All the furniture had been pushed up against the walls to make a space in the center of the room for the two chairs. *What was going on?*

With no preamble of "how are you" or "good to see you," Ella said, "Look him in the eye and tell him." Ella, stationed behind Ann's chair, was glaring down at me.

Ann raised her head, then her eyes. She had become a beautiful young woman. Tears filled her eyes.

"I'm going to have a baby," breathed Ann.

"Louder," said her mother, "repeat it louder."

She began to cry.

"Oh, don't cry Ann. Please." My eyes filled with tears. I wanted to hold her, help her. I leaned forward and put my hands on her hands as my dormant childhood affection for Ann overwhelmed me. We were just inches apart just like the day under the porch. How strange, I thought, for this to be the time and place to gently touch her for the first time. I glanced up at her mother. She was furious, her lips, her eyes twitching. Ann had lowered her head.

"It's alright Ann. We all do things that we wish we hadn't done."
The prolonged gulf of silence between us widened. Ann was looking
at me now, waiting for me to speak. "I've done the exact same thing,"
I said lamely. *Why? Why did I say such a stupid thing? There was no chance
of my getting pregnant. Or did she think I had done that to some girl? After all
it's what males are known to do, have sex and move on.* Even more absurdly,
I hadn't done anything at all. I was a virgin as pure and innocent as the
day I crawled out from under the porch on Carbon Street. I wanted to
say more, do more, ease her pain. I wanted there to be better words
but didn't know what they might be—*it's not your fault? It's life? It's a
learning experience?* Sheer nonsense.

"I want you to tell the rest of that family of yours," said Aunt Ella.

I felt boiled down, couldn't move, as though a bubbling cauldron
had swallowed Annie and me—the three of us. *What was going to happen
to Ann?*

"You can go now."

I didn't move.

"What?" I said.

"NOW!"

I rose to my feet, my arms hung uselessly at my sides. Ann looked
up at me, smiled weakly. I felt helpless. Tears began to run down my
face. I wanted, needed to hug Ann, but what can you do when you are
born into a family that never shows any affection. Instead I just stood
there speechless.

Eventually I found myself outside almost running the half-mile
toward my home in the light of an overcast afternoon. I knew I could
not, would not, tell anyone in our family about Ann, not to spare them,
but to protect her.

Over the span of time I have come to understand what happened
that day. Aunt Ella was angry, not just with her daughter, but also with
the family that proved so indifferent to her solitary struggle to raise her
three children. She wanted her pound of flesh from people that were
and would always be indifferent. It was the sins of the father, Ann's
father coming home to roost. I wanted no part in it except to reach out

to Ann. They moved away a short time later. And I now know, on that day, a final curtain began descending for me, on my father's family.

I've done things I wish I hadn't done. You've done things you wish you hadn't done. We all do things we wish we hadn't done. But then, there are things we wish we had done too.

17

I Didn't See It Coming
Age 9

It just never occurred to this Jersey-born kid how it all works. I was old enough to understand not everything is going to be to my liking, that certain compromises need to be made for the greater, long term, self-serving personal good, like doing something all your friends love to do and you don't. I just didn't understand how transparently bad I was at it until my friends told me to get lost. In my own defense, I did have a mitigating factor. But taking the long view, which I was eventually able to do, I realized it was an important experience overall and I took it to heart. So much so, that to this day, I have never done anything, like work at a job I didn't like, at least not for too long. This goes a long way toward keeping your sense of self in tack, but not your bank account. Of course, the alternative solution would be to become a better actor and never say anything derogatory about certain things your friends like, like politics or religion or the New York Yankees.

B Y MY NINTH YEAR on the planet I knew I didn't like baseball, never would like baseball. Really, never ever even wanted to like it. I had several good reasons for this, though some might think it unbelievable, unmanly and subversive, even sub-human, that I could be unable to grasp the beauty, grace, elegance, profundity, and camaraderie of this game, played with a hard leather sphere and a stick. I did have a favorite ball team, still do, and it wasn't the NY Yankees. All my friends were Yankee fans. Everyone I knew was a Yankee fan. Not being a Yankee fan put your social life in grave danger, if not your body. You could have been a Communist or a Republican and people would just have looked up at the sky and said' "Oh well." But, to say you liked the "other team" would bring down the wrath of the gods upon yourself. So, though it irked me, I knew better than to ever utter the Brooklyn Dodgers' name, except in my uncle Phil's presence. And to this day the Brooklyn Bums, as they were affectionately known then in some locales, is still my favorite team.

But that's not this story. This story is about playing baseball, not watching it. Here, in my own somewhat self-serving defense, is the whole unvarnished, heartrending story of how I failed miserably at baseball and barely lived to tell the tale.

In the days before Little League, my friends and I, without adult interference, played sandlot baseball, in a real sandlot, which once existed across the street from PS 12. There are seven houses in that space now, but then not even grass grew there. We scratched lines in the dirt for foul lines. Bases were flat stones or pieces of cardboard, whatever we could find. We kids just got together and figured out what to do with whoever showed up to play. The only requirement: bring a glove, a ball and a bat. There were usually about eight to ten boys, never the same kids, and never enough for full teams, or even three bases. Every time we played we had to choose up sides. Dougie Van Blarcom and John Van Koppen often did the choosing. Who got to choose first was determined by a traditional bat toss. Someone would throw the bat to one of the two boys to catch handle end up. Then they'd take turns stacking their grips single handedly above each other until the handle end was reached. That top person got to choose first. The progression of picks naturally worked its way in descending order of ability among the boys until it finally reached the least capable player, usually me or a total stranger. No one was ever excluded no matter how terrible they were, and I was quite terrible.

It was the spring of 1948 and baseball season had descended upon my friends the way rutting season must upon moose. They were driven beyond all reason and even recognition, to my thinking, in their desperate need to play baseball. There was no way around this for me.

If I wanted to keep them as friends I had to conceal my bewilderment, which I did quite well. Fairly well. Well. Not well at all.

There were three justifiable, rational reasons why I didn't like to play The Game. First, it was the only thing my friends cared about every spring, the only thing they thought about and the only thing they wanted to do. Second, I found it boring. Either you were standing around waiting for something to happen when your team was in the field (I usually was in right field, and as you know very few hits ever go to right field) or you were sitting in a batting lineup waiting to do something. The whole affair baffled me, and for good reason, which brings me to the third reason. I was cross-eyed.

Whenever the ball came toward me it would divide into two separate balls eight feet in front of me, presenting me with, at best, a 50/50 chance of hitting or catching the real ball. Since no one else in the world realized I was cross-eyed, including myself, I had no way of knowing this phenomenon was unusual. Quite the opposite, I was amazed that my friends were so proficient at such impossible feats!

Finally, one day in utter frustration, John queried, "Why can't you hit the ball, you shit?" This was my best friend speaking, actually yelling red-faced, with his arms flailing about over his head.

My response was also a question, "How do you know which ball to hit?" I shrugged meekly.

"WHAT? Just get outta here. You're messing' up my team."

There are definitely times when you sense you've lost control of your life, that some force has interfered, has finessed events for your salvation whether you like it or not. Well, this was not quite the case here. Unlike my experiences with the twelve demented live chickens my father brought home one day, which provided me with clear information about hen pecking, this situation was multiple choice. The purpose of life is to reconcile differing realities, or maybe life is just a sequence of non sequiturs.

To my great grief, that short exchange between John and myself stopped the game and left me standing speechless, with all my rabid, ball playing friends in a scowling cluster directed to me. *Was it time to go home for supper?* It was far too early. But I lamely said it anyway. "I have to get home for supper now." I turned and broke away from the snickering circle.

Of course this event, no, no not event, that sounds like a political rally. Tragedy? Too self-indulgent. Humiliation. That's it. Humiliation, cut me off from my friends.

At the time it seemed permanently insurmountable. All that night and the next day at school, in solitude, I tried to imagine what to do with myself. There was Mary, my other best friend. I could see her, but she would ask too many questions, such as, "Why aren't you playing baseball with your other friends?" And then she'd want to play Parcheesi or Hop Scotch. Who needed that!?!

By the end of that school day I knew I had to get away from everything, and anyone who could make my life more miserable, or deter me from feeling sorry for myself. I needed something new, something I had never done before, an adventure, and time to construct a fitting revenge.

My house was just two blocks from the Passaic River. During the flood earlier in the spring, a large, mangled willow tree had been washed down the river and gotten lodged upstream from the North Straight Street Bridge. I had seen the tree from the bridge.

In that instant I knew. *I'll go to the river, not to the bridge, but right down on the bank next to the water where I could check out that tree.*

In all my nine years of life in Paterson, I had never been down to the river. I felt giddy. *I'll keep it secret from everyone until I've had an adventure, better than baseball, an adventure that would make all my friends realize there was something else in life.*

The river may have been my recent discovery, but of course it had always been there, an almost irrelevant thing, ignored, not just by me but also by the whole city. There was an unspoken understanding that no one should go there—ever. It was a filthy, unsafe place. Plus, you had to go through the Colored Neighborhood.

My most common experience with the Paterson portion of the Passaic River, until then, had been quick glimpses from the bus as it crossed over the Arch Street Bridge on its way downtown. The river was just something, like everything else, framed by the bus window like an unintentionally blurred photo. From the moving bus the river appeared to be docile, and uniformly gray, except during the very early spring when snowmelt filled the river with khaki runoff from the farms upstream. Those were the only changes I was aware of. They seemed benign and irrelevant to me.

So I decided to go there. Not just because of the big willow that was stuck there, and not because I needed a change exactly, and not only because I was feeling sorry for myself, but because I wanted to understand what had happened, and mostly to figure out a way to get back at John and the rest of my baseball besotted friends. But really, because I felt split in two. Unreal.

The next day I ran home from school, changed my clothes and left for a section of the river a few houses upstream from the North Straight Street Bridge where there was a vacant lot on Water Street. It was filled with discarded furniture and scrubby Sumac trees that gave easy access to the river. At the back edge of the lot was a steeply pitched bank that led down to the river, covered in a mix of tall grasses, gravel, bits of trash, and broken glass. From the bus the river had seemed flat and motionless. Down here, fifteen feet below the word of the city, things were different. The opaque gray water was not docile and smooth but choppy and rapid. Along the bank, sparkling reddish-and-silver bits tumbled around in eddies among the rocks and urban debris. The air, uncluttered by the noises from the street, smelled cool and earthy. There were birds I'd never seen, sea gulls, swallows, and ducks, all just a few blocks from my house.

My boyish impulse required me to throw stones at the water, at the willow tree, and then at the birds, until I grew bored. Everything that had brought me to the river seemed to melt away as I became transfixed by the looping, soaring flight of the birds. I watched the gulls hover above the water then dive for fish and fight to keep their catch from other lazy, bullying gulls. The swallows amazed me with their erratic darting along the bank to capture insects. And then there were the ducks, with this year's crop of trailing young, nibbling at the water's surface. I sat on the bank. There was no one else in sight. Overhead the world of noiseless traffic on the bridge slid by.

When my legs grew numb from sitting I stretched and wandered upstream. I was a city kid getting a firsthand taste of nature. A strange, perverted version of nature, but nature that wouldn't quit, even though it had been mauled by the greedy city, and everybody else along its eighty-mile length. In June of 1918 this same Passaic River downstream near Newark, caught fire. The story made news throughout the world. In the 1930s the poet William Carlos Williams, in his epic work "Paterson" said the "untreated sewage from Paterson and dye waste from its mills was so strong that it often took your breath away." Dye waste from the silk mills that supplied yard goods to New York City's garment district had eradicated the golden carp in the river forever. This portrayal of the river was surely not the vision that Alexander Hamilton, the father of Paterson, saw when he looked into the future from atop the Great Falls. Nor would this river ever again be the place of the Leni Lenapi Indians, but it was a force of nature just the same, especially when it flooded.

It was the flood that occurred early in the spring of '48, after the big '47 December snowstorm, that got everyone's attention. We had about three feet of water in our basement that drowned the coal furnace and flooded both ends of our block trapping us there for several days. Adam Klinger, a boy in my class that lived down on Water Street beside the river, had water nearly up to the second floor. I remembered standing at the top of Stout Street, seeing him in his second floor bedroom window two blocks away waving at me. It was this same flood that had deposited the large willow tree in the middle of the river right across from the spot where I went to sit. Its twisted broken arms had become clogged with debris, clothing, and broken furniture. The stuck tree that had initially given me the impetus to trespass through the Colored Neighborhood was now an integral piece of a whole secret River World. I couldn't understand why, but my wounded baseball ego seemed less important. It was only a kid's game. This was real. A tree died and an island was born.

It became impossible for me to stay away from the river. Most school days found me returning to that spot near the bridge to watch, not to do anything, but just to be there, at the water's edge with the birds, and the stranded tree island, and the quiet.

Nearly a month had passed. I still hadn't seen anyone at the river. I don't know what kept me returning—baseball rejection, anger, or revenge? It was something unexpected, something bewildering and exciting, a feeling of expectation that demanded I be patient.

It was near the end of the school year. Soon the summer games of Ring-a-Levio and Capture the Flag, as well as the heat, would overwhelm baseball fever. *I really should get back to my real life. No reason to continue these trips to the river.* I missed the easiness of friends. *One more time, then I'll stop.* It was a promise to myself that I kept making. Yet I knew, I was not done with the river because the river was not done with me.

When I arrived at the Sumac trees I slowed my pace so that I wouldn't startle the birds. As usual, no one else was at the river. I went down to the water's edge to look for fish, check out the tree for any changes. Gravel had filled in around the branches. Plants were now growing there. It had become a real island. Then I lay back against the slope of the bank, cupped my hands about my face to close out the peripheral sight of the city, and waited for the birds to return. I wondered about the ghostly fish, living in such a murky, trash-filled world. The gulls were still circling overhead. Something was keeping them away. Off to my right, upstream, about a hundred feet or so, was a solitary Colored Man. He was sitting on a wooden milk case with his elbows resting on his knees, holding a fishing rod in one hand and the line in the other, staring into the water. I watched him for quite a while before my curiosity overcame my better judgment and compelled me to walk over to where he sat. In all the times I had gone to the river through the Colored Neighborhood I had never seen one negro. To see a man fishing, black or white, in the afternoon, seemed even more peculiar. Why wasn't he at work? I stood there timidly watching him fish for several minutes before I gathered enough courage to speak.

He was thin, had on patched, worn overalls, no shirt and was maybe in his forties. He had hardly moved since I first saw him.

"What are you fishin' for?" It was an innocent child's question

He didn't respond. I was standing about eight, ten feet away. After several minutes I asked again what he was trying to catch.

"Catfish," was his terse reply.

Not catching his tone, I asked, "What's catfish?"

"The only thin' big in the rivah."

His eyes never left the set of the line into the water. I sat down on the bank right next to him, to watch. Neither of us spoke. There were several fish in an old metal pail behind him. About ten minutes passed. "What do you do with them?"

He turned for the first time, to glare at my annoying presence and said nothing.

It was early summer before I went to the river again. It was a clear, cool morning when I reached the grove of scruffy Sumacs. As I moved through the trees I heard voices of boys ahead. When I reached the top of the bank I saw five Colored Boys spread out along the river's edge where the ducks and seagulls gathered. They were throwing stones at the birds. The birds had fled to the island but I could tell they were nervous. The stones were landing just short of their mark.

·   "Hey. What are you doing? Stop that," I yelled. My outrage had as much to do with territory as it did with seagulls. I too had thrown stones at the birds when I first went down to the river, although with my eye problems there hadn't been a chance of hitting one. But now these boys were in *my* secret place. The fact that this was their neighborhood eluded me.

The boys turned toward me. They were about two years older and a full head taller.

"What's that white boy?"

"Leave the birds alone. Why are you throwing rocks at them?" I now had their full attention, which I slowly realized was maybe not a good thing. They started to move toward the steep, grassy bank where I stood.

"This is our place, cracker, what are you doin' here?" Several boys reached down to pick up stones. I turned and ran.

The Colored Neighborhood was mostly along Water Street, a street no longer in existence, replaced by the pretentiously named Presidents Boulevard. I knew if I could reach the White Area, one block away, they would stop chasing me. I was fast for my age, fast, but not faster than the boys that were chasing me. I made it out of the Sumacs, ran to the corner and looked back to see the boys burst from the vacant lot a few seconds behind me. Several rocks whizzed past as I rounded the corner and ran up the street to the White Block. I crossed the next street. I was safe.

But no, I wasn't. They were still coming. If I could make it down the block, I could turn into my great uncle Phil's butcher shop, around the corner on my street. But I was going too fast to make the turn. The boys were right behind me. The traffic on the street was heavy. I judged if I timed it right, I could dart between the cars, and buy a few seconds. But my pursuers didn't wait for the traffic as I heard the screech of brakes behind me. I was going too fast to turn onto the sidewalk. Instead I flashed through the open door of the Tanis Hardware store, where I, and the five Colored Boys, landed in a thrashing heap amid a dozen toppled straight brooms. The next thing I knew the counterman had grabbed one of the brooms and was swatting at the juvenile ant war at his feet.

"What the hell do you think you're doing? Get out of here you niggers! Get back where you belong!" he said as he hit them with the handle end of a broom. He pulled me to my feet as they ran out the door. He didn't ask why they were chasing me and I didn't offer any explanation. "Those stupid niggers," he went on, "should know better than to come on to this street! You OK? Did they hurt you? I hope I didn't hit you with the broom."

I was a little scuffed up on the outside, but really felt incredibly stupid and humiliated on the inside. This was worse than my baseball humiliation. This time there was no mitigating factor of poor eyesight. This was totally self-inflicted.

"I'm fine. Thanks." Then I said, "I better get home now," though just like the other time, it was too early.

It had been strange, this journey from baseball bats to broom sticks. What was it I had hoped for back there in the sandlot? An act of bravado? A perfect plan of revenge? What I needed, at least, was better eyesight. I sensed the river and I were done with each other. The endless, free days of summer were beginning and I was back with my friends. And we were on to the next thing. It would be awhile before I could accept that life is a series of non sequiturs, until it isn't.

Without a doubt, there will come a day when you have a rude awakening. Mine was the day I went from being a blissful member of standing with my friends to being a pariah. Many years later I learned from a rather demented gentle teacher of Tai Chi, that life gives us the same lesson over and over, with more severity each time, until we get it. But at that time I was very young and malleable and easily bored with schemes of revenge so that I got it in four or five easy months, down at the river. Here is what I learned, there's no end to getting it wrong.

18

Astigmatism Stickball

Age 10

What's your take on reincarnation, evolution, or synchronicity? How about a step further—flying saucers? About a week before the events of Astigmatism Stickball occurred, my mother and I were walking down our street when we spotted a streaking brilliant, orange dot at about 11 o'clock, high in a cloudless, cerulean blue sky, over Al Mosca's store. As we watched, the object came to an abrupt stop, then changed direction at a crisp ninety-degree angle, moved a short distance to another instant stop and over the next five minutes, repeated the same maneuver several more times, in erratic directions, until it disappeared in a flash, over the distant horizon. If you are inclined to snicker discretely behind your hand in response, then pay attention as I relate the serendipitous synchronicity of my life with celestial world events. I am certain that what I experienced a week later on a hot summer day in 1948 Paterson, NJ, at Mr. Mosca's store, was a maliciously contrived farce, written by some bored space being. This one-act play contrived for three primary actors, four supporting actors, and numerous extras, I am sure came intentionally from the infinity of space specifically into my day. Or maybe there aren't any capricious space beings and the craziness descended on me for no reason at all.

M Y EYE PROBLEMS, WHICH were at the heart of my profound baseball dilemma, were finally getting addressed. It was during that same summer of '48 that my father realized something was wrong with my eyes. He asked me to tell him the time. We were in the kitchen. There was a large clock on the wall about ten feet away. I squinted at it and guessed the time. I was wrong. He went over to the clock and pointed at different numbers for me to identify, which I could when he did them sequentially, but when he changed the position of the clock and pointed at numbers randomly I didn't get one number correct. I was cross-eyed (exotropia strabismus). One eye turned inward, which had then caused lazy eye (amblyopia), meaning my brain was partially shutting down the use of one eye in order for me to see things up close. The remedy was simply corrective glasses, which greatly improved my vision, but not my image. Nor did they greatly improve my interest in sandlot ball games, which I avoided playing whenever possible, though I did have a favorite pro-team, the Brooklyn Dodgers. I loved the Dodgers passionately, devotedly and exclusively until 1957 when the team was moved to some obscure town on the west coast (Los Angeles, I think) and I realized that pro-baseball was just another business out to make a buck. As far as I was concerned it was an arrogant abduction. If you'd ask me today what ball team I like I will tell you, the Brooklyn Dodgers. They are exclusively still my favorite team. I would like to be able to say I never played baseball again. That I had the guts and determination to remain true to my convictions, but peer pressure proved to be more meaningful than my own intestinal fortitude. Like an eager young politician—you go along to get along—I caved. I no longer had the excuse of poor eyesight so I was trapped into continuing my less than brilliant baseball career.

It was now midsummer and for a variety of reasons (vacation trips, summer jobs, kids helping out in their parents' store) it was easier to get a few boys together to play stickball rather than baseball. Stickball, like skateboarding later on, was a socially unacceptable juvenile activity—too noisy, too oblivious of traffic or people walking by, or other people's yards. We usually played in the cool morning or late afternoon. I hated stickball too. I really did. It seemed even more pointless than baseball, a game it had only shadowy resemblance to. Stickball is a city game, for those innocents of you out there who grew up in the country. So maybe I should describe the game we played in Paterson, on North Main Street, in the summer of 1948.

A minimum of three players is needed. The bat is a cut off broom handle. The best ball is always a soft pink rubber ball about the size of an orange, usually a Spaldeen. There is a batter, a pitcher, and as many fielders as are available. A white chalk box is drawn on a wall about the size of a milk crate, which the pitcher tries to hit. If the ball hits within the box it's a strike, if not, a ball. Three strikes are allowed and then the players rotate positions until everyone has had a chance at bat. Or you could play teams if there were at least six players. There were no bases and no running, usually because there wasn't enough room or because of traffic if you were playing in the street. How far the ball traveled without being caught determined a hit. A short hit was a base hit and so on for second base and third. A home run was any hit that landed on a roof, bounced off the outfield building, or broke a window. In our games a broken window counted as a double home run. If we didn't get caught. The person with the most runs or bases won the game. We rarely played teams, and girls were never, ever allowed.

The place we used for stickball was on our block, next to Alphonso Mosca's Italian grocery store. The only open space on the street, a desperate location that consisted of a triple wide gravel driveway that sloped slightly uphill to dilapidated wood garages, next to a doublewide yard with a low, loop topped, wire fence between the driveway and the yard. The outfield building was Buddy Hemingway's house. They had moved there from the second floor apartment in my house, that spring. In all, the space was about eighty feet deep, parallel to the street. The foul lines were scratched into the gravel drive, and the batter's box was drawn on the sidewall of Mosca's store.

We only played this game when none of us could think of something better to do. This is what happened during one particularly memorable stickball afternoon. I believe Buddy Hemingway, Dennis Joosten, and myself, with a demonstrable lack of imagination, decided to play our own version of the game. Dennis liked to pitch so he took that position. I was batting because I had just gotten glasses and was intrigued with the novelty of seeing only one ball coming at me. I was even able to hit the ball often enough to keep Dennis and Buddy from making fun of me. Buddy liked to play the field which put him in his own yard, a good place to escape should the need arise.

We had some severe limitations. A smooth stucco wall is best for pitching against. However, the wall of Mr. Mosca's store was brick, which often sent pitches off at odd angles instead of back toward the pitcher. In addition to the brick wall there was that fence between the pitcher and the outfielder. We were always falling over it trying to catch hits. Then there was the lady that stood guard in her yard whenever she had laundry on her clothesline. Any foul ball that landed there she kept. Then there was the trouble with Buddy's landlord. Even though other kids played there, the landlord assumed that anything broken was our fault. There were unreasonable drivers and pedestrians who seemed to resent being hit by foul balls. And then there was Mr. Mosca.

The Mosca family had recently moved to our block and opened their grocery in what had been a vacant store. They were our token Italians, and they were considered very exotic, as were their culinary concoctions laced with pungent garlic. The Dutch—or so was the opinion of my family—had a great fear of garlic. Much like the Irish and the English, it was opinion of the Dutch that if your food wasn't boiled to death, it was inedible. They (my grandmothers, both of them) thought "it" would make you exude a pungent garlicky odor when you sweat.

Mr. and Mrs. Mosca ran their store with occasional help from their son Alfie. Very occasional. Mr. Mosca's father, Alfie's grandfather, a shoemaker, took over the shop next to their green grocery. Mosca's store sold only fresh vegetables and fruits, many of which were put out on display in front of the store.

Of all the disapproving people we stickball players had to deal with, Mr. Mosca, proved to be our biggest nemesis. Though, unknown to him, he and I shared a common dislike for the game.

It was thoroughly perverse that we played in Mosca's driveway. He had forbidden it because it kept customers away from that side of the street, but mostly because the ball thudding on his wall drove him crazy.

His favorite technique for chasing us was to throw rotten fruit at us. He had a good eye and a good arm, which was the main reason we three never changed positions. Dennis pitched, Buddy played the field, and I batted. Batting of course put me dangerously near the store, which was OK with me because I fancied myself the fastest and best-broken field runner in the neighborhood. Plus, I needed the batting practice for the next season of sandlot baseball. It was Dennis's job to warn me if he saw Mosca peering around the corner of the store. And Mosca was good at it—sneaking up on us. This set-up worked really well unless I became bored with swinging the broomstick. The result, my successful connections with the Spaldeen diminished exponentially, which meant the ball hitting the wall of Mr. Mosca's store increased exponentially. Every missed swing meant a thud. If there was a steady flow of customers Mr. Mosca didn't bother us. But if business was slow he would come after us, foaming at the mouth angry.

This problem proved to be nearly as intractable as the dumb fence. In response to Mr. Mosca's surprise attacks each of us devised escape routes. Buddy's strategy was simply to melt into his house. Dennis, not a good runner but a good jumper, would leap over the wire fence and run down the street to his house. I, not having such a safe haven at hand, would run back to the garages, climb over a fence and run through the laundry lady's backyard.

But on this particular day, my escape route was blocked by Alfie. He was our other significant problem. Alfie was large for his age and a couple of years older than we were. He had to help out in the store, which ruined his summer and made him permanently pissed off. Whenever we played stickball he would try to sneak out the back door of the store and force himself into our game. He was a stickball bully. He only wanted to bat, but Alfie's batting did have a mitigating factor, it meant less thumps on the wall. If we didn't let him bat he would threaten to get his father.

On this particular day, Alfie was hiding behind the cars parked up by the garages, throwing stones at us. I had been at bat too long and was floating along in one of my transcendental stickball shutdowns, when Mr. Mosca erupted from around the storefront. The sudden sound of Mosca's voice shattered my concentration on the void, causing me to hit Dennis's last pitch clean out of sight. With half the stickball evidence dispatched I adroitly dropped the bat and with a look of feigned innocence on my face, turned to meet Mr. Mosca's anger. It wasn't much of a ploy, but coming out of the void and hitting my first and only home run ever, didn't lend itself to quick thinking. Dennis and Buddy were already out of sight. I should have run but the image of Alfie lurking somewhere between me, and my escape route caused me to hesitate. Mr. Mosca grabbed me by the collar and shouted, "Where's 'a dat damna son 'a mina?" He continued on in Italian/ English as he dragged me around to the front of the store. I had no clear indication of what my immediate future might hold. However, it didn't seem to include rotten fruit. I knew it was sure to be serious, something just short of death, maybe permanent injury.

That was it. No more ball games for me of any kind. The gods of ball games had spoken and the message was clear, "Kid, you have no heart for the game, you don't pay attention and you're messing things up for yourself and everyone else!" Mosca was still shaking me and confusing me with his tortured English. All this shaking must have dislodged a sudden realization; Alfie hadn't tried to horn in on our game because he was hiding from his father. At that same moment Alfie's head appeared around the front corner of the store. His menacing look and his internationally understood gestures of foul language left no doubt in my mind what Alfie would do if I ratted him out.

So! It was his son Mr. Mosca wanted, not me the stickball player! I shrugged my shoulders and raised my right hand, palm up, in the best Italian body language I could contrive to show that I didn't know where Alfie was. But, not being very knowledgeable of foreign language, I failed. Mr. Mosca thought that I was pointing at his father's shoe repair shop. He pushed me to the front of the shoe shop where I caught a glimpse of the eldest Mr. Mosca sitting in the window working away at a large machine. I tried to tell him his son wasn't in the shoe shop, but thought of Alfie's possible revenge, and decided to seize this opportunity to get away. So I climbed the three steps into the store and entered into a serene world of leather smells. The store was about twenty feet wide by thirty feet deep with a tall wainscot half wall down the center of the shop. Along the right hand wall were a few seats for customers and a shoeshine stand. The air was cool. No one else was there. Mr. Mosca Sr.'s work area was on the left side of the shop on a slightly higher level, concealed behind the half wall. Nothing from the outside world intruded upon the tranquility I felt the moment the door closed behind me. I couldn't see Alfie's grandfather at work beyond the wainscot wall. But I began to wonder why Alfie's father hadn't gone into the shoe shop himself. Then I remembered Mr. Mosca was convinced that if he left the store for one moment he would either miss a customer or some kid would steal a piece of fruit. According to Alfie, his father had a fanatical preoccupation with fruit thievery. I may have failed at Italian body language but I had no doubt about the urgent reason Mosca wanted his son from the way he was jiggling around and holding his crotch. He needed to take a leak. But he could not—would not—leave his produce unguarded.

As I stood beside the four-foot wall I was confronted with another challenge for the day, Mr. Grandpa Mosca. When he climbed down from his stool in the window he disappeared from sight behind the wooden palisade of wainscoting. At his proudest moment in life the elder Mr. Mosca might have been just over five feet tall. He was now bent with age and could not see me over the wall and workbench. He began shouting in garbled English to locate me. I answered his call and moved toward the sound of his voice only to discover he had moved toward my former location. This we did again and then again. It was proving to be the most interesting stickball afternoon I had ever had. We finally located each other by waving our arms above the workbench wall.

Now what was I going to say to him? Ask him where Alfie was? I knew he didn't know. Ask about some supposed shoe repair? My family didn't use his shop. I stood there with my hands still waving in the air, when the realization struck me—Mr. Mosca senior did not speak English well enough for me to understand him even if we were face to face, nor could I use my recently acquired Italian body language to communicate with him because of the wall. He was now waving different pairs of shoes above the wall.

"No! They're not my shoes! I'm looking for…" it was useless. I could see Alfie's father through the door, glaring at me as he rapidly hopped from foot to foot.

"No! No! Please… I pleaded with the senior Mosca.

I emerged from the store with a pair of men's shoes neatly wrapped in brown paper, tied in two directions with hemp cord, not knowing what I could say to Mr. Mosca the Second about his son's whereabouts. He began yelling at me the moment I vacated the shoe shop in what I can only imagine was blue tinged Italian, while Alfie reappeared at the far corner of the store with a repeat of his earlier, silent menace.

Suddenly, Mosca spun around spotted Alfie giving me the finger, waved a fist at his son and made a frantic dash to what I suspected was the bathroom as Alfie took off in the opposite direction. As I turned away from the grocery store I spotted Mr. Mosca the elder, again seated in his window, smiling and waving at me as he returned to work. I stood there flummoxed for a moment contemplating my next move. In a flash I made a decision. It was probably not one of my best decisions, but what it lacked in quality was made up by its simplicity. I set the package of shoes down on the sidewalk against the wall of the shoe shop—after all they didn't belong to me—walked over to the grocery store and took a peach.

I had never stolen anything ever before, except a nickel I found in a forgotten purse of my mother's in the back of my bedroom closet. Other than that, nothing. At that moment a dark, snickering thing inside me whispered, "Take that peach." Stealing a peach accomplished so much. It fulfilled Mr. Mosca's obsessive fear of thieving children lurking just beyond his storefront, it made Alfie look bad, I got a reward for all the craziness, plus it went against the universal notion that all little boys before the age of ten were sweetly innocent. So I picked up that peach, took a bite, turned and walked a few slow swaggering steps past the shoe shop when I heard Mr. Mosca call out, "Hey! You come 'a back 'a here!" I panicked. Dropped the peach. As I took off running, the whole wacky afternoon repeated itself in my mind. *Everybody wanted something from me. I didn't want to play stickball, but did, didn't want to cover for Alfie, but did, didn't want to get caught by Mosca, but did, didn't want to look for his son, but did, didn't want to take those shoes, but did. The only thing I did want was that peach, and I threw it away!*

Of course Mosca couldn't leave his store so I slowed to a walk, and crossed the street in front of my house.

"I'm glad this day is over," I muttered as I entered the kitchen.

My mother was all dressed up. Where've you been? Did you forget we're gonna eat out tonight and go see *Abbot and Costello Meet Frankenstein* at the Fabian?"

There's getting it wrong, and you know it, and you take your punishment. And then there's getting it wrong to amuse the gods or imps or whatever ego there is out there that is bored with running the universe, and you go along with the fun.

19

Join the Club
Age 10

From the very first moment I suggested the idea it was downhill all the way.

IT WASN'T BUT A few days or possibly weeks later (I had to build up my courage after the stickball disaster), posing as a sweet, innocent little boy again, I went back to Mosca's and paid for the stolen peach. It was impossible to get around the neighborhood without him seeing me and I didn't like thinking of myself as a thief. During that time, Buddy moved away to Totowa and other than Dennis, there was no one else that would even consider playing stickball next to Mosca's store because I had told everybody what had happened.

I had gotten a pair of clamp-on shoe roller skates for my last birthday and found that I did quite well on them in just a short period of time. Most of my friends also had skates and so we spent that summer roller-skating. There were five of us. We met every day to play Tag in my neighborhood, at the end of the block. It was an anything goes, free-for-all. The game was half Tag, half Hide n' Seek. Every object and person, willing or not—people walking dogs, mothers with baby carriages, even wobbly old ladies—became part of our weave and dodge 'em strategy. Oncoming traffic, not a danger in our minds, was just an opportunity to skate across the path of a car so close your pursuer couldn't follow. Terrified pedestrians were forced to flee, often unsuccessfully, as we careened gleefully away. How no one was ever seriously injured remains a mystery. Fortunately, the street was narrow and congested, which kept traffic speeds down. The neighborhood shops weren't spared either. The Tanis hardware store on the corner, Mosca's fruit and vegetable store, even my great uncle Phil's butcher shop across the street had things on display on the sidewalks, which made them especially good for tight squeeze get-a-ways.

The game filled our brains, like dogs on a scent. Nothing else mattered. Nothing else existed. It was summer, and the adult world was an amorphous backdrop. Until, one day, as we met to start our morning to dusk game, we were greeted by Mr. Tanis, Mr. Mosca, and my great uncle Phil. We five skinny boys were suddenly confronted by these three large, looming men. My great uncle seemed to be their spokesman, my pinched-lip, keep-your-own-council, can't-hardly-get-a-word-out-of-him, great uncle.

"No more, or we'll call the police." That was it. He crossed his arms atop his bulging stomach for emphasis. Didn't even use the word "skating." All five of us stood there wide-eyed and silent, looking up at the three squinty eyed old men. The morning sun glinted off of my uncle's bald head.

So, we moved up the hill to Dougie's house. But it was just no good. We needed the congested, dodge 'em course of North Main. Plus, all the little kids and beginning skaters came out of everywhere wanting to be in our games.

"I know how to get rid of them," said John. "We'll start a club."

"What will that do?" I asked.

"You know, if someone wants to join they'll have to pass a test."

"A test. What kind of test? Like a written test? Like school?" Pudgy's face was all scrunched up into a question mark.

"Nah! What's wrong with you? Something scary to do."

We all agreed it was a real good idea but no one could think of anything really, really good and scary. We went from one lame idea to another: skate on one foot for three house widths, jump over a milk case, skate backward.

"Anybody can learn to do that stuff. It needs to be scary so my brother won't wanna try it," said Dougie.

"I've got it." No one paid any attention to me. They were all complaining about the little pissant kids in their lives.

"I've got it," I repeated. "I know it will work. It's really, really, scary."

"Yeah. Right. So what do you think is scary?" They all wanted to know. After my disastrous baseball debacle no one took me seriously.

"Skating down Haledon Avenue…" They all sneered at me. "From the top."

"Is that it?" Frankie snickered.

And then I let them have it, "…without stopping." I nodded thin lipped and squinty eyed (a technique I had just picked up from the three old men), looking around at everyone for their response.

"All the way to the bottom?" John said.

"Of course."

"OK! OK! That might work."

After a quiet second my friends began to gleefully goof on the image of the annoying twerps fleeing from us in terror as we tried to drag them up the hill. "Well. You really want in our club you worm? We'll wait for you at the bottom of the hill if you're still alive."

Dougie's younger brother was one of the biggest pests. He was a constant horror in Dougie's life—breaking his things, hiding them, telling on him. Pudgy's brother and sister were just as bad, driving us crazy, always in the way of our game, falling down on their cheap toy roller skates.

"I like it," said Dougie. Everyone agreed. "That'll scare the hell out of them."

Frankie, the moral ethicist in our group, and our token Catholic, said it wouldn't be fair to the twerps unless we all went down the hill ourselves. Ethics aside, we knew that the twerps wouldn't take us seriously if we didn't do it first. That made sense, so up the hill we went.

We never made it. Two blocks from the top we gave up. It was two steps up and one and one half back. Everyone had fallen at least once. The last block we pulled ourselves along, clutching front yard fences, exhausted.

"This is high enough," said Dougie. Everyone agreed. The twerps would never know that we didn't go all the way to the top.

"OK. Let's go," I said as I turned around and looked down the long, long. long hill.

"I think we should stay on the sidewalk." That was John's contribution. Everyone agreed. No one moved.

"Alright. On the count of three we all go." I said with sham bravado. No one moved, or spoke.

"This was your idea Jerry. You should go first." Once again everyone was in agreement. Except me. I was silent. They were all looking at me. This had not been a good year for me for endeavors in the out-of-doors. I had been cast out of sandlot baseball in the spring by John, (he was the one that suggested I go down the hill first), I had been run out of Water Street by the Colored Boys, and caught by Mosca playing stickball in his driveway, as well as stealing a peach, and had crashed two bicycles.

"What are you waiting for?"

I was waiting for all my years on earth to flash before my eyes. That takes time. We all have to face the unknown, the scary, at some point. I just didn't want to start so young. There was no way out of this if I wanted not only to save face, but also to restore my standing with my friends.

"I'll wait for you guys down the hill." I turned and let gravity take over. At North Fifth I was moving right along but not so fast that I couldn't check for cars. By Fourth Street I was barely in control, having just maneuvered an irregular slate sidewalk. I made it across the street just ahead of a turning car. The sidewalk between Fourth and Third was no better and I was no longer in control—arms flailing, ankles wobbling, mouth screaming. I tried to grab on to a no parking sign at the corner of North Second and nearly knocked myself down. I no longer had any idea what my feet were doing as I flashed across the next two blocks and veered out into Haledon Ave., cutting off a car, trying to avoid another rough slate sidewalk. I slowed to a stop at the corner of my own street. My left hand and arm were stinging from the pole, my legs shaking. I collapsed on the curb gasping for breath, but otherwise I was all right. I turned to look back up the hill for my friends. No one else was coming down the hill. Oh well! I'd finally had an adventure better than wimpy baseball. And I suddenly realized, I had my wimpy friends where I wanted them. It was another Molly Schwartz moment. "…nothing should never be a total loss" *if you live through it.*

I realize now that skating downhill for eight blocks wasn't a good idea. Back then there seemed to be no limit to my ridiculous inability to project future outcomes. I have also realized, as I grow older, and because of the law of symmetry, that I will probably suffer from short-term memory loss. This will be like coming home to my lame brain childhood—no looking ahead, no evaluating consequences. Only now I won't be able to look back. Though I shan't mind it too much if I can do it on roller skates.

Mike—Aunt Tyne's son

Eva Vis—Bill's sister

Jerry—three months old

Friend, Dennis—age ten

Roselyn & Bill—wedding picture

Jerry—two years old

John Whitehead—grandfather, Roselyn's father

Communist Uncle Phil

Ada—grandmother, Roselyn's mother

Ada and Roselyn

20

Hi Ho, Hi Ho

Age 8–10

In retrospect, the forties were a time of great social change for women, though fraught with irony. Because, as it is with such things, society was living with its feet in two worlds: vestigial Victorian conformity and the rapacious survival needs of twentieth century life. Women had gotten the vote in the 1920s but social change cared more about fashion and little about such advancements. My mother went to work outside the home, not out of any notion of gender liberation, but because we needed the money. And she always wore the correct outfit for "going downtown," definitely not "work clothes," though as soon as she arrived at work she'd change into her waitress uniform.

M Y MOTHER STARTED TO work when I was eight years old. I took it in stride. It seemed no more significant to me at the time than turning my head to look out of a different car window. She was the only mother I was aware of that had a real job outside the house, an actual-money job. Her first job was in Quakenbush's Department Store restaurant. Then at Popewynie's down the street then back downtown at the more upscale restaurant at Meyer Brothers' Department Store when I was ten. It lasted a short time. Then she switched jobs, under mysterious circumstances—something to do with me I think. She went back to work at Popewynie's Luncheonette down the street, five days a week. On Saturdays, she continued to help her parents at their store in West Paterson.

The only other wife in the family who worked was my aunt Fay. She was a waitress, nights, but that was out of self-defense. She wanted to spend as much time away from her husband, who worked days, as possible. Divorce would have been a more satisfactory solution but not socially acceptable, especially if you had young children.

There were other mothers that earned money to keep the family's nose above water. Mary's mother took in ironing that was done in her closet of a kitchen. There were times when the kitchen table would be lost to sight for several days, forcing everyone to eat standing up or balancing their plates on laps in some less congested nook of their equally cluttered house.

Most of the mothers I knew stayed at home, didn't take in work. It was the norm. For the first few years of my life my own mother rose earlier than my father and I to have breakfast ready and on the table every morning. Like all of the mothers then she wore a cotton house dress, a light, usually floral or plaid affair buttoned to the neck with a prim collar, elbow length sleeves, tapered waist with a skirt that flared out to mid-cafe, below which were white bobby socks and penny loafer shoes or even low stacked-heel shoes. Her summer versions were short sleeved with an open frilly collar. Sometimes she put on a ruffle edged cotton bib-apron to do heavy cleaning or baking. However, this assemblage was never permitted outside the house. Even a simple trip to a local store required a major change of clothes to something fit for the street. Going downtown required different, even more stylish clothing, and my mother was totally compliant, gleefully so, especially when it came to our visits to Great Aunt Tyne's house.

Going to my aunt Tyne's house required the most careful, time-consuming preparations. Tyne was my grandmother Ada's older sister and two more disparate personalities did not seem possible in the same family. It actually took me a number of years to realize they were in fact sisters.

Slim Ada, was meat-and-potatoes survival: practical and pragmatic. I never saw her dressed in anything but a white housedress, penny loafers, and white socks. The only dispensable item was her white butcher's apron she wore while working in her store. Aunt Tyne, by contrast, was a grand dame, a tall-but-chunky body with a personality that seemed preordained to rule over whatever or whomever she came in contact with. She dressed as though she were on the verge of something socially significant. She always looked magisterial, with her omnipresent pearls and high-heeled shoes and careful lipstick. It's not that she never wore house dresses. She did. Yet they were somehow more elegant, perfect, as if they had been purchased at Meyer Brothers' rather than Woolworths. Maybe it was the pearls that made the difference, that gave her an omnipotent aura requiring everyone to sit up straight and never place their elbows on the table.

My mother was overwhelmed each time she was to attend afternoon tea at Tyne's house. Did she have adequate clothes? Who else would be there and how would they dress? Could she wear the same thing two visits in a row? These were issues not discussed with me but I could tell by the intense flurry of preparation preceding each of these mid-week visits that something out of the ordinary was impending. What my mother wore was what every women visiting Tyne's felt compelled to wear then: best dress, seamed silk stockings, high-heel shoes, open-toed were my mother's most stylish, white cloth gloves, a hat with a veil and a pocketbook, as they were called then. My mother had several veiled hats, but the one that she favored for these visits, had a veil with largish polka dots that must have obliterated great pieces of the passing world. When she took my hand to cross the street I wondered if I was the one safely leading the way.

It was at this point in my childhood that I started to take an interest in women's hats. This interest began when I was trapped behind some fashion conscious women at a movie wearing a hat that blocked my view. The worst offenders were those hats with feathers that dramatically fractured the movie screen into quivering snippets with the slightest movement of the head. Unlike my hat, or all men's headwear, which according to social norms were to be removed indoors, women's hats were always permanently affixed for the duration of an occasion, and it was Aunt Tyne's afternoon teas that finally brought this to my attention.

In contrast to anything my mother would normally have worn during the day, the kind of hat required for one of these teas was startling. It wasn't just my mother either. All the women at Tyne's long kitchen table were wearing a variety of bizarre headgear, which was not removed throughout the afternoon. It took only a couple of teas before I understood that women's hats were the silliest of things, providing scant protection from sun, rain, wind or snow. I could tell by the degree of a hat's uselessness what type of event was about to take place. A kerchief, which my mother favored, meant a trip to a neighborhood store: a fairly useful object, a kerchief meant a woman didn't have to fix her hair before leaving the house but it didn't provide much protection against the weather. A small brimmed hat, even one with some fake fruit or flowers, meant a trip downtown shopping. This type of hat could be useful against the elements, but tilted toward the decorative.

In my case, such a trip to town with my mother required that I change my clothes too. The last and most bizarre type was the least functional and the most weirdly sculptural, even to the point of making a women's head look anatomically deformed. These ranged from casual tams or pillbox types worn at odd angles, to swooping assemblages of felt or straw with gigantic brims, festooned with feathers and ribbons, and veils, nearly always worn on the side of the head, defying gravity.

Naturally these hats were reserved for formal, public gatherings, and important social events, like a visit to my aunt Tyne's house, or the movies, or church, though hats for church tended to be less flamboyant but were no less of an obstruction. In church I longed for one with lots of feathers to be seated in front of me. I thought all this varied millinery as contrived trappings for generally contrived child-unfriendly affairs. But, then most things adult seemed peculiarly contrived to torment me, including some of the clothing I was compelled to wear. The worst, most torturous and loathsome were the short pants and knickers I wore until I was seven. All little boys did then. I just had to do it longer than most. The only exceptions were my Army and Sailor suits, popular during the Second World War, which I loved to wear because the long pants and uniform made me feel grown-up. It was what I wore to Aunt Tyne's teas until the order to cease and desist came down from her.

It was most likely when my mother began to work that these visits to my aunt's house came to an end. Women just didn't work when I was a boy—weren't supposed to. It was said they were taking jobs away from men just back from the war. Women were expected to stay at home, to ease everything along for their families. My mother would have dinner ready and have changed out of her housedress into going-to-the store garb by the time my father got home from work. There were some women in my family on my mother's side who also worked, but not outside the home. They worked in family-run businesses like my grandmother. As I said, when my mother really went to work it was outside the home. It meant we were poor enough to care more about survival than social status. My grandma Ada, sent to work at the silk mills at the age of twelve, must have come from a very poor family. I don't really know. What could I know about such a thing? No one would ever talk about it in any detail. When my mother went to work it opened up a whole new experience of the world. I got to know Molly Schwartz, next-door, who fed me lunch every day while my mother was at work and checked up on me after school. Molly had a broader vision of the future than my day-to-day struggling family had.

"You must go to college," she said repeatedly as I sat in her kitchen eating lunch.

In my father's family his mother Clara didn't work, unless you count raising six kids without a washing machine or a hot water tank or enough money. My German aunt Mary worked, she was a solitary German immigrant, until she married my uncle Neil. Actually she got him his job at her firm which he kept until he retired to tour the country in their Nashua travel trailer. I don't know what my cousin Ann's mother, Ella did. She must have worked to support herself and her three children after my father's brother and she divorced. Joe remarried and had three more children with his second wife. I'm not sure but I don't think she worked either. Gert, married to my father's older brother Pete, took in ironing like Mary's mother. Or maybe not, but what else could explain the mountainous stacks of clothes everywhere, more than one family could possibly own or need.

Once my mother broke free from her hermetically sealed container of housewifery she never looked back. To my knowledge my father never objected. He seemed relieved actually, though I noticed he started spending more time in the bar next store now that he had some extra pocket money. For once they were able to catch up on bills and even go out to a show or restaurant occasionally, even heat the whole apartment throughout the winter. And, my mother stopped threatening to make me wear play clothes to school. Wearing dungarees and sneakers meant you were poor. We even got a private telephone line—better for my father's business—and a second hand ten-inch TV set from my friend Buddy's father who had started a TV repair business.

My mother's work hours barely allowed her to get home in time to get supper ready, so I was given the job of helping out, putting dishes on the table, peeling potatoes, and trying to get my father home from the bar before our supper got cold.

It was a long time before I realized that my family lived hand to mouth. And while it was unusual, even in our blue-collar world for my mother to go to work, it had the unintended benefit of unfiltered freedom for me. It's when boyhood adventure really took off. It's also when I really started to look at things, figure them out and form my own opinions, mostly about childish things. But you have to start somewhere. And I loved doing it, wandering around inside my head, forming profound insights about women's hats.

21

The Kiss Off

Age 10

Do you know that irresistible feeling that comes over you, a kind of dark vision that closes out every reasonable thing but the light of a really dim-witted idea at the end of the tunnel, so insistent that there's room for nothing else in your brain until you've extirpated yourself from it by carrying it out? It was just such a situation I found myself in...again.

IF THERE IS SUCH a thing as a social vanguard my mother was in it, the first among her friends, waiting tables in the lunchroom at Meyer Brothers' Department Store, five days a week, from ten in the morning until four in the afternoon. This hardly allowed her to keep her first day job—me, the house, and my father.

Meyer Brothers' was considered the finest store in town, because of their high-class clientele and their high prices, so she made good tips, which made up the biggest chunk of her earnings. Her wages were miniscule since working at that store in their restaurant, according to my father, was considered a privilege by the storeowners.

One day during the early summer I thought I'd pay her a visit at work. As the sole member of the Haledon Avenue Skate Club—the only one to skate all the way to the bottom of Haledon Ave from the top—I was downtown roller-skating with three of the club wannabes. They were too chicken to skate down Haledon Avenue.

You remember how it is when you're a kid, things just pop into your head, like visiting your mother at work.

"I think I'll go see my mother while she's at work," I said to my three friends.

"What?" Pudge, put on one of his best faces, he looked like had just smelled something bad. "Why?"

"She just started workin' at Meyer Brothers'."

"So? Let's just keep skating."

"It's kind 'a strange. Like she's another person. I just wanna see her. She has to wear special clothes."

"In the store?" asked John.

"Nah, she works in the restaurant part."

There was a slight pause then Dougie chimed in, "Aaaah, you're too chicken."

"Am not! You're chicken," I said.

"This is different from Haledon Ave. I'll betcha you won't do it."

"Yeah, on skates," said Pudge.

I was already in too deep so I kept going. "On skates?"

"Through the store too. Or else."

"Or else what?"

"You'll have to kiss Barbara Liddell."

"On the lips," put in John. "In the playground in front of everybody."

The main entrance to the store was on Main Street. This elegant store, built into the slope of a gentle hill, went through to Washington Street, which was a flight of stairs up from the Main Street level of the store. The restaurant was off that upper level. The four of us were stopped outside the Main Street entrance.

"Chick-en, chick-en, chick-en, chick-en..." they chanted.

People were looking at us. We were standing in the middle of the sidewalk blocking the doors to the store. Besides, I didn't mind the threat. I really wanted to kiss Barbara Liddell, although I'd kill before I'd let my friends know. It's just that I didn't think she wanted to kiss me. I mean, after her mother grabbed my box of Whitman chocolates Barbara always snickered at me behind her hand.

"And if I do it? You guys have to skate down Haledon Ave. like me."

The stakes were now high for everyone. My friends looked at one another without a sound.

"That's way more than skatin' through the store," John finally said, his eyes squinting, his lips in an indignant pout.

"Is not. I could go to jail for this. Bauk-bauk-bauk-bauk," I chicken chanted at them.

"Alright. Alright. It's a deal. OK with you guys?" John said to the other two.

They nodded agreement, but I could see they weren't comfortable. I started toward the door.

"Wait. How will we know you did it? We need somebody up on Washington Street, and you have to come out of the restaurant's street door. Wait for us to go 'round the block."

"How will I know when to start?"

"Oh. Count to a hundred," said Buddy and they took off down Main to Van Houten Street to go around the block.

I immediately forgot to count. *This is a scary heap of silliness.* "No way out," I said aloud. *Should I try to walk through the store?* The first floor was filled with lady things: perfume, jewelry, cosmetics, clothing, hats. I'd be wading through all that stuff and women dressed in high heeled shoes, veiled hats and white gloves turning their heads to see what sort of small miscreant was intruding on their elegant world of pricey purchases, wearing roller skates no less.

No. I needed to get this done quickly. Having lost awareness of the time, I decided there must be a bit of the count left, so in finished up with ninety-eight, ninety-nine, one hundred, and off I went, crashing past a woman holding open a door for someone behind her. I glanced off her arm, nearly losing my balance, which propelled me forward, with my arms flailing. I careened into the cosmetics counter and a customer, where I saw an open perfume vial launched into the air. The main aisle, though fairly wide, was filled with preoccupied consumers. It looked like a pinball machine, with countless bumper guards and flippers for improving your score, and I did quite well since most of the human obstructions never saw me coming. The few lucky ones that managed to flatten themselves against counters only succeeded in reducing my total pinball tally, not their dismay. I didn't need to look back to understand the carnage I had created.

In front of me now was the flight of stairs that led up to the Washington Street entrance. I had a lot of experience with steps on roller skates. It was one of my better tactics for shaking off pursuers in a game of tag. Up I went. The landing was very wide. The Washington Street exit was just ahead with the restaurant off to the left. I hesitated then I thought, with that part of my brain that thought skating through a department store was a good idea, *I've come this far. I need to do it all, leave by the restaurant door not this one in front of me.* So I turned left across the landing and erupted through the dining room opening past the maître d' rolling ten feet into the room before I stopped. Walking toward me with a tray of dishes was my mother in a funny maroon and white dress, a white apron and a peculiar white, starched, lacey affair on her head. She let out a startled but decorous cry then asked, "What are you doing here?"

Like a deer in the headlights, I stared back. "Nothing." I answered. Then I turned to look for the door to the street. There was a velvet rope across the door and a sign on a chrome stand, which said, "Please use the store entrance." Knowing myself to be a well-behaved boy that always tried to do the right thing I turned back toward the opening to the store, ducked under the grasping arms of the maître d' and fled in the direction of the Washington Street exit with the maître d' in hot pursuit. Nearly at the head of the stairs, taking two steps at a time from the lower level, was a man dressed in a pin stripped double breasted suit, white shirt, a tasteful tie with a red carnation in his lapel—the store detective, looking wild-eyed at me. I must say that my rush to the exit looked like it was going to be a three-way photo finish. I flashed under the arm of an entering shopper, and as if in a Max Sennett movie, heard the head on collision of the two men behind me as they grasped at empty air. I burst out of the Washington Street door into my three friends clogging the narrow sidewalk.

"Hey, you didn't come out the right door. It don't count."

"Get outta here!" I yelled as I ricocheted through them in a rush toward home.

It's a little vague now, but I must have returned to the home of my parents that same afternoon, for I continued to finish out my childhood with them, though I have no recollection of any repercussions from that day. There must have been some price I paid. Admittedly this was quite a serious thing that I did, but like the trauma of a major accident, you remember very little, especially the actual pain. Soon afterword my mother switched jobs, my chicken friends, not willing to skate down the eight-block hill, because I came out the wrong door, went back to playing baseball, this time without me. And I spent the rest of the summer with my other best friend, Mary.

I have come to the conclusion that the difference between a memorable childhood and a total blank is the willingness to do anything with as little forethought as possible, as often as possible, for no possible good reason, except to be free, to be spontaneous and inventive, to excel at making your own mistakes.

22

Food For Thought

Age 10–12

A good subtitle for this tale might be "How my Life was Decimated by Scrabble, Glutted on Graham Crackers, Distorted by Riches, Derailed by Salvation, Perplexed by Strange Admonitions and then Restored by Scrabble," but that admittedly is too long. An even better subtitle might simply be, "Don't use me for Target Practice."

"IT'S NOT ALLOWED! IT'S not! It's a contraction. And besides, it's spelled wrong."

Mary Robinson lived two doors down the street at 95 North Main. She was the daughter of Lithuanian Catholics, and like myself was an only child, and if pressed to admit it, my very best friend. My other best friend that is. She was, after all, a girl and I could never let my other friends Douglas, and John know about her. I lived a double life—with them I did boy things, with her I did, not girl things quite, but sedentary-small muscle things. She was headstrong, smart, independent, fiercely competitive, and lots of fun. We squabbled continuously in a way that only a brother and sister can. My time with Dougie and John and Mary were spent in alternating clumps of time—days or weeks with just the boys and then only with Mary. The school year schedule was the strongest influence for my social flip-flopping. She went to Catholic school and I to public school. We tended to see each other during vacations or on weekends, usually at her house. Neither of us liked the hot summer sun, except when Nell, Mary's aunt, would take us up to the Lakeside Swim Club in Haledon, so we gravitated to serene, minimally physical exertions, table-top activities: Monopoly (our own rules which were the source of many arguments), Parcheesi (which she liked because I would get bored and lose), Clue, a detective game (which was only fun when three people played), and a variety of card games, Rummy, Casino, Hearts, and Canasta, which Nelly taught us. When Scrabble came out in 1949, it completely dominated our summer existence. Insidious Scrabble consumed us. Completely. We spent hours every day for weeks, playing the game outside in Mary's backyard, or when it rained, all snug on the glassed-in front porch.

But, out back in the yard under an impromptu tent affair devised by Alice, Mary's mother, was our favorite spot. The tent was constructed from two large white bed sheets, clothes pinned together over their clothesline then anchored to the ground with stones to keep the tent shape open. On hot days "Mary's Mother"—my childhood name for her—would wet down the whole affair, giving the tent a translucent coolness that saved us from the city sun. It was a magical space, as far away from the grown-up world as a tree house in the woods or a forgotten corner of an attic. The tent was just big enough for a small table and two small wooden children's chairs. It was a place of absolute perfection for our absolutely guileless, winsome selves, the cherished Scrabble game, and Webster's Collegiate Dictionary, and infusions of buttered Graham Crackers and sweetened ice tea provided by Mary's Mother.

However, regardless of how reluctant I am to spoil this idyllic, sugary Scrabble pastel, there was a flaw. I could not spell. And INFURIATINGLY, like salt in a wound, Mary could spell anything. Flawlessly. Time after time, my mangled spelling attempts were swept from the board by her unerring photographic index of correctly spelled words.

I was best at Monopoly (Monotony she called it), better at most card games, equal at checkers and Canasta. But once we got Scrabble my life became a Dante's Inferno of endless word challenges and lost turns. Most devastating of all were the times I couldn't even find the word in the dictionary. I once had to explain to my teacher, before the entire classroom with everyone listening, that I couldn't find the word in the dictionary because I didn't know how to spell it.

Occasionally I would suggest, feebly, "Let's play cards today." Knowing how passé she held that suggestion to be.

With a lock on my eyes she would say, "I want to play Scrabble."

I had suffered indignities, real and imagined, in my young life when I felt like an over turned beetle struggling to right myself. My baseball fiasco comes to mind. This was worse. She had me. A fly trapped in her web. No escape hatch, because the winner, which she always was, got to pick the next game, a rule that always carried over to the next day. "House rules," she would say if I suggested a different game—the arrogant, evil little despot. In Scrabble spelling was all, and I was absolutely nothing. Weeks of humiliating loses brought me to my knees, not a pretty sight, a prepubescent ten-year-old boy up against a flawlessly intelligent girl. So if I couldn't match her spelling ability what could I do? I needed to make an end run around her gloating superiority. I needed to play differently. I needed to use strategy. (Thank you, Uncle Phil, for teaching me how to play chess.) Mary always went for the glitz of laying down long words, trying to use all her tiles at once to get the big fifty-point bonus. That was her weakness. She never tried to do anything else. I realized that if I stuck to small words that I could spell (most of the time) and fit them into tight spaces like a crossword puzzle, I could create multiple scores with just a few tiles. And it worked. I started to win. Mary, crazed and livid, argued about the rules, now that her superior spelling ability was no longer a guarantee for winning.

"Baby words! You use nothing but baby words!" she flamed. "Is that all they teach you in your school?" she sneered.

My school, huh! I pointed out that she went to a school where the teachers all dressed like penguins and made the girls wear weird plaid clothes and knee socks. Yes! Now I was the one that was winning and gloating, still not a pretty sight, but much, much more to my liking.

Though Scrabble was the core of our frequent loud squabbles, these Scrabble squabbles often spread sideways into any subject, such as our schools, which of course effortlessly flowed out through the tent walls and reached Mary's Mother and her aunt Nelly sitting on the swing glider by the fence next to Charley's Bar and Grill. The wooden glider was a wonderful affair—two facing open slated yellow settees with flowered cushions joined to a slated wood floor that enabled the whole construction to be swung back and forth in a wooden framework, under a candy striped canopy, with fringe. It was an adult version of our tent, removed from the childhood world of interruptions and demands twenty feet away. Well somewhat removed.

"More ice tea? Some more Graham crackers?" Alice reached across our table and filled our glasses.

Mary and I were locked in an eye-to-eye mortal staring combat. I was winning the game but not the argument. *Ah! Where are you today Mary. Researchers have now proven that the ability to spell is genetic, and has nothing to do with IQ or education. So there.*

"You know good friends don't argue about religion or politics Jerry."

I kept my glare fixed on the spot where Mary's eyes would have been if her mother's arm and the pitcher were not between us slowly pouring out the iced tea. *Nice try Alice, but I'm not going to be the first one to break off the stare.* I didn't respond. I couldn't understand what Scrabble had to do with religion or politics, even though we were impassioned in our nit picking like two sixteenth century opposed clerics. *Why did she only tell that to me?* I had completely forgotten about the educational comparisons we had made just moments before, and so too, had Mary as things turned out.

"Do you understand?" Mary's Mother continued as she moved her arm out of the way.

I knew she was looking down at me, waiting for an answer but my eyes were still focused on Mary's reappearing face. I was not willing to lose another battle of wills. Mary looked at me, scrunched up her face, and stuck her tongue out at her mother as I swallowed a snicker.

"Well?" said Alice still staring down at me. "Snorting is not an answer Jerry."

Mary's facial antics continued behind her mother's back as I tried to stifle my laughter. "Oh," was all I could choke out. I let the sound of that single syllable trail off into a singsong ending, hoping it would convey comprehension. Mary's Mother stared at me impassively. Then after a prolonged silence said, "Good," then backed away from the tent.

We peacefully returned to the game, united in the knowledge that the real enemy was the Adult World. But within fifteen minutes we were Scrabble arguing again. Alice's arm bearing a full pitcher of tea reappeared through the tent slit. "Good friends don't argue about religion or politics," she repeated with some vehemence.

"Oooooooooh!" I repeated. Mary's Mother grimaced slightly and backed out of the tent.

"What does she mean?" I asked Mary. Mary rolled her eyes and shrugged. We went back to the game. In about thirty minutes Alice was back again. This time with more buttered Graham crackers and another admonition, directed at me.

Mary leaned over the table after her mother left and whispered, "Do you know what she means?"

"Me? No. I just asked you! She's your mother. You should tell me."

Alice had joined Aunt Nell back on the glider.

"Shhhhhhhhh! She can still hear you," said Mary.

"What's all that whispering about in there?" said Alice.

"See!! I told you," said Mary.

Up until that day Mary's Mother seemed as uninterestingly normal as everybody else's mother, but now, even though she wore the same old funny cotton house dresses as every other mother, she seemed mysterious, enigmatic, someone that bore furtive watching. And for the first time ever, I thought she might possibly be a person, not a food vending machine.

"NOTHING," we both yelled.

We returned to the game and within a few minutes forgot Alice's repetitive pronouncements. We were arguing again when the arm reappeared and added more crackers to the already overflowing plate. Not a word was said as we stared up expectantly into Alice's face. She greeted our stares with her own.

It's not just youth that's wasted on the young. It's also subtlety. Neither Mary nor I could tell if she was trying to warn us, scold us, or instruct us. Maybe it was just for me, since she mostly directed her declarations toward me.

"What's going on Mary? I thought your mother was normal. Why's she always coming in here and sayin' that stuff?"

Mary tilted her head and performed another scrunched face shrug. "What's it mean? What's it mean?"

I wasn't sure what normal was. Up until the age of ten I thought of most adults as talking wallpaper, as a staticy radio when they were angry. Then they were crazy. But wallpaper was the norm. I didn't even know how to define what Alice said that day. Normal, abnormal? It was certainly nothing I'd heard before. The conclusion I eventually came to was that her intentions were religious. Why? No reason, just a ten-year old's hunch. Mary and I had said something about our schools, a comparison, parochial vs. public. That's what I remembered a lot later. Anyway, Alice went back to being Mary's Mother and Mary and I went back to squabbling about Scrabble, but with one caveat. I was now secretly paying attention to Alice, and soon other adults, because of events that were about to take place. This exchange with Alice was a premature distraction, after all, I still needed to work on being a child and doing childish things as often as possible. We weren't up to whatever it was that Alice was worried about. Wanted from us. From me. Whatever it was, Mary's Mother never made it overtly clear. I thought it might be about our squabbling, but what did religion or politics have to do with that? She wanted something for herself, I thought much later, something that didn't gel with what was really going on. I felt uncomfortable, confused and to a lesser degree Mary did also. But still, I thought her family proved to be far saner than mine.

Until the day I beat Mary at Scrabble for the first time the grownups in my life asked little of me. Nothing serious—take out the garbage, say thank you, do your homework. But that day changed something. It was the smallest thing this wackiness of Mary's Mother, yet it changed how I understood—no, scrutinized—the grown-ups around me for the first time and forever. It wasn't the "what" but the "why" of what she did. Over the next few years, things happened that were similar enough to warrant special attention. Special things. Things that made me feel apprehensive, almost before they happened. There were always the same telltale signs, even before the words started. Something to do with the way adults moved to isolate me, and the way their eyes seemed to bore into me, into the center of my forehead. And when they started to speak their words seemed to slip around so I had no idea what was coming next or where the words were leading me.

My aunt Lizzy, who was really my great aunt, was married to Joseph Cerroni who worked for the ABC, (that stands or Alcoholic Beverage Control Agency set up by the government during Prohibition) he was a local agent that went from bar to bar to enforce the liquor control laws after the repeal of Prohibition. He was not a nice man. He beat and bullied his wife, tried to make other people look stupid, and as my father discovered, he took bribes from the bar owners. They never had children, although there were rumors that my mother was their daughter. (She volunteered this information to me out of the blue, then told me it wasn't true.) One day, a few months after the Scrabble skirmish, My aunt was taking care of me at their house. She had to go shopping so I was left alone with Uncle Joe. He paid little attention to me. I was in the living room kneeling on their luxuriously thick oriental carpet playing with some toys I had brought with me. It was a cool day. The winter sun was flooding the front room, picking out the intricate pattern and colors in the carpet, creating a magical fantasy landscape on which I was constructing a large complex of buildings, a city really, from my large cardboard box of American Bricks. The box contained many sets that I had accumulated over several years from birthday and Christmas presents. I passionately loved them and took them with me when I knew there wouldn't be any other kids around to play with. The pieces were modular red plastic about ¼" thick by 2" long by 1" wide. The outer ¼" edge was textured to simulate a brick surface. There were nubs on the top that fit into holes on the bottom of the next unit so that they could be assembled into a variety of building designs. Instead of using the bricks in the scale for which they were designed, I was treating each ¼" thick piece as a building story in height. This allowed me to build multiple groupings of buildings, to create a complex town of streets with a variety of building types. I had been working for several hours and had covered a large area with these structures. I had no awareness of anything else until I felt that sensation of someone staring at me. I looked up and through a large archway saw my uncle in the dining room, down on his knees in front of a large opened safe looking over at me.

"Jerry, come over here," Uncle Joe said.

I got up, went over to him and stood there looking down at him and the open safe.

"Kneel down here next to me. I want to show you something."

In the safe were stacks of money filling two large shelves. He pulled out a bundle opened it and fanned it out. They were all one thousand dollar bills. (Last printed in 1934 and taken out of circulation in 1968)

"Have you ever seen these before?" he asked, without pausing for me to respond. "What do you think? Would you like to have this?" waving at the safe.

My father was making fifty dollars a week a week. I couldn't even comprehend what he was showing me. I thought it must be make believe, like my city on the oriental carpet in his living room. Then I remembered being with my aunt one day when we went into a check cashing place across from City Hall on Washington Street, so she could have a thousand-dollar bill broken. He laid the fanned money on the floor between us, reached into the safe and lifted a small box out of a drawer and opened it. In the box was a ring. He took it out so I could see it better, wobbling it between his forefinger and thumb to catch the light.

"Here try it on. You like it?"

What could I say? I had never seen anything like it. He thought it was important, special, so I guessed, it must be important and special too. There was a stone setting the size of a lima bean on a band of gold. It was meaningless to me.

"You can have it. Someday this ring can be yours.

I felt unable to respond.

"In a few years when you are grown up I'll give you this ring."

"Yes?" I said, when I should have asked "Why?"

He didn't realize my "Yes" was a question. "I'll give you this ring if you will promise me one thing."

There was a prolonged silence as he waited for me to respond. I felt as if I were seeing and hearing him from under water. *What? What? What was he telling me?* Finally, I said the word out loud, "What?" because I didn't understand. He thought it was an answer to his provocative offer.

"I'll give you this ring and all this money if you'll look after me, take care of me when I get old.

I thought he was old already, which really alarmed me. I was sitting there on the floor next to him wanting to flee when I heard my aunt come into the house through the kitchen door. Without waiting for an answer he put the ring away, slammed the safe shut, got up and walked into the bathroom, closing the door behind him.

Around the same time that my uncle was offering me his deal, my father got struck by lightning. Until I was nine years old my father had tried every flavor of standard Protestant church available to us within walking distance of our house—Presbyterian, Methodist, Dutch Christian Reform (now known simply as Christian Reform) and Baptist, even Congregationalist for a few visits, the church his brother Pete went to.

"It's for you," he said to me one day. "I'm trying to find the right church." as if I had shown some interest in his search.

When you're ten, what do you really understand about the adult world of God or church or country? Not much. At least I didn't. At that age my life wasn't about concepts, it was about experiences. And of the three the only concrete one was church. I went there on Sundays and sat still on a hard wooden pew for hours. The day began at eight in the morning with a light breakfast, followed by the donning of my suit, tie, and polished shoes, a walk to church at nine for Sunday school, immediately followed by an 11:00 a.m. church service (back again on the hard pews) until 12:30 or 1:00 p.m., an hour and half for lunch, back by 2:30 p.m. for Young People's meeting, followed by

Prayer meeting at 4:00 p.m., followed by a potluck dinner, followed by a church social which usually ended by 9:30 or 10:00 p.m., leaving me numb and exhausted.

But then my father *really* got into religion. For whatever reason, those stalwart protestant churches didn't resonate for him. Then he discovered a small fundamentalist church two blocks away with lots of resonation. For my mother and I it required a vast amount of resignation. Not only was church attendance still an all-day affair, there were additional unique requirements beyond being a decent, God-fearing person, that spilled over into the other six days of the week, that dominated life in a way the other churches hadn't and left little to no space for being yourself or permission to experience anything else. Then a day came when my father sat me down at the kitchen table and asked me, "Would you like to live forever, go to heaven when you die?" I wondered silently if I died that day would I be ten years old forever? I can't say I didn't see this one coming. Still, I was getting that trapped, confused feeling again.

My mother's parents, upon learning of my father's new religion said they wanted to speak to me.

"We need to talk to you."

I started to get that fluttery feeling in my chest. "What about?"

"It's about your future. You're our only grandchild and we're concerned that you get to do what's best for you in the future."

MY FUTURE! My future at the age of ten was about riding my new bicycle and praying that I didn't have to stay in church all day Sunday.

I sat there guardedly waiting for them to continue. Where were they going with this? I was pretty sure they didn't know Mary's Mother, the master of indirect admonitions. I just didn't know! Maybe it was my family's laconic tradition, then again it could also be the emotionally repressed Dutch heritage, or even adult-babble-talk, or me. I eventually decided it wasn't me, I think.

"We're Baptists. Always have been," and then they paused.

As far as I knew they never went to church. The closest my grandfather got to a religious experience on Sunday was to bend his elbow at the Hillcrest Tavern in the pursuit of liquid, not Holy spirits, while my grandmother stayed home talking to her canary and drinking Red Rose Tea.

"We'd like you to stay in the family tradition."

What in the devil do you do when you're ten years old and adults behave like this? A huge part of me felt like they were in a dead heat tie with my uncle Joe's maneuverings.

When I was twelve my uncle Phil, the American Communist Party member, told me I must commit my life to "the struggle" between the working class and the rich—*like me with my uncle Joe maybe? That struggle?*

That made five. Five behavior modification plans for my life all within a two-year stretch. Was it water fluoridation, or lingering radioactive fallout from all that above ground nuclear testing America did in the west, or the ethers of the universe conspiring to befuddle me, or was it just the way the world was, the way people are when they spy a malleable prepubescent child (or should I say an easy mark) to exploit for some supposedly noble good of their own creation. After some considerable time, the conclusion I came to, including my Communist uncle Phil's sincere proposal, was religion. You know, anything that will not tolerate a second opinion.

My hunch about Alice's behavior was right! It was religion. Even my uncle Joe's bribe was religion. They all were trying to create a hedge against the vicissitudes of the future—their physical wellbeing future, an economic future, and the social fabric future, the going to hell future. None of it was about, or for, the ten-year-old me. And since it wasn't about me they all had to use the same persuasive devises, fear, guilt, bribery and a better life to come, the basis of all truly effective religions. Of all these persuasive demands only two proved of value to me, Alice's "good friends" admonition, the most useful for getting along with people, and my grandparents warning about my father's fundamentalist religion, which created an irreconcilable conflict in me, but was prophetically correct and once more, another long story.

As I look back on that day that I think of as "The Day of Alice," not the "Day of Scrabble victory over Mary," I have an inkling of

Alice's concern, for that is what I think it was. Back in the forties the lines of separation were quite clearly delineated between blacks and whites, Jews and everyone, Protestants and Catholics. It was truly the time of "don't ask, don't tell" if you wanted to be polite and get along. Everyone was slightly on edge and in denial about the dysfunctional American melting pot. Alice was probably just trying to get out there in front of a bias problem that lurked everywhere. I don't know but, God, I could have told her that she didn't have anything to worry about. My Protestant religious proclivities were to stay home on Sundays. My father's multi-church switching in the preceding years had left me feeling like a mashed piece of candy in a sampler box of confections. I was not about to explode with rage against her Papist daughter with my own soul suffering from an identity crisis. I was clearer on politics, for a ten-year-old, because my entire family voted for Democrats except my Communist uncle. But then everybody I knew voted for the Democrats, probably the Robinson family too.

Well, all this is just speculation. I don't know with any certainty, what motivated the good heart of Mary's Mother to give us too much ice tea, buttered Graham Crackers, and homey advice. Then again, why did she only look at me when she repeatedly stuck her nose under our tent? Well she did smoke Camel cigarettes.

Now that I have had the good fortune to live through a sizable chunk of my life, I realize that it wasn't my family or church that helped me understand the world. It was Alice Robinson. Without even trying, without blackmail or preaching or bribery. She was just hardworking, honest soul making the best of her minimal existence with dignity and without complaint.

23

The Worm Box

Age 10

Isn't it peculiar though, how the mind makes associations that defy reason. What do you do with them? Keep it a secret? You don't want to seem strange as you suddenly find yourself staring off into space. That's what happened to me, many times, as a child. There was only one person that would call me out on this, Mary. Now I realize everyone has had these experiences of queasy suspicions, dredged up by the unconscious mind. The trick is learning which ones to act upon.

ALICE'S HUSBAND, ROBBIE, MAY have earned his living working in a silk mill, but it was Alice that held the family together, including her sister Nelly who she had taken into her family, though I'm not certain how that came to be. The Robinson's first floor apartment was too small to accommodate Nelly. So she rented the front hall room on the second floor from May, the owner of the house. Nelly never married. Her face was badly scarred from small pox. She rarely went out.

Nelly, so gentle and kind and patient, seemed like a benevolent visitor to life, as if she were about to depart. She spent endless hours teaching Mary and I games and telling us stories about her childhood in a Lithuanian farming community near Hoosick Falls, New York.

The most elusive, unknowable person in the Robinson family was Mary's father. I think his name was Charles but everyone called him Robbie. I don't recall ever speaking to him. He was either working the night shift at one of Paterson's weaving mills or asleep in his bedroom off the living room. On weekends he slept on the living room couch with his back to the room, the green WWII shades drawn, while a ball game droned out of the console radio in this liquid twilight atmosphere. Alice demanded that Mary and I tiptoe through the house, speak in a whisper, even when he was in his bedroom. Which was why we were confined to the glassed in front porch or the backyard. I was afraid of him. Maybe not so much afraid as uncomfortable.

The couch he spent his weekends on was next to the bathroom. When on my way there I wondered apprehensively, should I move quickly past this reclining Buddha or tiptoe slowly on my way through the living room. He seemed lifeless. Could he be dead and alive? I sometimes stopped within an arm's length to listen for his breathing. The hiss from the ball game on the radio, with its volume set to sooth, masked his breaths. I tried to imagine each day, every week, week after week, of his life. How could a life turn out that way? I tried to picture him as a boy. I couldn't. He must have been curious about life and the world, as all little boys are. How did he grow up to work all night and sleep all day? I never heard his breathing. I never saw him move. I never ever saw his face.

I must have mentioned him to my Communist uncle Phil, the family's token radical. He knew Robbie from the neighborhood. He explained how difficult it was for men like Robbie, uneducated, born poor, coming of age during the Depression, with no options, stuck in a life of numbing survival, working for mill owners that didn't give a damn about anything but their profits.

Every time I saw Mary's father asleep on the couch I thought my uncle was right about the mill, and Robbie, but there had to be more to this person, or depressingly less than a sleeping worker ant. My uncle's answer wasn't enough. It was too impersonal. I wanted to know Robbie. That person right there in front of me on my way through the living room. There was a great mystery here. How does anyone's life turn out? How would my life turn out? Would I, curious about life and the world, grow up to work all night and sleep all day in numbing isolation?

I had Alice to thank for this new vocation of watching, with her provocative litany of "Good friends don't talk about politics or religion." There was an edge of apprehension in her words that had made her dimensional, that made me curious and attentive in a new way about the parallel world of the adults around me.

Alice was an unremarkable remarkable person. A wearer of ubiquitous house dresses, a messy housekeeper, an excellent preparer of fish—she deboned her boney trout by leaving the dorsal fin on until the right second of doneness when she would yank the fin, back bone and ribs out in one movement—a skilled gardener that had the most beautiful flower garden, a fine cook (I loved her stuffed cabbage), a realist that augmented her husband's salary by taking in ironing. She was simply the anchor of her family. A clear minded person, not educated, not sophisticated, that showed me that it was possible to maneuver through the randomness of life with dignity and pragmatic clarity and unflappable patience and the importance of holding your cards close to your chest. My uncle tried his best to save my body, my father my sinful soul, but Alice showed me the true meaning of faith and conviction, not by words but by example.

It wasn't until that Scrabble summer that I became aware of the life force that impelled Alice. She may have been Catholic by birth and habit but her true religion was fishing, and I discovered she had converted the entire Robinson family to her core belief. They too, like ecstatic converts, loved fishing, including Robbie. According to Mary, fishing glowed in their collective mind's eye like a longed for journey to the Promised Land. They knew every major and minor fishing spot (shrine) in north Jersey, what could be caught there and at what time of year. They also used coded names for these places, I suppose, to protect them from profane use by the sacrilegious. This included me. I guess they feared I might tell someone. Each one of them had their own tackle box equipped with an assortment of hooks, lines, spare reel parts, and lures, hand tied by themselves, including Mary. Often Alice, Nelly and Mary could be found at the kitchen table devoted to this task. Their tiny railroad apartment was filled with but three types of items: the things they needed to get through each day, ironing, and fishing equipment.

This equipment was incorporated into, on and under every surface and pile of dreary necessities and fresh ironing. The only uncluttered seats were Robbie's couch, sometimes three kitchen chairs, and the toilet, which was always bracketed by two lid level stacks of all the fishing news available on the planet for the last several decades. A visit to the necessary room for anyone in the family could last up to several hours. For anyone else the trip was fraught with the dangers of tripping on something in the dimly lit rooms or getting impaled by a piece of fishing gear. Even someone as familiar with their house as I was didn't fare any better for the piles and the paths changed, often daily.

I tried repeatedly to penetrate the arcane mysteries of their world. Mary would only stare silently at me whenever I dared to broach the subject of fishing. It seemed very curious the way the Robinsons held their mystical world of fishing aloof from everyone else. Like a group of silent monks, they kept the gates to their sacred monastery closed to the rest of the universe. Only the most determined could have gotten in. In this regard I fell short. It was frustrating to see Mary drop everything, including me, when I was there, in her house, to tie fishing lures with her aunt Nelly.

"What is it about fishing that's so good?" I asked Mary. I had watched the colored man down at the river fishing, just sitting for hours. He was fishing for food. "Is it for food?" I asked her.

"No."

"Isn't it just boring old fishing?"

"No."

"What then?"

"Cause it's so peaceful. An' we get out of the city."

I had actually tried fishing. Buddy, my upstairs friend asked his father if I could go fishing with them on the opening day of fishing season. Begrudgingly his father agreed.

Having never fished before, I watched with great intensity, the elaborate preparations for this expedition. By the time we left the house it was nearly noon. Had this been Mary's family, they would have been fishing several hours. After a ten-minute drive we arrived at a park with a little, narrow, docile trickle of a brook, no more than five feet across. We parked in a parking lot. Buddy's father went into the men's room to don his elaborate fishing gear—hip high rubber boots, a hat snagged with many, many fishing lures, a vest with multiple pockets for tools and smokes, a basket over his shoulder to hold the captured fish, a big knife on his belt and a determined look on his face. We walked across the grass to the trickle, he took out his rod and reel from a beautiful wooden box, assembled them, walked a safe distance away from us and began to fish. Buddy and I were on our own. At least I was, for I had no fishing equipment and none had been offered. I found a stick, got about six feet of cord, found a safety pin in my pocket, baited it with a ball of white bread and caught an eighteen-inch pickerel, the only fish caught that day, within five minutes. No one spoke to me for the rest of the afternoon. I never went fishing again. It seemed too boring.

I wanted to understand this fishing thing that existed between them, that indefinable force that seemed to make them secretly more alive baffled me. I didn't have anything like that in my family. I wasn't interested in my uncle's politics and I didn't want to join my father's religion and I didn't want to be anywhere near my uncle Joe. No. I wanted to go fishing with the Robinsons. I wanted a second chance to see what I missed out on my first time. What more could anyone want or expect of a ten-year-old boy.

One afternoon Nell and Alice were sitting on the glider facing each other, gently swinging back and forth, in a rhythm synchronized to the sounds of the ribbon looms emanating from the factory behind their house, soothing their way through glasses of iced tea. Mary and I were ensconced in our tent with an obliquely slotted view of the adults through the dampened sheets. We were preoccupied with a life and death interpretation of a Scrabble rule, on the verge of physical blows when Alice, seated not twenty feet away on the glider quietly said "Oh!" Unlike my own "Oh" which usually trailed off into feigned comprehension, hers carried the true light of revelation. We forgot our game and widened the tent opening for a better view. Alice with her hands holding both sides of her head was attempting to stand on the swinging floor of the glider. Unable to keep her balance, she fell face foreword into Nell's lap. Nelly, always the supportive dignified person in their family, was trying to help Alice up out of her awkward position, while attempting to slow the glider by dragging her foot along the ground. But as soon as Nell had Alice up she fell again. Mary and I were now outside the tent looking on as Alice struggled to leave the still moving glider. At this point she was the only one that knew what the problem was. She was staring at a small, cement terraced area between her kitchen wall on the right, Charlie's Bar and Grill on the left and the end wall of her bedroom where Robbie was sleeping. Alice, with her hands still at her temples was looking down into the alcove of space. She took a tentative took a step forward. I followed her gaze to a low wooden structure about three feet wide, a foot deep, and six or so feet long nearly invisible in the shadows cast by the buildings. It was the worm box. All winter Alice saved coffee grounds, egg shells and vegetable scraps and other closely guarded secret ingredients, which she mixed into the soil that filled the wooden box—her red wiggler worm box. Red wigglers were the ultimate bait for catching bass according to Alice and while some in the family debated the merits of other baits (a minor internecine doctrinal dispute) in the end, they all used Alice's worms. By this time in spring, the box was literally a writhing mass of fish bait, which many people willingly traveled a good distance to purchase.

By now all four of us were standing in a row looking down into the worm box. Alice's face was drawn and drained of life. Nell was rubbing Alice's shoulders while Mary muttered "oh no" repeatedly. Someone had stolen every one of her red wiggler worms: coffee grounds, eggshells, and all. Though I was only a wannabe fishing acolyte, it felt to me like a barbarian had pillaged the sacred treasury of their monastery. We stood there silently for quite a while except for Alice's deep rasping sighs. It felt awful. The worm box had been transformed into a ransacked coffin.

It was a thing beyond my control, but it reminded me of Frankie Fratelli's bother's funeral the year before, this same time of year.

"Can I go to Frankie's brother's funeral?" I asked. My mother was washing dishes. I was at the kitchen table pretending to do my homework but really thinking about my friend and that maybe I should go to his brother's funeral.

"Who's that?" She asked.

"I'm not sure. Georgie I think."

"Who's Frankie?" she clarified.

"Oh, he's a kid we play tag with after school."

"Are you his friend?"

"Who, Frankie?"

"No. His brother. What's his name?"

"I'm not sure. Georgie I think. He never plays with us. I don't know him that well. I mean knew him. They live over on the corner of Jefferson Street and North First."

"And you want to go to his funeral? Fratelli. Sounds Italian. They must be Catholic." Her back was toward me. She was struggling to keep the dishes from falling over in the drying rack. The sink was an old white cast iron monolith on metal legs crammed into an alcove next to an old sealed up fireplace. "What happened?" she asked.

"Frankie said he was playing stickball in the street. He got hit by a car."

"That's awful. His poor mother. If you didn't know him why do you want to go?"

"Frankie's my friend and he's real upset because of his brother. Thinks it's his fault."

"Are you sure?" She was facing me now. "You really want to go?"

"Can you go with me? It's on Saturday morning."

"No. We're going to your Grandparent's store that day to help out. Besides, I don't think it's a good idea anyway. You're too young."

I knew it was a weird thing to ask. I'd never been to a funeral before so I dropped it. Changed the subject. Waited a few minutes then asked, "Can I go over to Mary's to play on Saturday instead of going to the store? They said they'd take me fishing if it's OK with you."

"You know you need to cut the grass this Saturday," she said.

"I cut it last week. It won't be so bad. They never asked me to go before. It's really special."

On the day of the funeral, three days later, I didn't go to Mary's. Instead I went to the funeral on my own. I didn't tell anyone. I waited for my parents to go to work, got dressed up in my Sunday clothes and walked the few blocks to Saint Michael's church by myself. I had never been to a Catholic church before and I wondered what to expect. As of that moment my Dutch family was going to the Dutch Reformed Church and though I wasn't clear on the technical differences between these two Christian churches, I knew that some of my family's ancestors had died in Holland during the Reformation at the hands of Spanish Jesuit priests. I wondered if things had changed much since then or would some wily Jesuit pick me out at the funeral and make me disappear along with Frankie's brother.

This is crazy. *I'm talking to myself,* I said to myself. *I am not afraid to go. I just don't know what to do when I get there.* My first funeral and I didn't know how to act in a Catholic church. I stopped walking and started to turn around. "I'm a little scared," I said out loud. "Only a little."

There was this book that we had heard about in Sunday school. One of the boys got a copy of it called *Fox's Book of Martyrs* with drawings showing the different ways Protestants were tortured and murdered by the Catholics. One scene I remember in particular. We were sitting in the back of the church waiting for service to begin looking through the book.

"Wow! Look at this one."

He turned the book so I could see. "Oh no! That's awful. What's it say?"

"Ah, let's see, 'Jesuit priests interrogating a living martyr while pigs fed from his bowels.' He's still alive! How could they do that?"

"I can't believe it," I said. But I did, for it was right there in front of me in the book. This thought was not helping me get to the funeral. There was a vague nausea beginning in my stomach. I tried to put these images out of my mind. That happened a long time ago. It can't happen today. I'm going for Frankie I reminded myself. Poor Frankie. His mother always had him out looking for his younger brother. Georgie was always disappearing.

I had gone over to Frankie's house to see if he wanted to play tag the day George died.

"Have you seen my brother?" he asked me the day of the accident. He was frantic. "He was supposed to go to the store for my mother. She's furious."

"No." I said, "You wanna play tag?"

"I can't." he said as he turned and ran off.

But I know where he is now, I thought. *Everyone does.*

The interior of the church was dimly lit and cool. Diffused light from the stain glass windows fractured the brilliant morning sunlight into a scattering of colors, which softened everything they touched. The glittery, golden alter, filled with flowers and candles, was magical and unlike anything I had ever experienced in church before. The service had started. There were many people there, sitting together in the rows at the front of the church. I was relieved that no one saw me enter as I slid into a seat on the isle behind the last occupied row. I began studying the backs of heads to see if I could locate Frankie.

"Where is he?" I said under my breath. "Where is he? Where is he?" The vague nausea returned joined now by a dry lump in the back of my throat. There wasn't one other kid in the entire church. I wanted to get up and run away but instead I sank down into the pew.

I'm little. Maybe no one will notice me. They'll just look over my head and I'll be able to sneak out after everyone leaves.

The service ended. The priest moved to the side of the coffin and indicated that we should come forward to say goodbye to Georgie. Each row stood and filed by the open coffin to pay their last respects.

Why are there no other children here? Where are you, Frankie? It was a day for talking to myself. I was alone and stuck fast. If only I could have found Frankie we could have gotten out of there. I came to let you know, Frankie, I didn't think it was your fault.

Before I could comprehend what was happening the row of mourners in front of me stood and began to move forward. The last person in the row, a large young man, seeing my hesitation, motioned for me joint the line. I was the last person on the last row and I had no idea what to do or what to expect. I wanted more than ever to escape from the church but I was too frightened. I hid behind the enormity of the man as we moved to the front of the church. *I'll watch this man. I'll do what he does.*

He knelt down on a cushioned bench next to the box, folded his hands around a string of beads, and closed his eyes. He crossed himself, leaned forward and kissed the dead boy on his forehead.

"I can't do that! I can't do any of that," I muttered. I moved up next to the man and looked down at Georgie for the first time. He was dressed in a suit and tie. People had laid individual flowers in the coffin with him. He looked so small lying there. The suit was too big for him. There were flowers all around the coffin. The sweet flower fragrance mixed with the earthy smell of incense was overwhelming. There seemed to be statues and gold woodwork, and lit candles everywhere. It was dazzling, beautiful, disorienting. The immediate family was standing off to one side next to the priest comforting Georgie's mother. She started to moan. I eyed the priest in his vestments and wondered if he was a Jesuit or did they only wear plain clothes now, like the Gestapo, to blend in with the crowd. It was difficult but I finally forced myself to look at Georgie. There were large granules of orange makeup on his face. The makeup ended abruptly at the jaw line so that his neck stood out whitish and waxy against the unnatural orange color. *Why is his head turned away to that one side?* You couldn't see his face clearly. I forgot about doing anything. I didn't kneel, didn't cross myself, had no beads, didn't close my eyes or even try to pray. Without thought or physical effort I saw my hand float through space toward Georgie, so small in that wooden box, as if to test the emptiness I felt before me. The ability to turn away had left me.

A large strong hand reached out and grabbed my wrist. "Why are you here? Who did you come with?" said a stern male voice.

"I'm a friend of Frankie's."

"We don't want any children here. Who did you come with?" his voice soft and angry.

"No one. I came by myself."

"Get out of here. NOW."

He was still squeezing my arm. Unable to move I stood there looking up into his face. We stayed locked in that terrible moment then he pushed me away. I ran through the obstacle course of departing mourners to the sunlight and the fresh air, turned right, slowed to a walk and started my usual counting of steps to the next corner in an attempt to crowd out the images lodged there.

For many years afterward I tried to erase the memory of the four of us looking down into Alice's worm box, tried to stop my mind from going further into one of the more unfortunate things I ever did as a child. Not just for me but for George's mother. For years I felt forever stuck with that intangible reality of real, intangible death. At times I would get close to stopping those memories, but then an impulse I could not resist, that I could not stop, repeated that awful childish rhyme—the worms crawl in, the worms crawl out...

24

Miss Sickles

Age 10

Caution Children at Play, is a street sign found in most residential neighborhoods, which should include 'Against All Odds.'

IT WAS SATURDAY MORNING and Dennis and I were hanging out of his attic window, which looked down on North Main Street at the corner of Haledon Avenue, shooting at birds with our peashooters. The birds had gotten wise to us and were staying away, so we were bored, early in the day.

Occasionally, when we were bored we would make up scenarios. What-If-Stories we called them. Usually these stories were about people we knew or characters we'd seen in a movie. If we liked the What-If-Story we'd improvise on the idea by acting it out, sometimes for the rest of the day or even longer. But sometimes we just made up stories to change our mood, pass the time, not be bored. It could be either of us that started the idea, but the stories were always collaborative.

So I started to tell a What-If-Story. "What if a car coming down Haledon Avenue, all the way from the top of the hill lost its brakes part way down."

I was slumped against the wall by the attic window. I leaned toward Dennis and opened my eyes wide for emphasis. Dennis glanced at me and then looked thoughtfully out the window at the quiet street. "It could then fly across North Main, just missing' all the traffic, jump the curb between two parked cars, skid across the sidewalk and up the concrete stoop in front of my great uncle Phil's butcher shop."

Dennis, trying to figure out where the story might be going asked, "Are you mad at your uncle?

"He's all right, I guess.

"Sounds like you don't like him."

"He doesn't talk much. It's not about him. It's just where the car would go." It was a scrap of a thought, like a film clip, taken out of context that had flickered across my mind with no beginning and only a suspicion of what was to come.

"And then?" asked Dennis.

"The car's going too fast to be stopped by the stoop so it smashes through the door, and one of the plate-glass windows sending wood splinters and glass everywhere in the store."

"Where's your uncle?"

"I guess he'd be behind the meat cases, or in the back, in the walk-in meat cooler. What do you think?"

"Behind the meat cases," said Dennis.

"When the car finally stops it's between the meat cases and the wall of canned goods."

The meat cases ran the entire depth of the store on the left side and shallow shelving paralleled the case on the right hand wall.

It was a clear May day and the sun was flooding the attic floor with a pool of warm light near the window. The rest of the attic receded into darkness where I looked to collect my thoughts, "My uncle, saw the car comin' so he ducks down. Then when everything's quiet he comes out from behind the case.

"He's hurt, right?" Then Dennis, answering his own question said, "Nah, just covered with dust and bits of glass. Just little minor nicks. That's all. On his bald head."

I picked up on my last thought, "Yeah. He's out from behind the case… to see what's happened. But there's not one scratch on the meat case and not even one can of Campbell's soups knocked from the shelves. There's only inches to spare on each side of the car." I paused for a second.

"Is that it?" asked Dennis. "That's not enough."

"No. Not yet. How's this?" I asked. "The car's front bumper has stopped a foot away from the rear wall."

"And there," jumps in Dennis, "trapped between the bumper an' the wall is evil Miss Sickles."

Miss Sickles was our sixth grade teacher. "Yeah, and she's pinned like an animal with her arms spread out against the wall, bug eyed, and terrified, and gasping for air," I added.

"Is she hurt? Somebody should be hurt after all that. What about the driver? Who should that be?" I asked.

"I know! I know!" said Dennis, "Sammy Voss's mother. She must hate Miss Sickles after what she did."

"Yeah. That's a good one, that's perfect." I said as the story picked up its own momentum.

"Are you OK, Miss Sickles?" says Great Uncle Phil.

"Yes I think sooo… get me out of here," I say imitating Miss Sickles' pleading, squawky voice, "Get me out of here! Help me! Move this car away!"

Trying, but not succeeding to stifle his amusement, Dennis suggests that Mrs. Voss leans out the car window and says, "Not until you say you're sorry for what you did to my son, not until you promise you won't terrorize your class anymore, then I'll move the car."

"Just think," said Dennis, he let loose a volley of peas at some sparrows that had returned to the telephone lines. "Just think of that usual rock hard angry look on Sickles' face breaking into little pieces.

Dennis and I nearly fell out of the window in hysterical laughter as we goofed on that mean spirited plague of our lives. It was so easy to do. She looked and acted every bit the part of a wicked witch. She had a large lumpy nose with a large hairy wart on one side. Her wiry black hair, pulled back in a bun, was streaked with gray and never altered. She wore thick wire framed glasses, dark drab cotton dresses, which sort of concealed her tubular plumpness. Only her ankles and feet seemed normal in size and shape, but preposterously out of scale with the rest of her body. But she overcame this discrepancy by wearing sturdy, black, laced up shoes with a solid stable low heel. She was a classic. Heaven knows that stereotypes and classics don't exist but she truly was one, a classic nineteenth-century tyrannical spinster schoolmarm alive and well in our mid-twentieth century classroom. Even her mannerisms conspired to complete this vision of an educational inquisitor. She carried an eighteenth-inch oak ruler at all times, not for reasons of instruction but for purposes of correction. Had Tasers been available then she would have used that instead. Her teaching technique, like a shark unable to be at rest, was to parade up and down every row in search of any mischief-maker while she droned on about such things as diagramming sentences—one of her passions. And if by some chance some part of your anatomy appeared to be inattentive, such as a jiggling foot or glazed over expression, you would have to extend your hand to be struck with the flat of the ruler, second offensives for the day were rewarded with a blow from the rulers edge which raised red welts on the back of your hand. She was considerate enough though not to hit your writing hand, or girls, more than once. Anyone that exceeded the double infraction law was made to stand in the punishment corner in the front of the room. Alas, poor Sammy Voss, with his sweet openness and a natural dreamy look, prone to say whatever came into his mind at inappropriate moments, earned Miss Sickles endless attention. So much so that she grabbed him from the punishment corner one day and smashed his head into the blackboard with such force that it cracked the slate top to bottom, requiring a trip to the nurse's office to stop the inconvenient flow of blood he had the effrontery to produce.

Dennis, inspired by our What-If-Story collaboration, leaped away from the attic window and began to imitate her walk. It was the determined coming-to-get-you-with-the-metal-edged-oak-ruler-walk, with the ruler hand held high, head and body tilted slightly back, BB-eyes squinting down that warty nose to focus on the annoying insect child through her bifocals as she stretched out each step like someone defying the existence of a mine field—clump-flump, clump-flump as the sensible heel and then the sturdy thick sole of each inflexible, laced shoe descended upon the fir flooring. Dennis was perfect. PERFECT.

He had every nuance, every snarly, unpleasant twitch memorized. I collapsed against the attic wall while Dennis devastated me with his flawless impersonation. I turned to the open window in self-defense for some fresh air and relief.

"Dennis, come here! Come here! Quick! It's her."

He ran to the window and crouched down beside me. "What is it?" he asked.

"It's her! It's Sickles!"

"Where?"

"Crossing the street. She's headed toward my uncle's store." She stepped up onto the concrete stoop, opened the door and went in. We turned to look at each other. "Did you see her?"

"Yeah"

"Are you sure it was her?"

"Yeah it's her. It's that silly frumpy walk of hers."

We sat there staring at each other for several moments. We both reached for the box of dried peas at the same time, took a handful each and turned back toward the window to wait.

It was quiet. There were few vehicles or people on the street. She was the only customer in the butcher shop. A few more minutes passed before our sixth grade nemesis reappeared three stories below. She stopped just outside the door on the stoop to put something into her purse while juggling a shopping bag. The doorway was set back under the second floor preventing both a clear view and a clean shot at our target. At last she took a final fatal step forward into the open warm Saturday morning. The peas caught her mid-stride as she attempted to step down from the stoop. In that split second before her foot reached the slate sidewalk we heard her scream and watched the bag of groceries arch gracefully through the air above her head as she brought her arms up to flail at the space about her face.

"Bees! Bees!" she yelled.

Dennis and I jumped up from our crouched positions by the windowsill as we watched Miss Sickles and the broken bag of food spread themselves out on the sidewalk in front of the store. She lay there on the ground like an overturned turtle with her dress up around her waist while her arms and legs paddled the air in a futile attempt to chase away the non-existent insects, still screaming, "Bees, bees!"

We staggered about the attic, hunched over clasping our stomachs whooping breathlessly with laughter. I went to the window to get one more look. My great uncle had rushed out of his shop to help his fallen customer. Under calmer circumstances, with two strong hands this would have been a formidable task, to right that rotund mass, but Great Uncle Phil in his haste, wearing his bloody apron, and still clutching his butcher's knife in one hand, made the whole affair look like a grade B horror movie as he unsuccessfully struggled to stay up right, dodge the flailing limbs trying not to cause any more harm. Never before had one of our What-If-Stories included other people. It was a whole new dimension that we needed to explore. We collapsed again on the attic floor, and best of all, a little tidbit we couldn't wait to tell the others kids about: Miss Sickles wore knee-length bloomers. God, she really was old fashioned. After nearly a full school year of torment at her hands we had stumbled onto a perfect revenge.

We looked at each other while the yelling, the laughter, and the uncontrollable tears caused us to collapse onto the floor, and then we simultaneously froze, and went colorless.

"What the hell have we done?" said Dennis.

"We're dead. Let's get out of here before they find us."

Instead of a discrete departure we stumbled and frantically fell down two flights of stairs into the rear yard. Mr. Tanis, working in his hardware store on the first floor, stuck his head out the back door. I caught a glimpse of him as we hopped the fence into the neighbor's backyard. I didn't think he saw us. At least I hoped not. We emerged from the alleyway on North First Street at a run, but soon slowed to a normal walk as we headed west.

"We'd better not go to my house. That's the first place they'll look."

"Yeah!" said Dennis, "Yeah, you're right. Why don't we go to the falls?"

"OK. If the river's low enough we can get out on the rocks at the bottom of the falls." I said. Then I thought, "I'm hungry, are you? Why don't we go to Libby's by the falls for a dog all-the-way and a birch beer soda too? You got any money?"

"Sure," said Dennis, "Sounds good."

It is so true, at least for ten year olds, that out of sight is out of mind, or so it was for us. We walked slowly on without saying anything until we came opposite the house behind mine. Without a moment's hesitation, like homing pigeons, ignoring the conversation we'd just had, we turned in the alleyway, climbed over the fence into my own backyard. I took the skeleton key off the nail in the back hall and let us in. Both my parents were at work.

"Why'd we come here?" said Dennis.

I just shrugged and grimaced.

"We need to do somethin' that makes it look like we've been here all morning," he said.

"Let's play with my Lincoln Logs set. OK? If we work fast, we can make it look like we've been here a long time."

"OK," said Dennis.

Neither of us mentioned the fact that it was really stupid to go to my house. We dumped the large cardboard box of logs onto the living room floor and set about jointly building a large fort. The young afternoon began to drift by as we lost all track of time. It wasn't until the knob on the front hall door bashed into the plaster wall that I knew someone else was in the house. Dennis's mother walked into the room jolting Dennis and I from our Lincoln Log tranquility. Immediately behind her was a police officer.

"What were you two trying to do, kill Miss Pickering?" she glared down at us.

"What do you mean?" said Dennis—since it was his mother I let Dennis do the talking.

"You shot peas at her!"

"No," said Dennis, "We were shooting at the birds on the wires."

True…true. Well half true anyway. "Quick thinking Dennis," I said to myself, though it wasn't what we had planned to say. Actually we hadn't planned anything. Too late now. Maybe she'll go for it."

"They took her to the hospital in an ambulance because of you."

"Oh no." I said under my breath. We were still sitting on the floor. Dennis was looking up at his mother. I was watching the policeman. This is way, way too serious. I felt like an upside down turtle. My mouth was dry and my stomach queasy.

"Get up! You're coming with us now."

Does she mean me too? Neither of us responded.

She reached down and jerked Dennis to his feet. The policeman moved toward me.

Oh God! We're both going to jail!

She turned her full attention on me. "This is your fault, Jerry Vis." She made my last name rhyme with rice. "Look at me." She was spitting mad. "You put him up to this."

I sat there with my mouth hanging open, trying to remember how or if I had done that. "I didn't ..."

She cut me off, "You're nothing but trouble."

Wait a minute, who did she say? She said Miss Pickering, not Sickles. Miss Pickering was our art teacher. "Did you say Miss Pickering?" I felt myself transformed from an inverted box turtle into a lumpy piece of dog doo. My eyes bulged out at the policeman looming over me as he fingered his handcuffs. I really liked Miss Pickering. She was the best, and I knew she liked me. She told me I was the best drawer in all her classes.

Dennis's mom repeated, "The hospital...they took her to the hospital. And it's your fault. I never want you to go near my son again. You're never to see him or talk to him."

This was a triple whammy. First, it wasn't only my idea to shoot at her. Second, it was unfair. Dennis and I had such fun together. We were such good friends. And third, I'd have to stop going into his parents' deli. Every day on the way home from school I stopped at their deli for my most favorite treat—a dill pickle. I'd pick up the tongs hanging on the side of the pickle barrel and select the biggest pickle I could find, paid my nickel and ate the pickle as I finished my walk home.

In that one instant I lost my good name, my good friend and my favorite treat. Not fair! Triple not fair!

As quickly as they had come, they left—the policeman, Dennis's mother, and now Dennis. I sat there shivering on the living room floor staring at the open door, wondering why I wasn't going to jail too. What were my parents going to do? What was I going to do about Miss Pickering? I tried to alter the memory of that morning so everything would turn out better. What-If it was a warm spring morning and we were in the attic over Dennis's house making up What-If-Stories and then we went to my house and we spent a long time building a fort with the Lincoln Logs. There. Done. Better? No, not really. I started over—it was a warm spring morning and we went to play at the falls… No. What if I had just stayed home that day?

We never saw each other again outside of school. Miss Pickering was all right. Just some bruises. I avoided her as much as possible. I tried not to talk to her or make eye contact. I wanted to tell her how sorry I was but I never did. Now there was a fourth thing to add to the other three. I was chicken and really, really sorry. Five things.

Miss Pickering never said anything to me, and my parents, miraculously, never brought it up either. A few days later my childhood resumed its course. After all, I was a callow youth, and the entire thing faded into the dark hole of repressed embarrassments, until an epilogue occurred to tidy things up—or not.

One Friday Miss Sickles lost it. About an hour before the school day was over, one of the boys in the back of the room farted—a long drawn out raucous affair, while Miss Sickles was flump-walking toward the front of the room. It took her several seconds to react as she was lost in a rapturous explanation of when to use who and whom, or some such thing. For about forty-five seconds there was dead silence, then like a distant but irrepressible wave, faint sounds of snickering began, first among the girls, that grew into a tidal wave of hysterical tears-running-down-the-faces-of-everyone-in-the-class-laughter as the fragrantly modified air spread throughout the room.

When Miss Sickles reached her desk she spun around with her eyes and cheeks bulging out, hyperventilating through pursed lips, while rapidly smacking her own left hand repeatedly with the oak ruler.

"That is quite enough. Whomever is responsible for this tasteless disturbance come up here now."

No one spoke. Everyone knew it was Matchec, the Polish boy, who probably had had cabbage and sausages for supper the night before. We could always tell when he had cabbage and sausage, although he usually kept things somewhat under control. But this time he couldn't or wouldn't help it. Instead he exploited this rich but fleeting resource as best he could, as a weapon of comic relief and no one—no one—was going to give up this stealth attacker to Miss Sickles.

"Stop this noise. Everyone sit up, fold your hands in front of you on your desks and keep your eyes to the front of the room. You will stay like this until someone tells me what rude person disrupted my class."

No one moved. There was almost an hour before the school day ended. At 3:20 p.m. the final bell rang. A few kids got up to leave.

"Sit down. I didn't say you could get up," Miss Sickles bellowed. "I said you would sit there until someone told me what I want to know, and that is what you are going to do."

Her formidable presence worked its will upon every child in that room. No one dared move or even twitch as she moved up and down the rows maliciously swatting the air with the threatening, omnipresent oak ruler. The school grew silent as all the children and teachers in the rest of the school left for the day. Another hour passed. My legs and arms started to ache with numbness from not being allowed to move.

"Well?" was all she said at random intervals. It was now a test of wills and this time everyone in the class, without a sound or a vote or any communication, had united against her. It was the French Revolution redux. There were now muted sounds from concerned parents in the hall looking through the small square of glass in the door. More time passed. Why, I wondered did no one come to our rescue? Were we to sit here all weekend? Why didn't any parents come into the room? It was now nearly 5:30 p.m. We had been sitting there for over three hours. Then the door to the classroom opened, the principal entered the room, stood with his back to the class and spoke inaudibly to Miss Sickles. She looked at him and shook her head. He left the room. A few minutes later two men in white uniforms entered the classroom, took Miss Sickles by each arm and without uttering a sound, escorted her from the room. For a brief moment none of us moved. We sat staring in incomprehensible disbelief as parents silently came into the room to help their traumatized children to their feet.

Strangely, no one ever mentioned her again. I think everyone understood that such an act could bring a curse upon us, that she would return to inflict revenge. The next day we had a new teacher, devoid of oak ruler. And although Dennis and I stayed friends, we never again saw each other outside of school.

Children live in present time. It's what Dennis and I were doing that day in the attic, fantasizing, just improvising in the moment. Play-acting. It is, after all, the nature of children's fantasies to try, unconsciously and metaphorically, to understand the real world that lies ahead. But Dennis and I were so lost in the moment that we never knew we crossed a sharp edge into unintended consequences.

Miss Sickles too, caught up in a fantasy, crossed that edge of unintended consequences. But she was already an adult with nowhere left to go.

25

Something Gained, Something Lost

Age 10–12

I'm writing this while sitting on the porch of a hill top cottage on Monhegan Island, Maine, watching Monarch butterflies dart through a field of September wildflowers. The sky is clear, the air calm and warm. In the distance, below, is the syncopated rhythm of island houses, beyond, is the harbor and eleven miles of tranquil seacoast waters that lie between the island, and the shore, and much further still, resides the beginning of this century old story. How did I—do we—get from there to here?

BORN IN 1916, MY father Willum Hendrik Vis, or Hendrik Willum Vis, no one is sure which is correct, not even his parents, answering to the name Bill, was the fifth born in a family of six. Only Bessie, his sister, brain damaged at the age of three from a malfunctioning kerosene heater, was younger. Pete, a year older, was his best friend and his nemesis, always competitive. Joe, the third oldest, seemed to be the family contrarian and jokester, continually at violent odds with his older brother, sober Neil, the only one born in Holland, the country of origin for the family. Eva, the second born, the happy one, was her mother's favorite.

I was ten years old before I learned of her early death, years before my birth, which explained one mystery about my grandmother. My grandmother seemed isolated from the rest of the family. She walked with stooped shoulders, her head perpetually hunched down, and at first, before I learned of Eva's death, I thought my grandmother Clara behaved and walked that way so as not to draw attention to her five foot ten height. Her husband Hendrik, after all, was only five foot four and I had commented to someone in the family that, "I think they made a peculiar looking couple. Why did they get married?" as if appearances alone constituted a reason for or against matrimony. "No," I was sternly and imperiously informed by my German aunt Mary, Uncle Neil's wife, "She valks dat vay 'cause of da greeef she carries from da death of her favorite kinder," which didn't make sense to me then. It does now. And maybe it was the reason for her posture and the overwhelming stoic sadness that perpetually emanated from her. No one provided any other possible explanation. No one else ever mentioned it.

My father's at-arms-length-family seemed to have come to America for obscure or obscured reasons. Though I inquired often I was never given a detailed or consistent explanation for their need or desire to emigrate. Grandma Clara did have a married brother in north Jersey. I never met him or his wife. Only saw their son, my second cousin Gerard, once, maybe twice. They lived in Midland Park, at the end of the bus line that passed in front of my house, which might have been the reason for my father's family to settle in the Paterson area, to be near them. We never went to their house or they to ours. Why did we never see them?

My grandmother only spoke Dutch. Her husband, a solemn, aloof individual, a smoker of stubby black Dutch cigars who would only eat after everyone else had finished, rarely spoke in any language, let alone respond to any of his grandchildren's curiosities. So what information I did acquire arrived in short dismissive sentences from one and all of the other family adults, as though they were giving directions to a disoriented stranger while impatiently rushing to catch their bus.

Bill, was the studious one, (this according to my mother) who had the best grades of any one in his family (source, mother) which was a serious bone of contention with his year older brother Pete. (This also according to my mother.)

Oh, yes, another explanation for their coming to America: Hendrik, in the Dutch Queens Mounted Guard was to be posted to the Dutch

East Indies. Clara, his future wife said, "It's either me or the colonies in the East Indies." That was the totality of that explanation, completed in less than a minute.

A whiz at math, Bill's teacher would call on him, "Let's ask the little Vis boy," to provide answers to questions no one else in the class could answer. He could solve the math problems in his head as they were being stated—multiplication, division, fractions, algebra, geometry.

Another plausible explanation for their journey to America: Hendrik married Clara against his family's wishes. The Vis's were successful bankers in The Hague, while Clara's family was not at all significant. I've never verified this. I did hear that the family in Holland lost most of their holdings in the war, bombed by the Germans, though the American Vis's did receive an inheritance of $75,000 in the fifties from an aunt in Holland. A very considerable amount then, but a mere pittance of what they would have received had they returned to Holland to live.

Willum Hendrik, aka Bill, played the violin so well by the age of thirteen that Hendrik Willum, his father, and Clara, under the advisement of their son's music teacher, were going to send him home to Holland to further his studies. That was in 1929.

And here is another expat explanation: Hendrik and Clara were married in haste and left for America in disgrace. The inference being Neil was conceived out of wedlock. This my mother told to me spontaneously out of the blue one day in my twenty first year. I could never figure out how she found this out which made me think, for no rational reason, that it must be true.

But the times were against Bill, not him personally but the whole generation that came of age in the depression. By his fifteenth birthday he dropped out of high school to work full time in a grocery store on Washington Street in downtown Paterson. He dropped out of school because the family needed the money to help meet their basic needs. Of all those in his family, his job was the only one with an opportunity for full time employment, an upgrade from his part time position after school, to work ten hour days, six days a week, for twelve cents an hour.

Of which his mother allowed him to keep fifty cents each payday. Not until I was born did he stop helping his family. By then he was driving a bread truck for Dugan Brothers out of Clifton, still working six days a week. Then he drove a bus for the Public Service Bus Company, and then he painted houses, and then he sanded floors. And so life went along. He and his wife Roselyn stayed in the old neighborhood, rented a five-room apartment from Roselyn's aunt Hazel. So, all that intelligence and all that talent and promise just lay there, trapped in that time, locked in by diminished opportunity and circumstances of survival. His was not an especially tragic story. Quite commonplace then, which makes it all the more poignant, just another minor casualty of an age that had failed its people—the lost generation of the Great Depression. There may be worse things that happen to people—wars, diseases, accidents that make it into the news. But a house that rots into the ground for lack of resources is no different from one that an arsonist burns down in the night. He no longer played the violin. He just worked and worked and worked with little time or energy remaining to build a different future. And then he began to drink. He became, as it is euphemistically known, a functional alcoholic, never missed a day of work because of his lately acquired avocation. He was a conscientious provider for his family, a responsible husband and father, but no frills, no soothing softness, with no respite from his tedium. Nothing special. Nothing that was like playing the violin had been.

So he drank, as many people do, to feel something other than a suffocating dead-end survival, to feel their existence transformed for the moment by the minimal effort of draining a glass, and he went to church perhaps for the same reasons, hoping to find—to feel—something that gave his life purpose and meaning and a longed for respite. So he sampled many different churches, as long as they were main stream Protestant, but he eventually returned to the most agreeable and undemanding one, Charlie's Bar and Grill, right next door. Like many life patterns his drinking started small, a few Friday night beers after a week of work and an occasional Saturday night dancing at the bar with his wife, then a quick beer on the way home every evening. After a while it became my job to go next door to get him for supper. One day Charlie, of Charlie's Bar and Grill, asked if he would open the bar in the mornings before he went to work. Of course he'd be delighted to help out, and as a fringe benefit, the opportunity for a free, quick pick-me-up or two to start the day. This all occurred over a seven-year period, the transition from church hopper to barfly. My mother refused to go out with him any longer. Since he only wanted to go to Charlie's it meant he was now drinking alone. Still he kept his job, wasn't overtly mean or abusive to his family, just never home, only to sleep and eat at night. I remember going to my friend Johnny's house seeing his father on the living room sofa drinking beer. One time he had come home drunk, hit both his wife and Johnny, wrecked the kitchen in the process and was muttering to himself, when I got there, having an argument with an invisible person, and I wondered if my own father could be like this, become this.

On a Saturday night, some weeks before I saw Johnny's father lose it, my parents were next store at the bar. My father came home to check on me. Since they were just next store there was no babysitter. He woke me up for no practical reason by tickling me. It went on too long. I realized he had been drinking. "STOP! STOP! STOP! STOP! STOP!" I screamed, "You're hurting me." He was wobbling about over me, giggling. I thought, what would make him stop? I yelled, "I hate you," repeatedly until the words finally penetrated. He froze, stared down at me in my bed, turned and left the room and the house without any response, to my complete surprise and relief. And in that moment I wondered, did I mean it?

A few years later, on just another Friday night, I went next door to the bar to bring him home for supper. "I'm not hungry," he said. "Go on home and eat without me. I'll be home in a little while."

Suppertime was a silent sullen affair with my mother. I went to bed at nine and still he wasn't home. Sometime in the night I heard voices coming from my parents' room. Our two bedrooms were joined by a door, which my father had removed in order to keep my room warm. The dining room and living room had been closed off for the winter to economize. We were using the cook stove in the kitchen, which adjoined their bedroom, instead of the coal furnace, to heat the remaining three rooms. It was my mother's voice and another unfamiliar one, not my father's but a man's voice in their bedroom, that woke me.

"What's wrong?" she asked. Her voice seemed thin and strained.

"He's got acute indigestion."

"How do you get that? Did he eat something?"

"No. Drank too much."

In an attempt to maintain some privacy, my father had put up open shelves in the connecting doorway so I couldn't walk into their room. I was kneeling on the floor, peering clandestinely around the edge of the doorjamb through the book lined shelving to see what was happening. My mother was sitting on the edge of the bed looking up at the doctor.

"He'll be alright won't he?" she whispered imploringly.

I leaned further into the doorway and looked at the motionless form of my father in the bed. His face seemed whiter than the sheets.

"How long did he throw up? Was it greenish with black chunks in it?"

"A couple of hours and then he passed out."

"And what color was it?"

"Like you said. Shouldn't we get him to the hospital?"

"No point," the doctor's voice carried a tone of laconic indifference.

"What should I do?" asked Roselyn.

"Nothing. Just watch him. Make sure he doesn't strangle on his vomit.

"Is he just drunk? That's it isn't it?" she asked hoping for some assurance.

"He's had too much to drink, way too much. He's not just drunk, he's poisoned. The green fluid is bile. The black chunks blood. It's too late to pump his stomach so there's nothing anyone can do." He took out a pocket watch. "It's about two a.m. now. In another four hours he'll either be dead or alive." His tone had turned impatient and aloof as he prepared to leave.

My mother's eyes were darting about the room. She started to speak several times in an attempt to delay the doctor's departure, anything I realized, not to be alone. Without another word the doctor turned and left. It was understandable. Ours was a poor blue-collar neighborhood and this doctor had seen more than a fair amount of men trying to drink their way through an unrelentingly numbing existence.

I was still at the doorway, slumped down now, with my back against my bedroom wall, waiting for my father to throw up, to hear if he was choking on his vomit. My mother never knew I'd heard what had been said. I could hear her in the next room pleading, crying angrily, "Don't you dare die!"

I wanted to help her but I was frightened and confused and vaguely angry, afraid to let her know I had heard something neither she nor he would want me to know, and that I didn't want to know. At some point I got back in bed, laid there trying not to think of the last hour. It was late Saturday morning when I awoke. I peered around the edge of the doorway once more to see if he was alive. He was propped up against the headboard, his face a pale green, his breathing short, shallow, and raspy. The house was silent. My mother was nowhere to be found. I felt a rush of panic. Where was she? "What now?" I repeatedly said to myself.

The rest of that weekend was a haze, but the issue of near death was never mentioned, at least not with any implication of its seriousness. "Your father has a bad cold," my mother explained. That was the extent of it. On Monday he was still in bed when I left for school, his complexion no longer green, just ashen. I thought, he's not going to die, but butterfly feelings lingered in me.

When I came home from school for lunch he was sitting in the kitchen with his arms resting on the cold Formica table, supporting his head. He didn't look up and I didn't say anything nor did my mother, and that is how things stayed for the days and weeks ahead, no one talking, no one interacting, like strangers on a sidewalk, avoiding eye contact. Our everyday lives resumed—school, work, and domestic chores. I drifted back into my independent childhood adventures and within a short time lost the intense awareness of that night, my mother got a waitressing job in Meyer Brothers' Department Store, and my father stopped opening Charlie's at my mother's insistence, but not his evening beers after work. He reminded me of his own mother, internalized and remote, while my mother became uncharacteristically decisive and assertive. I stayed out of the way. I was at a loss to understand how I got up that Saturday morning in a different reality then the one I went to sleep with the night before. I sensed I had a lot to learn.

Several months went by. Life was now a veneer of fabricated calm. Intuitively I asked that the door between our bedrooms be put back up. "Why?" my parents wanted to know. I couldn't tell them anymore than they would tell me what their whispered conversations were about. But the door went back up.

One morning a Mr. Hagar stopped at our house. He was a colporteur working out of the Seventh Day Adventist church a few blocks away on the corner of North Second Street and Haledon Avenue. He was following a calling, is how he described it later, to sell religious books and give out tracts to non-believers. To my mother he seemed to be the answer to her prayers. She purchased a set of books written by the church founder, Ellen G. White and gave them to her husband. Though we were a steady Sunday-go-to-church family we never attended any one of them long enough to became members. It was during this period that my father completely stopped going to any church while my mother and I began to go to the First Baptist Church on Washington Street, for her own sanity I suppose, as well as the hope that her husband would join her. She had a lovely, sweet soprano voice, tried out for the choir and was accepted. The musical program was quite ambitious, which required two rehearsals a week. She didn't want to leave me home with my apathetic, morose father so I went to choir practice with her in the evenings. I suppose it would have been possible to leave me with Uncle Phil and my aunt Fay upstairs, or one of our other neighborhood relatives, but then she would have had to explain too much. It was fine with me since I loved to sing, so I sat there next to her and learned the soprano part of the music too. Mr. Werner, the choirmaster became curious about my presence. One evening after practice he stopped us and asked if we could stay a few extra minutes.

"I noticed Jerry," he began, "that you seem to learn the music well enough to sing without looking at the sheet music. I think I can pick out your voice but I would like to ask you to sing all by yourself for me. Would you mind?"

I said it would be fine with me. After my debut in Mrs. Levy's fifth grade class, singing alone had become a cinch. The choir had been working on Bach's "Magnificat." The church had a large organ, which was only used during church services. I loved the sound and the vibration of the organ, a carryover from the Fabian Theater I imagine, that rumbled throughout the old, dark wooden interior, but during practice we stayed in the rehearsal room with the piano. I wanted to sing with the organ. So I asked, "Could we use the organ?"

"You like the organ? It's a fine idea but the church is unheated during the week and the organ is cranky when it's cold. We better stay here, OK?" He struck a note on the piano for me to start and I sang the soprano part acapella.

"That was perfect," he said. "You have a wonderful voice and an excellent ear for the music. Tell me, would you really like to sing with the organ?"

I didn't know what to say.

He turned to my mother, "It has always been a dream of mine to have a children's choir, but I have never been able to find anyone to do the solo work. Your son is perfect for it. How do you feel about that?"

"It would be fine. What do you think Jerry, would like to do that?"

"Would I get to sing with the organ?" Organ or not I was thrilled. I loved the music and suddenly, everything about it, down to the musty old woody smell of the church, but mostly the feeling of being transported into a perfect expanding universe of music.

"Yes, but we would have to see if your voice is strong enough to be heard over the organ."

Well what can I say? Life was getting layered in complexity. My father had almost killed himself and my parents were behaving peculiarly, I had a best friend that was both a girl and a Catholic, that I had to keep secret from my other friends, I loved singing in church but didn't like going to church, preferred sitting under a tree, or going down to the river or looking at the night sky or building models rather than playing baseball or any sport—most certainly baseball—my grandparents, my uncle Joe, and my uncle Phil all wanted me to be something other than what I wanted to be even though I didn't know what I wanted to be. My life seemed fragmented into pieces that had to be held apart from each other, yet I was having fun if I ignored my parents, at least my father, and various family adults, saw Mary anyway—she was the only one I could talk to, and just be myself with as long as I didn't seem to be too Protestant—show just enough interest in baseball to keep my other friends, slept in church after the singing was over. And the end result? I concluded that life was a maze. I started drawing maze puzzles that I gave to my friends to solve. None of them cared to do it. I concluded that adults were meddlesome, especially relatives, and to be avoided without letting them know what I thought, and realized that if I gave each of these different people a little bit of me, the smallest bit possible and didn't give them a hard time, they were happy and I could go my own way. And that is what I did as often as I could.

I said yes to Mr. Werner. He formed the children's choir. I became the major soloist and loved it as much as any ten-year-old could love anything and I continued to sleep in church, after the choir sang of course.

Unbeknownst to me, my father, a nonreader, was reading the entire set of religious books my mother had purchased for him, reading with a vengeance. He stopped drinking, at least he cut down considerably, and he called Mr. Hagar for some one-on-one information about his church. My mother and I continued to go to the Baptist Church during this period while Willum, father and husband, molecularly absorbed the writings of Mrs. E. G. White.

It was Friday night and we were getting ready to go to choir practice.

"Did you know that you're going to church on the wrong day?" he pronounced to his wife.

I was about to put my coat on but sat down instead. This was one exchange that wasn't being spoken in a whisper and I was all ears. My mother, blind-sided by her husband's disruptive non sequitur, looked about the kitchen and didn't respond.

"It says in the Ten Commandments that the seventh day is the Sabbath, the day of rest. That's Saturday. You're going to church on Sunday, that's the first day of the week."

Up until his recent flirtation with death he too had been going to church on Sunday.

"That's when we always go to church. Everybody goes then," said Roselyn. "That's when you used to go too."

"Well it's not right. Jesus worshiped on the seventh day and there's no place in the whole bible that says it was changed by him or God or anybody."

"Where are you getting this from?" challenged my mother.

"From the books you bought me. It says the Catholic Church changed it from Saturday to Sunday to distance the church from the Jews." He paused. I figured it wouldn't be a good idea to mention this to Mary. "And I've been talking to Mr. Hagar. He wants me to go to his church this Saturday."

"When did you see him?"

"Last Sunday. He stopped by when you were at your church."

"Saturday! Are they Jewish?"

"No! They're Protestants. Why don't you come with me tomorrow? The church is an easy walk from here."

"I never heard of any Protestants who went to church on Saturday. I go to the First Baptist church downtown. I'm in the choir. Your son's in the children's choir. Why don't you come to my church this Sunday instead? You could hear him sing. He's got a solo this week."

My mother had been standing the whole time with her coat draped over her arm ready to leave. Both parents stared at each other, silently. "You know I help out my mother and father at their store Saturdays. They count on me."

"So don't come this week. Come next week. That'll give you time to tell them you can't make it."

Roselyn broke eye contact. "Put your coat on Jerry. We've got to leave now or we'll be late for practice."

I knew she had said something to me. I even thought I knew what it was—put my coat on. I couldn't move.

In my family where never a harsh or a disagreeable word was ever spoken, in my presence at least, I found their words overwhelming and upsetting. It occurred to me that my father was coming out of the cloud he had been under since the night he almost died. But he wasn't the same as before. He was excited…no, more like agitated. And this transformation was plummeting down on our lives like an avalanche. I didn't understand it. Not yet.

Over the next few weeks things got better and worse. My father quit drinking. Cold turkey. Came straight home from work every night, and began attending the Seventh Day Adventist Church on his own, two blocks away, regularly, on Saturdays, while we continued on Sundays at the First Baptist Church.

Sometime during this transitional period, when I was at my grandparents' butcher shop they had asked me not to go to my father's "peculiar" church. Ever. We were at the kitchen table. They had given my mother a task to do out in the store. I wasn't sure what was coming but seeing them sitting down together at the kitchen table was peculiar. On good days they continually sniped at each other, otherwise they avoided speaking at all or through a third party.

"Will you promise?" my grandfather John Whitehead asked.

What should I say? My mother was helping customers out in the store. That now familiar feeling of a beetle pinned to a mounting board overwhelmed me. I nodded weakly, not really certain what I had agreed to, or rather what it might mean. What was I supposed to do?

Grandfather stood, walked over to the buffet, opened the top drawer and took out a large dusty bible. "This is very important to us and to show you how serious we feel about this we want you to swear on the bible."

Who were these people? They looked the same but now as I sat there staring at them across the kitchen table, their eyes penetrating, faces pinched, they were barely recognizable, less meaningful, and simultaneously more dimensional, requiring more careful observation than I was ready or willing to invest.

They were still talking, taking turns though I had drifted away into my own uncomprehending thoughts about all the adults in my life and how strangely peripheral and trapped I felt by their demands. Mr. John Whitehead reached into his pocket and withdrew a pocket watch and placed it on the table in front of him. "This was my father's gold watch," he said. He pushed it toward the center of the table. "I wanted to give it to you when you grew up but I want you to have it now," he said to me. "It's yours for doing the right thing."

He slid the watch and the bible across the table to me. "Do you promise?"

I felt queasy. I needed to get away, to the river, to the giant magic willow tree at Tippy's house before it had been cut down, anyplace else.

"You may not understand what we're asking you to do today, but one day you will and you'll thank us," said Mrs. Ada Whitehead. "Please promise us. Swear on the bible."

And I did. And I felt awful and confused and conflicted because it was an oath against my father. *Why did I do what they asked?* I didn't know them anymore, or what it might mean if I didn't keep my oath. And now there was a piece of me that I didn't know any more.

I heard the bell over the door in the store ring as the last customer left. My mother, finished with her work, came into the kitchen. Using this interruption, I got up without speaking, went into the sitting room and got out the Brady Civil War folios with pictures of disemboweled and limbless dead soldiers. I wanted to blot out the whole morning. And it worked for a bit, until I heard the word "promise" sweep through the doorway from the kitchen and settle between the gory pictures and myself.

"Promise us that…promise us you will…promise you won't let him…"

I wasn't sure I had done the right thing but my mother agreed happily to the same promise at once, even though there was neither Bible requirement nor a second gold watch proffered. They pushed on. Hard. "We told you not to marry him." It seemed I managed once more to be in the right place at the wrong time. I leaned back and looked through the doorway into the kitchen. My grandparents, still seated at the table, had their backs to me. My mother seemed frozen in mid-stride opposite them on the other side of the table with a tea cup in her hand that she had just gotten from the dish rack at the sink. I watched her face change from agreeable to pained and conflicted. Not a rebellious person, nor confrontational, she always tried to make the best of things, to make adjustments, to work things out, smooth them out. This situation was not about to get worked out. There was no adjustment that could satisfy both her husband and her parents.

Months went by. Nothing changed. Her husband kept after her to go to church with him. She kept going to the store on Saturdays. The air in our home grew dense and gray. No one argued, or fought or cathartically lost control. But everyday life became coldly mechanical. Then one day she stated, "We're not going to the store this Saturday, we're goin' to church with your father." Which we did. And the following day, though he had said he would go with us, we went to the First Baptist church without him, and the next Saturday we were back at the store.

There was the usual mid-morning lull at the store. I had just come in from cutting the grass to wash up in the kitchen sink. It was a luscious blue day and the canary Aunt Tyne had given her sister Ada was singing its head off. The one that never sang.

"Do you know what your father did?" asked my grandmother.

I had no idea. She had just made a cup of tea for the two of us, buttered some saltine crackers and sprinkled them with sugar. My mother was out in the store putting out a new supply of socks and T-shirts on the dry goods counter, my grandfather preparing meat orders for home deliveries that afternoon. I didn't say anything. I just looked at her across the maple kitchen table. It felt like this tête-à-tête might be heading for another biblical-gold watch moment.

"Your father told your mother if she didn't start going to church with him he was gonna start drinkin' again." She poured both of us a cup of tea, put some of the crackers on a small plate and pushed them across the table to me. "That's the kind of man he is." It was a gilded cracker moment.

She sat there looking at me, waiting for a response, but I didn't know what to say, what to think. I didn't want or like any of this. What do you do with information like that when you're ten years old? What do you say to the grown-ups that want to claim you for their side in a tug of war set in a landscape of landmines?

I wanted this all resolved. Yet nothing got resolved. In self-defense I retreated into a solitary world of giant jigsaw puzzles, building speedboat models of my own design and drawing Western landscapes from my imagination. We kept going to the store on Saturdays, church on Sundays and my father, as threatened, started drinking again.

Mr. Hagar dropped by one week in the afternoon, ostensibly just to see how we were doing. I came home from school and found him sitting at the kitchen table talking to my mother. I felt like I was covered in slime.

"Would you like a cup of coffee?" my mother offered.

"No. We don't drink coffee," he said piously.

Her words were uncharacteristically cold and clipped. "We?"

"Adventists," he responded, "coffee's bad for you."

"Is there anything else Adventists don't do?"

"Yes, but that's not why I stopped by." He continued, "We've missed your husband at services. Is there something wrong?"

It was the right question. It overrode her irritation with his meddlesomeness and cut to the quick of her dilemma.

"He's started drinkin' again," she revealed.

"Why?" he asked. "What caused him to backslide?"

The next week we went to the Adventist church with my father on Saturday and every Saturday thereafter. And so there was no more choir for us, no more Tippy O'Neal or Willow Way for me, no more Saturdays at my grandparents' and no more Charlie's Bar and Grill. It was an amazing turnabout. He stopped drinking again and was baptized into church membership. Our lives took on a surface calm.

My mother was still working as a waitress to augment my father's income, and though it had helped financially she felt she couldn't earn enough for them to get ahead. At that same time my uncle Phil had decided to sell his two ice cream stores, one in Wayne and one on the corner of North Fourth and Haledon Avenue. He asked my mother if she would like to take over the one on Haledon Avenue. My parents made an offer the next day and Phil accepted.

Perhaps they were trying to get their lives back on stable ground, maybe the store seemed to offer a way forward, or a way to distract them from their thinly reconciled differences, but whatever it was it worked. The shop was a great success. Roselyn, with her husband Bill's part time help, soon turned it into a luncheonette that was serving an overflow crowd breakfast, lunch and after school kids, five days a week. The narrow space contained a counter on the left with about ten stools that ran the length of the narrow store. On the right were several small tables for two. Occasionally Uncle Phil would stop in to see how they were progressing, but really to schmooze, have a *cup 'a cauffee*, and if I was around, play a game of chess.

My mother's intuitive sense of design, with her husband's practical skills, soon transformed the sterile space into a charming, warm environment. She hung lovely floral café curtains in the window, painted everything inside and out with fresh soft colors, kept a clutter of lush potted plants in the window and brought in fresh flowers every day, reupholstered the stools and chairs, made all homemade foods and baked goods. She made it a policy to serve only the freshest of everything. If a pot of coffee sat for more than an hour she threw it out and made a new one. The store became a haven for me during that time, only a block from PS 12. I would stop there several times a week, after school, for some ice cream and a few games of chess or checkers with anyone of any age. The store soon became a gathering place for after school players. The luncheonette, with my father's help behind the scene, was now earning more than his floor sanding business and their lives were actually looking up.

It was my father's common remark at that time that "God has blessed us, and our store, as a reward for going to God's "True Church." And my mother agreed it did seem to be so. And then one day, "I'm quitting the sanding business," Bill announced to Roselyn, "to be a colporteur." After speaking with Mr. Hagar, he felt God was also calling him to spread the "true word" of God.

"Every nation on this earth must hear the true (Adventist) word of God before Jesus, his son, will come again to gather the righteous home to heaven," said Mr. Hagar.

My father explained that Mr. Hagar would help him get started. "I'm going to begin in Hawthorne," he said.

Hawthorne, the next town over from Paterson was a lot more convenient and accessible than becoming a missionary in central Africa. Already Christianized and known to be predominantly Roman Catholic, but not aware of the "True word of God," according to Mr. Hagar,

"What about the store?" Roselyn asked. "You'll still help out there won't you?"

He assured her that he would, but this new venture would demand a bit more of his time initially to get organized and operating smoothly. He might need to cut back on his support for a while, but eventually he'd be making a lot more money doing God's work than he ever did floor sanding. Mr. Hagar, he pointed out, supported his family selling religious books, and he could too.

I was crossing Haledon Avenue, walking with my friend John from Jefferson Street.

"Who do you have next year?" asked John.

It was the last few weeks of our seventh grade year. "I got Mr. Farrell next year," I said.

"Me too!" said John. "He's the best."

There were several eighth grade teachers but everyone wanted to be in Mr. Farrell's class. I couldn't believe how lucky I was to get assigned to his class. I was so excited. John was the only one of my friends that got the same assignment. Mr. Farrell's classes always did exciting projects and he was so friendly and cheerful all the time. After tyrannically insane Miss Sickles in the sixth grade and Miss Pickering in the seventh, whom I liked very much, but, after the pea shooter debacle that Dennis and I had gotten ourselves into with her, I couldn't look her in the eye. Though I had done well in both grade levels, I felt happy and relaxed about school for the first time since fifth grade.

Afternoons at the store always slowed once the after school rush of kids left for home. I started to concoct ice cream creations for my new chess-playing friends.

"I got Mr. Farrell in eighth grade next year," I told my mother while making a "Dusty Road" sundae—butter pecan ice cream with hot fudge, fresh whipped cream, dry malt dust and a cherry.

"Oh, Mr. Farrell?" she was cleaning the griddle with her back to me. "Is he a good teacher?"

"Oh yes. Everyone wants Mr. Farrell. His classes go on field trips. They do great projects and there's lots of art."

"Well it sounds wonderful. I'm glad you're so excited," she said. "I shouldn't have let you make that sundae. Too close to supper. Remember you also have to get home and get cleaned up for church tonight."

On Friday nights there were church meetings for everyone to attend, Young Peoples Meeting for kids in the basement of the church, which included a question, and answer period where I struggled to stay alert, as like one of Pavlov's dogs, the mere entry into a church, any church, triggered an almost immediate sleep response in me, and Prayer Meeting for adults up in the main church with its strange carved female figure salvaged from an old ship hanging from the ceiling, with homemade angel's wings added, bearing the Third Angel's Message on a scroll, the New Testament message of Jesus's second coming.

The Adventists, believers in the literal interpretation of the bible's Ten Commandments, went to church on Saturday instead of Sunday. This also meant that no work or diversion from religious behavior was tolerated on that day. They followed the biblical reckoning of starting the Sabbath day at sundown, not at midnight. So Friday night sundown was the start of the biblical Sabbath. That ended the next day at sunset. This, I realized from my fleeting interlude as a budding astronomer, meant the Sabbath day varied in length throughout the year. I wondered if those meandering winter minutes were added back in during the summer. I heard of an unfortunate group of Jews living in northern Russia that happened to see the sun set on a Friday night not to reappear again for a month.

If anyone had asked me at the time I would have told them I would prefer to fall asleep in the Baptist church rather than the Adventist church. Besides, we only went to Sunday services at the Baptist Church and the music was a whole lot better. The choir director at the Adventist Church was a dissolute ex-alky jazz trombonist and the lead soprano his toothless shrill voiced wife. There was a smallish compensatory organ though no one was skilled enough to play it.

If perchance I had a twinge of guilt about my solemnly sworn-on-the-bible oath to stay away from the "peculiar church," along with the proffered gold watch, it didn't last long because I hardly ever saw my grandparents anymore and I lost the watch before that summer was out. Such ethical, (or is it moral?) exactitudes also got lost in the everyday glee of my tenth summer on the planet. I'm not sure what my mother thought about her oath-breaking dilemma, but then she hadn't sworn on the bible. She just chose her husband over her parents.

Two months had passed since my father started selling religious books. Two months of little to no time for the luncheonette.

"With God's help it will work out. I just need a little more time," he told his wife. Another month went by. His old pattern returned. Once again he was never home for supper, not because of alcohol but because he was still trying, without success, or any outside help, to sell fundamentalist Protestant books in the town of Hawthorne. My mother, unable to handle the store without his help closed it down. She was waitressing again. Once more down the street at Popwynie's Luncheonette. My father, without any job prospects, gave up on selling books a few weeks later. We were poor again.

It was near the end of summer. My mother and I were in our bright cheerful kitchen with its green ivy pattern wallpaper.

"I can't believe summer's almost over." I was watching my pet salamander, Beauregard, trying to escape from his aquarium tank. "Dougie Van Blarcolm's going to be in Mr. Farrell's class too, with me and John. Both my best friends."

Our backs were toward each other. I was sort of talking to myself, not really expecting a response. So I wasn't paying attention until I heard, "...so you won't be going back to 12'sies this year."

I turned and walked across the room to stand next to her at the stove. She kept cooking. The room seemed dark, shrunken, with no way out. I needed a way out. I also needed to know, "Why not?"

"Your father and I…"

I formed a visual image of my missing father stretched up tall next to my mother with his shoulders pressed back and his eyes staring straight ahead, nodding solemnly, not looking me in the eye.

"Your father," there was a pause, "and I," she repeated, "have decided to send you to the Adventist church school for your last year in grammar school."

"What? But I'm going to be in Mr. Farrell's class."

Her response was, "Something, something, something," ending with, "and it's for your own good."

Ah, yes. It was the classic "father knows best." And mother too? To say I was disappointed is like saying being paralyzed from the neck down is an inconvenience. To this day I do not know why I didn't say anything, show some emotional response, have a tantrum, rebel, smash something, not that such behavior would have changed anything, instead I said, "I'm going over to Mary's house."

"There isn't time. You have to get ready for church," she said as I closed the door behind me.

I had to have time to think, to absorb what I needed to absorb and a safer place to do it. I should have known better than to go to Mary's. She knew me too well. But staying in my house was not a good option.

"What's wrong?" she asked as soon as she saw me.

Of course I said, "Nothing." Then there was a long pause. "Do you want to play Rummy, Mary?"

"No," she said. "It's almost time for supper. What's wrong with you?"

Mary and I were competitors in everything, but the bottom line, we were childhood soulmates. But, just then, all I needed was distance from my mother's words, not a sympathetic ear. Not yet. Not then.

"Don't tell me nothing when it's almost time for supper. Aren't you supposed to go to church tonight? What's goin' on?"

"I'm not going. I'm staying here."

"Are you in trouble?"

"My parents are sending me to their church's school."

"I go to Catholic school. What's wrong with that?"

"Nothing, I'll just stay here a little while then I'll go home."

My mother was now also a baptized member of the Adventist church and I was outnumbered and on my own.

I never rebelled, never acted out, I just slowly succumbed to the pervasive presence of the church in our lives with its self-assured clarion beliefs, not by intent, but by benign design, thus no one could ever be held responsible for its meddlesomeness. Except me. I felt responsible because I swore on the bible and promised my grandparents I wouldn't go to that church, my now nearly fugitive swearing on the King James Bible that they both used against me.

The next day I saw my friends Dougie, John, Pudgy, and the twins Jonathan and Jeffery. I told them what my parents had decided. They didn't say anything. Which meant it wasn't cool. I knew that, but I was trapped between two realities. It wasn't something guys do, let other guys know you're scared, upset. To them I was just whiney and wimpy. Plus, it was just one more weird change about me they had to absorb. During the past year, in an attempt to try on the garment of my father's church, I told them that the world was about to end, that Jesus was going to come back to earth in a cloud of glory and save only the most deserving, which would number about 144,000 righteous souls (not great odds if you were a gambling man) before God the father destroyed the planet with fire. These tenants along with other half understood minutia of the Adventist church, created a response in my friends that was a uniformly blank stare. These ideas weren't something I came to naturally, whatever that might mean. It was more like trying to wear an ill-fitting coat someone had draped over me. Most of my friends were main stream Protestants, which means, if you care to parse the word, they were supposed to be persons of Protest, originally against the excesses of the Catholic Church, but in reality, their denominational beliefs now functioned as an interchangeable collection of affable and comfortable religious notions that, I might add, I found more to my liking.

Next week class started in the one-room school in the basement of the Adventist Church. There were fifteen children from church families ranging in age from five to twelve. I knew a few of the boys, not too well, from attending Sabbath school before church service. Of course there was no art, or music, or gym, or woodshop, or field trips, or music lessons, or movies, or exciting projects or Mr. Farrell, only a single teacher that instructed us older students to help the younger ones with their lessons. The Paterson branch of the Adventist Church serviced an area about twenty miles in diameter. I was the only student that could walk to school, which meant that I lived in that blue-collar part of town, which meant I was not middle class, which meant I was suspect to many of the parents of my classmates. Ironically my parents were trying to remove me from the secular environment of public school while the parents of my classmates saw me as a contaminating secular influence on their children, which I probably was.

Class started at 8:00 a.m., twenty minutes before PS 12. We were required to be at the school thirty minutes before lessons began. In the beginning I was never able to meet this requirement, my resistance to the place always made me late. We were several weeks into the new school year. I had made friends with the other older boys and decided I would try to get to the school earlier to play catch in the small macadam playground. I went back for a ball up against the chain link fence at the sidewalk along the Haledon Avenue side of the property. As I caught the ball I saw a group of boys from my neighborhood coming up the street on their way to school. Among them were Dennis and John, John in Mr. Farrell's class. I hadn't seen him in several weeks, not since I had told everyone that I was going to change schools. I called out to them, "Hi guys!" They were nearly at the edge of the playground. There was no response. Dennis gave me a quick sideways glance.

The sidewalk was quite wide. As the boys moved nearer I saw them whispering together, then they veered away from the chain link fence toward the curb. At this point they were opposite me. I knew them all. John, one of my best friends, having been in school together since kindergarten, wouldn't look at me. I called out his name. "JOHN!" No response. He kept his eyes straight ahead, his face blank. I watched as they reached the policeman at the corner and then cross over Haledon Avenue. I remember standing with my fingers laced in the chain link fence above my head, watching them disappear up North Second Street toward 12sies. Mr. Soper, the church schoolteacher had called for everyone to come in for beginning prayer. It was time for class to start. It was time to let go of the fence.

For the first eleven years of my life I was free to be myself. Then I learned that all things come in paired opposites. This awareness is not original to me, but when it's your turn and it's your first time to find this out, it's a catastrophic derailment.

26

Relatively Pink

Age 9–12

My uncle was a dreamy leftist in America, the land of the free, when it was hazardous to one's wellbeing. His wife thought, in her generous moments, he was a contrarian, his daughters a loveable, distracted, heretic.

For me, he was that moment of opportunity that often comes to us when we are young, before we are wholly formed, that invites us to make the very best of the irrational path of our lives.

MY TENTH YEAR WAS a busy year. It was the year that I realized that there are malevolent and benevolent people, and that most of them haven't a clue about it, especially the ones that matter, the ones close at hand.

A few months before my ninth birthday, my uncle Phil appeared in my life just as I was beginning to peer over the wall of my parent's protective fiefdom. The Hemingway's had moved from the second floor to a house down the street next to Mosca's store. Their old apartment sat empty for a while until Phil, his wife Fay and their two daughters, desperately in need of a place to live, moved in. They had just been evicted from their apartment down the street, and although the eviction wasn't technically my uncle's fault, it was his fault. He was actually my second cousin and though they had only lived a block away, they were a complete unknown.

After a few encounters I knew I wanted to see him more, not because he was friendly, which he was, not out of an obligation of birth, which there was, but because he was so open, as curious and as clueless about life as I was at the age of nine. We were equals in that way. He never talked down to me and I always took him seriously. I accepted the totality of him, as he was and he was reciprocal, sometimes childlike, sometimes not.

His father and stepmother, survivors of the 1913 Paterson mill worker's strikes, lived down the street over their butcher shop. It was these very same flummoxed relatives that I had been given to at the age of two months.

The house we were living in, and Phil and his family had just moved into, belonged to his stepmother, Gramma Hazel, my great aunt. And though he had been ejected from the house right across the street from the butcher shop, she could hardly have turned him down, for ultimately her husband's blood proved thicker than her good common sense.

He was more than well-educated for that time and our neighborhood, going to college during the Great Depression. He became both a Civil and a Structural engineer. After his schooling, Phil worked for Passaic County in New Jersey as a Civil engineer. He also owned an ice cream parlor, a luncheonette and a vegetable truck farm, some of it simultaneously, none of it in any particular order, for purposes of pragmatic survival or paranoia. He was, after all, a member of the American Communist Party. I know because he showed me his membership card when at the age of nine I asked for proof. Most people thought of Commies, as they were known then, also Pinkos, as dangerously un-American because they were opposed to capitalism.

The only thing that mattered more to him than provocative conversation was something to eat, or maybe I should say anything to eat. A typical example of the latter would be the lunches he made to take to work. They consisted of two slices of white bread—I rolled a whole slice of this bread into a half-inch doughy ball and used it to catch my first and only fish—two slices of white bread slathered with any one of Campbell's soups straight out of the can. His favorite weekend treat at our house on Sunday mornings was a Jewish hard roll from Verp's Bakery, with the soft inner part pulled out and the crusty remains thickly mortared back together with butter and ketchup. In my family I was the only one to take up this epicurean delight, which I am somewhat embarrassed to admit, has through the years morphed into one of my security foods, along with bread and butter pickles with milk, confessed here for the first time.

Outside of his politics, Phil was a typical American. He loved all things sweet and all things salty and fatty. He especially loved Coca-Cola. Though according to him, his outsider politics made him more American than most because the minority views he often expressed were keeping freedom of speech alive in the land of the "relatively free." His wife described his free speech as conversational hand grenades.

Working for a company only serves their advantage. A worker is only a necessary evil for the company and should be dispensed with whenever possible was one of the most common grenades that rolled off his lips.

One day I took the long way home from school to stop by his store on Haledon Avenue for an ice cream cone. He was sitting on a soda case in the sun, leaning sideways against the storefront drinking a Coke. I asked him what he was doing. "Stripping paint off the storefront," he said with a bored air.

I was confused. I could see some nurdles of paint on the sidewalk but no tools or any indication of how the nurdles got there. He smiled coyly, took a swallow of soda, then poured some Coke on the windowsill, silently raised a finger and wordlessly indicated for me to be patient. After several minutes he took a putty knife wrapped in cloth out of his pocket and removed thin slurry of paint from the wood.

He added, "It works best if you have a hot day and direct sunlight." He then asked if I wanted a Coke with my ice cream cone. I said, "Yes." When he came back out with the soda and ice cream he handed me a putty knife and a soda case to sit on.

"You can stay for a bit, can't you? Help me strip some paint? You know how to play chess?" in a rambling nonstop, fast-mutual-back-scratching sort of way.

"Yeah, and no," I said with a smirk.

"In that order?"

"Yup," I answered.

He went back into the store, got another soda case and chess set and started to teach me the game. We sat there sipping cokes, playing chess and randomly stripping patches of paint until suppertime.

As I was leaving he asked, "What do you think of the game?"

I told him it was complicated but I really did like it. I liked the way it felt trying to figure out the next move.

"Calisthenics for the brain," he said and without pause continued, "Do you know about the Greek Civil War?

Phil had a personal quirk, an irritant some called it, a gift to my way of thinking, for terse political nonsequiturs that he inserted like lightning strikes into the flow of most conversations.

"No." I had no idea what that was.

"When you think you know we'll play again," he said coercively.

I began to stop by the store a couple of times a week, to buy a nickel ice cream cone and, I hoped, to play chess. Not that that really mattered. There were kids in my class that I could play chess with now, and I could have gotten ice cream nearer to my house, but no other grown-up in my life asked such questions or spent time with me in that way.

"Got an answer?" He meant what he said. I looked at him blankly. "About Greece.". After waiting a bit, he continued, "Oh well, since you're here why don't you help me strip some more paint."

Our method of paint stripping left the store looking like it had a blotchy skin disease.

Striping paint off the front of his store was completely out of character for this human who was catastrophically inept at any physical effort, skilled or otherwise. Even the minimum skill that paint stripping required. I don't think he was interested in stripping paint. It was the idea of using coke that appealed to his innate curiosity. It became obvious after several months that the only time Uncle Phil tackled this project was when I was there. And, even when I was there we never accomplished very much because we talked nonstop and drank most of the Coke.

The adults in the family thought Phil was self-centered, oblivious to reality, distracted, dysfunctional, uncouth, even deranged, and he probably was all of those things if you were more than nine years old. To me all the grown-ups in my family were a bafflement. Most of them acted as though they had an infallible ability to see things as they really were, which in their impatience left no room for Phil as he really was— an eternally curious child, trying, just like me, to patch the deranged, inscrutable bits of life together. For instance, instead of working as an engineer, which he also did from time to time, Phil dove deeper into the entrepreneurial world of small "c" capitalism. Seemingly contrary to his professed belief in Communism, he purchased a second business, the Alderny Wayne Milk Bar, a luncheonette on the corner of Ratzer Road and the Hamberg Turnpike in Wayne, NJ, which, he readily explained to the family or anyone else, freed him from corporate conformity.

In time, the interests of corporations will overwhelm our democratic government in America. That's what happened in Germany. That's Fascism when the two join forces.

There were two hospital-white, barnlike rooms in the new luncheonette, antiseptic and uncomfortable. Esthetics were never a concern for Phil. It was a place for a quick lunch or some ice cream. It was apparent to most people that Phil, a man of the mind, only used his eyes for navigational purposes. The first room had an el-shaped counter with twenty stools, a short-order kitchen and several chrome and Formica tables for two. The other stark-white room, also painted by Phil to let the public know there was a new owner, had suspended, dusty, bare florescent fixtures, puke green linoleum tile floor and a dozen mismatched tables and chairs of various sizes.

Business was so-so on weekdays, good on Saturdays and nonexistent on Sundays so he didn't open then, but he couldn't stay away. After Sunday morning coffee at our house—his wife Fay never joined us—he would get in his Buick Roadmaster and drive up to the luncheonette for the rest of the day to "fiddle with the equipment in his new playground," Aunt Fay's words.

One Sunday he said to my father, "Why don't you come up to Wayne for dinner this afternoon? My Treat. Tell Roselyn. Fay and my daughters will be there too. My treat. My treat."

This invitation seemed a bit odd to my parents, but Phil did possess a large streak of sincere generosity that would erupt without warning, blindsiding everyone into hoping he was a normal, non-self-involved human being.

He did the cooking. The food was simple but good, the gathering relaxed, the conversation mostly convivial. We sat in the dining room at a table in the middle of the room. Phil's wife preferred the dining room away from the clutter of the luncheonette counter. Uncle Phil liked gadgets. The "latest gizmo" Fay called them. "They make life better," he would say repeatedly to his wife. "Not mine," was her usual rejoinder. Money was the issue for his wife. Unfortunately, Phil's sense of well-being didn't come from dollars. His relationship to money was like that of a distracted Beagle wandering from one scent to another. He changed professions without warning and he was an impulse spender. The latest rub for Fay, she had to quit her good paying waitress job to help the struggling luncheonette.

As the months went by, the counter space filled with new restaurant equipment that wasn't warranted by his customer volume. First a large commercial doughnut maker appeared, then a twenty-pound capacity potato peeler, a bread dough maker, a replacement deep fryer that sat on the counter uninstalled, and other wonders that also sat there, unused after the first burst of enthusiasm waned, until there were only five free spaces left at the counter for customers.

These Sunday meals always started with shrimp cocktails, an item never found on the menu, followed by beef in some form, with gravy and potatoes. But once the food machines started arriving, the meals consisted of the shrimp cocktail, Phil's favorite, followed by a single course of biscuits, or French fries, or doughnuts, dependent of course upon the latest acquisition. I enjoyed these food odysseys prepared on futuristic machines. No one else did.

It became Phil's pattern that when we arrived at the luncheonette he would be behind the counter fiddling with the gizmos, hoping to lure someone over to him. No one ever responded. Instead everyone avoided eye contact, went into the other room to find Fay, and talked over his noise as if he were some inconsiderate neighbor at the beach with a loud radio. Except for me. I reveled in gizmoness.

After a couple of Sunday meals of Shrimp and mechanized food my aunt Fay started to bring picnic foods to compensate. We could have all stayed home and had the picnic in our backyard, but we kept going to the Wayne Milk Bar.

I'm not certain if it was short attention span, an argument with Aunt Fay, or boredom, but he was now staying in the other room fiddling with the equipment throughout the meal. Without Uncle Phil's conversational grenades, I had no interest in the adults and left the table to watch Phil and help him run the machines while the grown-ups sat around their table trying to ignore us in the next room. I think I was working the doughnut maker when I asked, "Why'd you buy all these machines?"

"I like to play," said Uncle Phil. A sly smirk flickered in his eyes.

"Ah, come on. You're too old."

"Am I? Really?"

"Aren't you?"

"If I thought I was too old to play I'd be sitting down at the table in the other room."

"They think you're acting strange."

"I know. Childish too."

Occasionally when he would join us at the table he'd revert to his typical behavior and erupt with things like, "If corporations make a problem for us while solving a problem for themselves, they haven't solved the problem." Or, "The Capitalist system exploits our natural resources and exploits its workers with no regard for either," crammed into the middle of someone's sentence. He couldn't help himself. He had a vision of the future, perpetually in front of him, that he believed in, a heaven on earth, that he had to share. And like an evangelist out to save us all, it would have been at odds with his essential nature to be something other than a bearer of the TRUTH. "Why make small conversation?"

Aunt Fay never sat near him or responded to anything he said.

"Yeah. We've heard it all before," was the general response of everyone else.

Another time I asked why he kept getting new machines.

"Because I'm an engineer. I like to see how other people solve problems."

"So why don't you work as an engineer then?"

"Because I don't want to be owned by a boss. What do you want to be when you grow up?"

"I don't know yet. Why?"

"It's important to figure that out. You shouldn't do anything that makes you feel used. That's not easy."

A few weeks after the initial chess/paint stripping session at the Haledon Avenue store I had stopped by for some ice cream. He sold a brand called Doeville, a local company that made the best, creamiest, densest ice cream. "Here's one of the small ways that American companies cheat us," Uncle Phil said.

If you're going to live in a Capitalist country, you need to pay attention.

"For example," he said, "Everyone sells their ice cream by volume when it should be sold by weight." He continued, "The big ice cream companies force air into their ice cream to give it more volume and so reduce the weight, that means the amount. They also tell you how much to charge so their ice cream stays competitive with other brands. The Doeville ice cream I sell now weighs more by volume, which makes it a better buy. When you scoop a major brand ice cream it compresses. It loses volume, by forcing the air out of it, the air that you paid for when you bought their ice cream." So he started weighing the ice cream he sold. "That's why I switched to Doeville ice cream," he said, "It doesn't compress very much." His business went from losing money on ice cream sales to making money.

"So have you found out about the Greek Civil War?"

"Yeah," I said.

"Uh-huh. And?"

"The Communists are fighting the US backed government."

"Do you know who's winning?"

"I don't know. Do you, Uncle Phil?"

"Not yet. It's pretty even so far. We'll have to wait 'n' see. How about we play chess. Do you have the time?"

In the summer of 1947, Uncle Phil bought a Buick Roadmaster and then proceeded to lose it in the blizzard at the end of the year. Misplaced, would be more accurate. It was a four-door Buick with wide, whitewall tires, and a straight eight engine. As a result, he got up much earlier for weeks so he could look for the car before he went to work. I found the car a few weeks later, three blocks away, on North First Street, peeking out from under a huge pile of snow on the way home from the Snow Fort debacle. "Oh! Good! I've been wondering where I parked it," he said, "Now I can sleep later." And he left it there until the snow completely melted revealing a sodden mass of barely legible parking tickets for blocking snow removal.

At the time he was working for the county. I asked him in tactless childish innocence, during a pause in his heated political exchange with my father, why he worked for a government he thought was corrupt. His answer went something like this—*It's a great place for me to hide, there's a witch hunt going on for people that belong to the Communist Party in this country. Besides most of the physical projects of government tend to benefit the general public, to some degree. So working for the government, is a lesser evil than for a company.*

"Corporate owners are greedy. They want to pay as little as possible for a chunk of your life, which they take home as profit"

"I keep a low profile, do a good job, keep to myself and hope to be ignored."

It made a lot of sense, but it did sound like an unusual career plan, nor was I totally convinced he could keep a low profile, since his interactions with people were politically evangelical. And I thought Aunt Fay, his wife, might have had a hand in this also as she preferred a steady income to Phil's forays into the uncertain world of commerce.

In order to work for business institutions, you need to conform, to bend your personality to the company environment and ethics. That eventually overwhelms your identity, narrows your world view and in time, lowers your ethics to their level, their bottom line. He repeated himself often, with the sincere, heartfelt, religious enthusiasm of a true believer.

The McCarthy era of looking for Communists in government, in Hollywood and everywhere was only a few years away.

I watched my father struggle politely, early every Sunday morning, over coffee, with my uncle's impassioned pronouncements.

"The worker's revolution is succeeding in all of Europe."

My poor incredulous father, unaccustomed to having his cursory political views tampered with, finally became so incensed one Sunday morning that he told my uncle, in glorious, though heated, patriotic terms, to leave the house and never, never, never ever, ever, ever, ever come back with his un-American, bullshit is what he wanted to say but I was in the room, talk. Undaunted Uncle Phil, always infuriatingly calm, went on with his monolog, unable to stop mid-thought, while my father physically escorted him backward across our kitchen and out the rear door, and as he slammed the door in his face told him, again, to never, never, never come back. Fifteen minutes later Phil came down the back stairs from his apartment, and without knocking on the back door, walked into our kitchen.

"We've run out of coffee upstairs. You don't mind if I finish my hard roll and coffee? Could you reheat the coffee?"

My father, still walking in circles around the kitchen exclaimed loudly what should be done with someone like Phil, let out a yelp, and walked out the door that Phil had left standing open, to pace around the back yard, hitting himself in his head while yelping continuously in a weak attempt to gain control of himself.

There were times though, when these coffee cloches were not so strident, when these two men toned it down to work out the implications of their opposing world views, the real red meat stuff—social welfare vs. charity, labor vs. management, communism vs. capitalism, humanism vs. religion, and how did these right/left ideas really address the inequities in our country, and who did they benefit the most? I could not, not be there for every second of these exchanges that were better than anything else I could imagine. I tried to hang on every word but the subtleties rushed by me. At times they used me as their focus. What would my future be, how should I be educated, what values should I be taught? I wanted to join in but my child's brain wasn't up to the task. What I was able to understand was that there existed an exciting world of ideas, that conflicting ideas could create a new landscape in the mind.

Uncle Phil, my second cousin, son of Great Uncle Phil, the butcher down the street, had absolutely nothing in common with his father. Phil Sr. was a meat-and-potatoes man when it came to matters of intellect. Keeping it simple was not a choice. It was a belief. A true American, he didn't like controversy about issues of national pride. His son was a Communist. They rarely spoke. The real rub for his father, he had paid for his son's education and look at the result.

Phil Junior had nothing in common with his wife either. Two more mismatched people could not be possible. Uncle Phil lived in his head. Fay in the beauty parlor. His interpersonal skills were like that of a seal that would surface momentarily to scan the turbulent waters of his domestic life, then dive for cover. If fashionable, immaculate Fay didn't intervene he would wear the same slacks and pullover zipper shirt endlessly. He did slightly better with his two daughters, Phyllis and Connie, until they got older. Phyllis, named for her father, was most like him in maneuvering the vicissitudes of life. Connie, more like her mother, practical, realistic, with a stylish flair. Phil was predictably unpredictable. He passed through everyone's day with the force of a train that willy-nilly, and frequently, left its track in pursuit of a more interesting destination.

In 1952, Phil bought another new Buick, a maroon convertible. A beauty, a true American dreamboat that could hold seven. The day he brought the car home he took everyone out for a ride, with the top down, sans politics, unless you acknowledged his euphoric expression of love for this General Motors creation.

All capitalist manufacturers make products with built in obsolescence. They create the most saleable product not the best product.

It did seem somewhat subversive regarding the intent of the Workers' Revolution, positively so, and confusing too. It gave everyone in the car a relaxed moment of hope about Phil's future. Except for Fay.

My family's first and only vehicle was a '41 Chevy panel truck that my father used in his floor sanding business. Whenever we went somewhere as a family I had to sit on a wooden milk box in the back of the windowless truck. It was an embarrassment to me. I dreaded the possibility that one of my friends might see me getting into the truck all dressed up. It was at the age of eleven that I learned the obsessive power of lust. It began innocently. I began looking for my uncle's Buick convertible on the way home from school. It wasn't always there but when it was I would walk back and forth, in a discreet way of course, sometimes even on the opposite side of the street so as not to draw attention to myself, as I wallowed in the fantasy of ownership. Despite all my uncle's econo-political admonishments, *Capitalism wants you to think that buying things will give your life meaning*, Phil, like many preachers, didn't always practice what he preached, plus I was a natural born American consumer-in-training, and I couldn't wait to pursue this avocation when I grew up. I would buy a Buick convertible too.

In our blue collar neighborhood, a car like Uncle Phil's was easy to find. It was the only new car. And not just new, luxuriously special. The light glinted off of that maroon tinged mound of steel, chrome and American knowhow, like none other on the street, so richly appointed that I thought of it as a chrome car with paint trim. The hood was long with a sleek space age ornament, a chrome Buck Rodger's space ship bursting through the circle of time and space. Below that was an aggressive, carnivorous looking grill of thick chrome teeth and chrome bumper below. Behind the hood a sleek, revolutionary, one-piece windshield trimmed in chrome swept rakishly up to the white convertible top, which opened and closed effortlessly by the touch of a chrome electric button. An elegant swoop of chrome down each side of the body gave the whole car a feeling of power and movement. All the windows were electric trimmed in, of course, chrome. The interior was soft, cream-colored leather with red piping. The rear was detailed with a large chrome symbol and name on the trunk over another giant chrome bumper and chrome duel exhaust pipes. I thought of it as our car. My family's car. MY CAR.

I was discreet though. As I moved down the street I did my best to stifle any outward sign of pride or interest. I'd rather have suffered from chronic postnasal drip than drool in public. I was cool, I was discreet, and I was on my way home from school one day when I saw Benny Taylor, coming down the street toward me. He was two years older than me. He lived across the street and was the last person that I wanted to see. Unfortunately, I had foolishly told him in a fatheaded moment, that the Buick was my father's, because Benny, seemed sophisticated and I wanted to impress him. I had made a point of showing him the car. *He was impressed.*

"Is that really your car? Wow that's really neat," and for a while we hung out after school together, but those few years of difference were more than I could handle. One day he challenged me to a speed jerk-off contest for which I was ill equipped, both physically and mentally, being both prepubescent and naïve.

So that's why I slipped into the neighborhood ice cream parlor and ducked down behind the greeting card cabinet next to the comic books, hoping he hadn't seen me. I instantly lost myself in selecting a comic when his two legs appeared next to me.

"Hey! What happened to your uncle's car?" asked Benny.

Unwilling to look up from the comic book, dreading what I knew was coming, I had to make a quick decision. Should I bluff my way through or should I be humiliated?

"What do you mean? There's nothing wrong with our car."

"That commie uncle of yours ruined his new car."

There was just enough ego left in me to give it another try. "It's our car. My father just loans it to him."

"Oh yeah! Then how come I never seen your father drive it?"

So much for my being cool. I got back to the main subject. "What? What happened?"

"Come on. I'll show you!"

As we drew up next to Uncle Phil's car, symbol of luxury and success, my body wilted. Piercing the back of the convertible roof of this otherwise pristine new Buick were the legs of his surveyor's tripod.

Benny, chuckling, started to say something. But I just put my head down, turned and went home without a word. I had to know. What happened? I looked without success for the next few days for my uncle and the car. Both were missing all that week. Saturday morning the car was finally parked in front of our house with the tripod still through the roof, but Uncle Phil wasn't home. Sunday morning, he came downstairs for his usual "cauffee-and." He and my father were discussing the upcoming election. "I'll vote Socialist this election but I won't vote Communist," said Bill Vis. Well that was a turnabout. They started to discuss the disappointing outcome of the struggle in Europe, the Greek civil war in particular. There was a slight reflective pause in the conversation so I jumped in, "Uncle Phil! Uncle Phil! What happened to your new car?"

"Ah….what…? Is there something wrong with it?"

"Yeah! There's a hole in the roof!"

"Really? A hole?"

I was struggling to force his mind back from the brink of class struggle in Greece, straining to drag it west across the Mediterranean Sea, past Gibraltar, over the North Atlantic to Paterson, New Jersey, to his Buick in front of our house at 99 North Main Street.

"Why should there be a hole in my roof?

This man had the amazing ability to transform convoluted abstractions into simple comprehensible realities for me and was equally skilled at converting simple observable realities into mysterious abstractions. He had been driving around most of the week with his tripod poking twelve inches through the canvass roof. Was this the man who taught me how to play chess, how to be observant of intricate historical relationships, how to plan your moves ahead, the same man with a week old unobserved hole in his car roof? Did he never look in the rearview mirror? No. He drove as if he were the only moving object in the world, always at the same terrifying speed, a fast forty miles an hour through city streets and a slow forty on the highway, while carrying on an eye to eye conversation with anyone in the front seat.

As Phil, my father, and myself were standing next to the car I saw an utter look of amazement and confusion etched on Phil's face. "When did this happen?" He turned to me for help, for an explanation.

"I don't know. I saw it this past Monday." I shrugged. "I guess you forgot you stood the tripod up in the back seat and then you put the top up." I felt foolish giving such a simple-minded explanation, but what else could have happened?

There was a long silence while he looked at the roof, then he looked back at me. He turned and moved next to me. His eyes looked pleadingly into mine. I could feel the enormous effort of his mind as he tried to penetrate this mystery.

"Oh," he said quietly to me. He left the tripod and the roof undisturbed, turned and walked quietly back into the house to have another ketchup sandwich and a cup 'a cauffee.

A few days later my mother and Aunt Fay were in our kitchen talking about the recent Phil antic when Fay told my mother why they had moved upstairs. It seems when they were living over the saloon on the corner by North Straight Street, Phil trained their cat to use the toilet instead of a litter box. And while he was at it taught the cat how to turn on the bathroom sink faucet for a drink of water. One morning after everyone had left the house the cat turned on the water and at the same time knocked the rubber plug into the sink. Sometime in the middle of the afternoon the ceiling over the bar collapsed. The owner gave them one week to move out.

After we stopped going to the luncheonette, I rarely saw Uncle Phil. His usual Sunday morning visits became infrequent and he often seemed distracted and internalized when he did show up. A few months later Fay stopped working at the Wayne Milk Bar. She got a good job waitressing at a theater club and kept all her earnings. Phil closed the luncheonette and sold the Ice Cream Parlor on Haledon Avenue to my parents. He also sold the truck farm up on the Paterson Hamburg Turnpike in Wayne to the tenant farmer that had been running it for him and got a job working as an engineer for the state. He worked as a site engineer on the Jersey section of the Palisades Parkway, which is how the transit came to be in his car. He did eventually patch the hole with some cellophane tape as well as other bits of the car's body parts he knocked loose over the next few years. His Buick no longer stood out in our blue-collar block, freeing me from any responsibility of feigned ownership.

Uncle Phil Whitehead taught me the importance of critical thinking, not what to think, though he did try, inadvertently, from time to time. He was, after all, too unplugged from day to day reality to be a role model. Yet I was sure his understanding of world dynamics and how our government and corporations collude, was accurate. He just never convinced me that his alternative to these conditions was workable. I asked him once when I was much older, "What's the difference between a corporation that builds a refrigerator that falls apart in five years or a planned economy that turns out a mediocre refrigerator that only lasts five years?" I could read his mind, as he looked me in the eye—smart-ass kid. It was mostly his own fault and I loved him for it.

27

It's A Multiple Choice Question
Don't Miss It If You Can
Age 12

None of the above. I once had a teacher that loved to give tests using multiple choice questions where None of the Above appeared most often as the correct answer. They became predictably common. If it hadn't been for my uncle Phil I might not have caught on to that teacher's cleverness. Sometimes the best way to deal with a problem is to study the instigator.

I HAD JUST COMPLETED eighth grade at the church school and was trying to accept the idea that my parents were going to send me to a Seventh Day Adventist boarding school in New Market, Virginia, in the fall, to start high school. Not surprisingly, I was failing at the task. Miserably.

Their decision came at me from nowhere. Almost nowhere. After my father had nearly killed himself with alcohol, which scared the bejesus into him, he then put his total energy into religion, which really did save him, but from my point of view, made him unrecognizable. Now he was fixated on changing my life, which up until then seemed pretty OK to me. Until then I had been living an autonomous boy's life, discretely so to a large degree. I wasn't rebellious, did my homework, ran errands, helped out around the house, a minimum to be sure. No one asked for more. Earned some pocket money with odd jobs.

In that time before my father got religion I did pretty much what I wanted, like most boys. I had a great new bicycle, was going to movies whenever I pleased, was singing in the Baptist choir, which I loved, hanging out at Charlie's Bar and Grill with Molly and the Mills Brothers (on the jukebox), and was actually starting to improve my baseball game. The sudden interest from my father to mold me turned my life into a grade-B horror movie, not a sanctuary of salvation.

"This change is a part of God's plan for your life. Try to accept that it's God's will," my father said to me when I didn't respond with joy at the news about Virginia.

Did my father really expect me to believe that, that it was God's idea, not his to send me off to school in rural Virginia?

"It's important that you give it a chance. Pray for understanding. We're sending you there for your own good. "

What my father didn't know was that Uncle Phil had gotten to me first, years ago, by treating me like an adult, talking to me intelligently, revealing a larger world of ideas and awareness about life's struggles and potential and that most precious of abilities, critical thinking. But the three practical things that served me the best were what Molly Schwartz and Alice told me about this distressing state I believed myself caught in, and the behavior of my great uncle Phil, the butcher—nothing should never be a total loss, don't talk about religion or politics if you want to get along, and keep your own council.

"It'll be a good change from city life to country. You can work on the school dairy farm," my father added.

Now there was a selling point. Work on a farm. Had he forgotten his family's Clifton dairy debacle or our backyard chicken fiasco? Farming did not run in our family genes.

Throughout the summer I heard, "Are you praying for understanding Jerry?"

Who was this strange man that had hardly been present in my life during the first eleven years?

It was just after supper on a hot August day and I was sitting on the steps of our front porch with my father and my uncle. We were eating ice cream cones from the soda fountain down the street. Another father-son pep talk about Virginia was underway. With his usual abruptness,

Phil interrupted my father's soliloquy on his view of a quality education, and explained that a good education teaches you how to use your mind, how to make value judgments, not how to conform. As they make you do in religious schools was the implication, which even I understood then. But my father wasn't having any of this. His days as a Socialist and a rational participant in world events were over, exchanged for the "Truth" of his new found religion. I sat there between them on the steps, looking out into space, trying to shrink my immediate world down to the size of my double dip chocolate ice cream cone, as they stared at each other over my head.

Uncle Phil, never understanding when he had exceeded the bounds of social restraint, thankfully, went on, "Remember those times we talked about your son's future?"

Nothing. No response.

"How old are you now?" he asked me.

"Twelve," I said.

Phil nodded thoughtfully. "Remember what I said to you once, there are three kinds of leeches at work in the world. They create nothing of value and give nothing of real value back. Can you guess who they are? "

I couldn't.

"Bankers, lawyers and theologians," he continued. "Given the opportunity all three will take your money, limit your freedom and steal your soul."

Silence. I knew my father wanted Phil to go home, but he was home, sitting on the front porch that was as much his as my father's.

I got up from the steps and walked back on to the porch to finish my ice cream in peace when a moving van pulled up in front of our house. A beautifully tailored colored women and a small girl in a pretty dress and pigtails with bows got out of a taxi and began carrying light things from the truck into the ground floor apartment next door while two colored men did the heavy work of moving furniture and big boxes in. We were now all standing at the porch railing watching as each trip to the apartment passed within three feet of us along the side of our porch. No one spoke though my father cast side-glances at me. I could feel a mounting level of discomfort. They were the first Coloreds to move into our neighborhood, and the first sign in our neighborhood of the northward migration of Negros from the south after the Second World War. My only contact previously had been with the five colored boys that chased me out of their narrow neighborhood by the river two blocks away. My uncle motioned to the woman to stop so he could welcome her to the neighborhood. My father bristled, folded his arms across his chest and scowled at him.

"I wonder where she's from? Sounds southern don't you think?" Phil said in a detached tone to my father, but he had gone into the house, I thought to find my mother. Moments before, no one was around. Now neighbors miraculously appeared from everywhere. My father returned with my mother to join Uncle Phil and I on the porch. Her face was ashen.

"Look at them," referring to our neighbors, "You'd think they'd never seen Colored people before," said Phil to the air.

My mother looked at Phil incredulously. For me, it was a welcome relief, better than talking about the surreal idea of going to a religious boarding school in Virginia.

"I don't know what kind of an education you're going to get down there at that school," my uncle said, "but just being in the south school will be an education in itself."

My father turned once more to scowl at Phil. It was my uncle at his irritating best. He the irreligious Communist was the calm, compassionate and welcoming one while my devout Christian father, standing rigidly, arms still crossed, was alarmed, angry and resentful.

In 1952, Brown vs. The Board of Education, the historic case about racial segregation in schools, was underway in the Supreme Court.

Two weeks later I was bundled into a borrowed 1949 Dodge sedan with all my clothing and my new roller skates and whisked off in an eight-hour drive to Shenandoah Valley Academy, in the middle of farm country, two miles from New Market, Virginia, population seven hundred and fifty.

The campus of this Adventist school consisted of three southern colonial style structures for its three hundred students, a boy's dormitory, a girl's dormitory and the combined classroom/church building. Then there were the dairy farm buildings for the cows. There were a few individual residences for staff and off in the distance, what I thought was an abandoned wreck next to the Shenandoah River, its siding falling off the walls, the front porch roof partly collapsed, the paint mostly on the ground, was in fact, a housed rented to a colored family by the school.

The first few weeks were one of massive cultural adjustment. Not to the south, which my uncle had tried to prepare me for, but to the perceptions my fellow student formed of me in the first few weeks.

Though I was from Paterson, New Jersey, a number of the more devout students thought, being so close to Sodom and Gomorrah, New York City, meant I had to be sinful beyond redemption, an evil influence in their midst. This I found strange since I wasn't the only kid from New Jersey at the school. I did wear my hair in the latest urban teenage style and didn't own any blue jeans. The first few weeks I was often met with, "Oh. You're the kid (demon possessed implicit) from New York City." I was not only in another B horror movie, I was home sick too.

It was ten o'clock at night, early in November, when the boy's dean woke me. "Tha's a phone caw'al from someone up No'th." In the two plus months I had been there I had not received one letter or phone call from home. My father, I learned, thought it would be better that way so I could adjust to my new life. Groggy from sleep and forgetting to put on my bathrobe, I shivered my way downstairs in my BVD's, apprehensive about what I might hear. I sat down behind the dean's desk.

"Hello?" I said.

"Jerry, you need to come home right away."

I didn't recognize the voice. "What? Who is this?"

"It's your uncle Phil. I want you to come home this weekend. I need to talk to you."

"What's this about?"

"It's very urgent. I don't want to tell you over the phone."

"I don't think I can come home this weekend. It's not allowed unless it's an emergency. Is it?"

"I can't tell you over the phone. Not over the phone," he repeated.

"Is it about my parents?"

He didn't respond. Then, "When can you come home?"

"We have a Thanksgiving break in two weeks. I can see you then. Can it wait?"

"It will have to. Come upstairs on Friday morning after Thanksgiving. Please, don't tell anyone. We'll talk then."

"OK. I'll see you then, Uncle Phil."

The entire time Mr. Feder, the boy's dean, weirdly stood about five feet away, his arms folded across his bulging stomach, listening to my conversation, continually scanning my entire body as I sat shivering in his cold office.

My parents sent a money order for the trip home a week before the Thanksgiving break. Up at five Wednesday morning, I walked two miles into the village to get the bus from New Market to DC, then caught a train to Newark, and another bus to Paterson. I was out of money so I finished the last few blocks on foot, nine o'clock at night. My teary-eyed mother met me at the door.

"I was getting worried. Have you eaten?" she asked.

I had eaten something but I told her no. I had had a forbidden-by-the-Church, hot dog, fries, and coke supper at the bus station in Newark. She got something together quickly and by the time I was finished my father came home from a job he had promised to complete before the holiday.

The next morning, we were all up early to help prepare for the day. My mother's parents were coming to our house for Thanksgiving for the first time. I helped set the table with the best china my mother had purchased one place setting at a time. Each piece was trimmed with a wide band of turquoise, and edged with silver to match the sterling flatware, also purchased on lay-away, and rarely used. The best tablecloth and napkins, freshly pressed, were laid out on the mahogany dining room table with all its leaves in place, and complimented with the extravagance of fresh flowers from the florist and candles in silver holders. She had made a traditional turkey meal even though my now vegetarian father objected.

My grandparents arrived a half-hour late at two thirty. They seemed stiff and distant, my mother ill at ease, and my father sulky and silent. We sat down immediately to mechanically eat four courses with my father pointedly refusing to eat the meat. Only my mother and grandmother spoke, small talk, about the butcher shop, customers, the dinnerware, nothing about missing my mother's help at the store, or how things were going for me at school, or my father's business. My mother had made her father's favorite angel food cake with vanilla butter icing for dessert. "I'll go start the tea and get the dessert," she said.

Her father looked at his daughter as she left the room, then at me and said the first words spoken by him that day, "Our lawn needs raking. Why don't you come up Saturday to help?" His tone turned acid, Oh! I forgot. Your father makes you go to church now on Saturdays." The two men locked eyes.

"I made your favorite treat Pop," said Roselyn, as she reentered the room carrying the cake.

He stood, "No. We have to leave now. The Timmerman's asked us to join them for dinner at five."

I awoke the next morning after eight. Our house was quiet except for muffled sounds coming through the ceiling. I knew it was Fay yelling at her husband. It was a price we paid for living in a two-family house, listening to these all too familiar sounds never acknowledged for what they were. Not a good time to try to see my uncle I thought. I lay in bed for another hour to wait them out. I knew Fay would be going to work at some point. Their disputes, my parents word, were always quite bloodless. They always started the same way. Phil, sedentary by nature, would be seated somewhere while Aunt Fay would pace and fume and shout, waiting, wanting and wishing just once for her rotund husband to respond. But Phil, ever caught off guard, always astonished at the spectacle of his wife before him, seemed like a box turtle being worried by a fox terrier. By ten o'clock, fight or not, I needed to hear the reason for that late night phone call to Virginia. I dressed impatiently. I could hear my mother shuffling things around in the dining room, dealing with the residue of Thanksgiving. I walked out of my bedroom into the dining room.

"Where's Dad?" I wanted to know because I didn't want to see him.

"Gone to work."

"He wanted to talk to me?"

"You were sleeping. Tonight he said."

"Is it important?"

"He said so. Do you want some breakfast?"

"No thanks. I'll just get a glass of milk."

"Are you sure?"

"Yeah. Uncle Phil said he wanted to see me this morning after Aunt Fay went to work. I'd better get going."

"What about?"

"I don't know."

"I think I hear her. She's just leaving now," said my mother.

I stopped to listen. The ceiling wasn't grumbling any longer. At last, after two weeks, two days and two more hours in bed I needed to get this over. With nagging curiosity and false determination, I crossed to the living room door jerked it open and rushed out into our chilly front hall.

The cold air assaulted me like a pail of ice water freezing me with indecision. I slumped back against our living room wall. *Why the phone call from my uncle?* A break between buildings across the street allowed a fragment of late morning sunlight to puncture the glass in the double front doors. I could see my breath. *My uncle and my father aren't speaking.* As I stood with my back against our living room wall my breath disrupting dust motes languidly circling each other in the slanting white light distracted me. My mind blissfully emptied. I could hear my slow breathing but not one other sound, not the traffic in the street, not my mother's tuneless humming as she worked, nor any sound of life from the floor above. Intuitively I knew it was too disruptive this disturbance by my breath in the ethereal world of whirling dust. *It'll be bad luck to move through that whirling dust, like, step on a crack, break your mother's back*...any flimsy reason to not go upstairs. It felt as if I was choosing between my father and my uncle. But I went. I dropped to my hands and knees below the sharp edge of the light and crawled across the floor to the other side of the hall, leaving the lazy tranquility of the sun lit dust motes undisturbed. I stood in the shadow of the far wall, looked back for good luck, to make sure there was no turbulence then started up the darkened stairs. The hall light above wasn't working. I groped along the railing toward my uncle's living room door, blinking hard to squeeze the sunlight from my eyes, found the door by brail, knocked several times and waited. I knocked again. Someone, Uncle Phil I imagined, just inside the door, was shuffling about. Once more I knocked and called out. "Uncle Phil!"

Never fast moving, he abruptly jerked opened the door, startling me.

"Oh! It's you Jerry. Why are you here?" Not waiting for a response he said, "Come in. Come in." He hurried me into the center of the living room. "Nice to see you though. Look. What do you think?"

What he had in mind was a mystery to me. The only room for mystery in my mind had to do with that urgent phone call. A quick look about the room told me that an invading army had just ransacked the living room. The floor was littered with the exploded remains of several large cardboard boxes. Shredded tuffs of wood excelsior, used as packing material, lay strewn about the carpet and stuck to the upholstered furniture and drapery.

"Is Aunt Fay home?" I asked in self-defense. I didn't want to become collateral damage in their morning battle.

"No, no, no..." he said reassuringly, to both of us it seemed. "No, no one is here. She went to work hours ago."

I wondered who I had heard yelling just a few minutes before.

"Well what do you think?" he repeated.

Since it seemed safe enough to stay, I thought I'd better invest some energy in this riddle.

"It came early this morning just after everyone left." Which I knew wasn't true. I was sure it was this mess that caused the angry words

I heard through the ceiling. He pointed at the hall wall. Next to the entry door was an overstuffed armchair, then a longish low table, and another armchair. Aunt Fay kept her Life Magazines stacked atop the veneered mahogany table, several months at least, and her prized hand painted table lamp. Hand painted by her. The base of the lamp was patterned in the style of a Greek Corinthian column. On this base were the figures of two Flamenco dancers welded in an embrace of flowing limbs and locked eyes. There was a bizarre craze at that time among all the mothers that I knew to buy and paint plaster figures of all shapes and sizes. Fay had gotten hers from Woolworths 5 & 10 on Main Street downtown along with small bottles of paint, brushes, and over glaze. The plaster portion of the lamp was an impressive thirty inches tall. The base was painted gold, and the large flowing dress was crimson with a floral pattern picked out in bold contrasting colors. The male dancer's clothes and hat were the traditional black. An elongated curved lampshade brought the whole assemblage to a monumental conclusion, which in Aunt Fay's opinion had earned it a place of honor in their living room.

What my uncle was pointing at was a large cloth fronted box perched precariously upon the stack of magazines and tilted against the lamp.

"Sit there," he indicated to a sofa across the room.

There were small bits of plaster paint chips lying on the table, the shade was bent back into the wall and the bare-lit light bulb was doing its best to harass my eyes just recovered from the blinding hall sunlight. He reached down to a slim box lying on the floor. It contained a three-record set of Raymond Massey as Abe Lincoln from the play "Abe Lincoln in Illinois," by Robert Sherwood. "Listen to this." He placed the first record inside the top of the mahogany box. That solved part of the riddle. The sound seemed to erupt from several places at once.

"Fantastic isn't it? It's like he's right here in the room with us. Isn't it?" He turned the volume up louder. "Latest thing, high fidelity sound it's called. How do you like it?" he shouted.

I didn't respond. I nodded. He smiled. Taking this as overwhelming approval he played all three tedious records.

"Do you like Mario Lanza?"

I liked the Mill's Brothers. I liked Bill Haley and the Comets. I liked Fats Domino. I had no idea who Mario Lanza was. "Yes, I do." I said. I knew that it was better to go along with my uncle whenever he was caught up in the thrall of the moment. There was certain inevitability about an exchange with him. The sooner you went with it the sooner you could get past it. He loaded the hi-fi record player with the disc of Mario singing his favorite Italian melodies. The record finished. Phil removed the record from the player, and as he turned it over to play the other side I asked, "What did you call me about the other week? You said it was urgent."

"Call you?" he asked looking at me. He was having a difficult time lining up the hole in the record with the spindle on the turntable. "I said it was urgent?" he continued.

"Yes. Urgent. You said urgent. And you wanted me to come home right away."

"Really! Why would I do that?" he said to himself. He was still fumbling about with the hi-fi, his head twisted away from the record player. He was staring at a spot to the right and slightly above my head. I listened to the spindle scraping back and forth across the delicate record grooves like a nail over a washboard. I thought of my aunt Tyne's instructions for handling records.

"But I told you I couldn't come until Thanksgiving and we agreed to meet the day after, in the morning. That's today, NOW."

I could tell that this sounded familiar to him. He took Mr. Lanza out of the player and dropped him on the carpet under the table.

"You had any breakfast?" he said unrepentantly.

I wasn't sure if this was a legitimate question or a change of subject. "No, I haven't." It was nearly ten.

"Let's go get something to eat then. OK?"

I got up and reluctantly started toward the kitchen. I anticipated that he'd offer me some reheated, stale coffee and a soup sandwich.

"Not here. There's nothing here. Let's go out. I'll treat you to some hash and eggs at Bickford's."

On the way out the front door I grabbed my coat and told my mother that Uncle Phil was taking me out for breakfast. She gave me a peculiar look and asked what was going on. "Later," I said.

His Buick was parked up the street. When I opened the door a precarious stack of newspapers toppled out onto the sidewalk. It took us five minutes to clear away the mess and empty out the floor area before I could sit down. He just added the debris to the rest of the piles in the back seat. Bickford's was a cheerless overly bright, antiseptic place across the street from the Eire Lackawanna train station by Market Street. It was my uncle's favorite hideout from his wife and I speculated the FBI. He said the government was spying on registered Communists, tapping their phones, even bugging their homes.

What in the world was that phone call to Virginia about anyway?

It was about ten thirty. The restaurant was empty. We sat at a table by a window facing the train station. The same harsh sunlight sliced through the crystal clear glass and ricocheted off the light tile floor and white walls. Every crevice of the restaurant glistened like a well-crafted vacuous sermon. My uncle hadn't spoken a word since we left the house. Our coffee arrived and he put five teaspoons of sugar in his cup and stirred it around and around. I said nothing. He said nothing. Round and around the spoon went. I could smell the sweetness of the mixture. It seemed like a groove must certainly be engraved in the bottom of the thick tan coffee mug as he continued stirring. He let the spoon go. It coasted to a stop then he looked up.

"What do you want to do with your life?"

The waiter brought our hash and eggs, put them down at the same time. The plates thumped loudly on the table and skidded perfectly into place in front of us. What did I want to do? I was not even thirteen. I wasn't concerned with my future except finding a way to deal with those holier-than-thou students back in Virginia. "I don't know." I said.

"You're really talented in art," he said while he buried his corn beef hash in ketchup. He grabbed the spoon out of his coffee and began stirring the pile into a bloody looking stew.

"Yeeessss?" I responded, trailing out the single syllable, surprised by this unexpected observation. And this I thought coming from a man that had just decorated his living room with excelsior and mangled boxes. It was true. I did have some talent, always drawing and making things, doing paint by number paintings that I painted my own way.

"You think I should become an artist?"

"A talent is a wonderful thing." As he said this he took his two over easy eggs and mashed them into the hash with the side of his coffee spoon until the heap turned a nasty purple color from the added yokes.

"It shouldn't be ignored. It should be developed."

I sat there poised on the edge of my chair staring open mouthed into the visionary future that my uncle saw for me. There comes a time in every young white middle class American male's life when the secret door of opportunity, as promised by years of schooling and third rate Hollywood movies, cracks open, beaconing for you to slip quickly into a promised gleaming affluent life. As a blue-collar kid I sat speechless waiting to see where this idea was going. Uncle Phil had all but devoured his food and was now eyeing my as yet untouched plate.

I finally asked, "How should I do that? I mean how could I earn money becoming an artist?" It seemed that my uncle was about to offer me something as he scraped his plate clean.

"I can help you," he said.

Intuitively I knew I should act, that this opportunity, if that's what this was, though unexpected, was there for the taking. Molly Schwartz would say, "If luck walks through the door offer it a seat."

"What do you mean?"

Uncle Phil leaned forward over the table, looked directly into my eyes and said, "You must emigrate to Russia."

"Do what?!?" My voice cracked.

"Look. You're a poor boy from a blue-collar family. Even if you could somehow afford a college education you probably would wind up working in advertising or making Hallmark greeting cards. Your talents would be exploited for someone else's profits and you would end up squandering all your ability and training on drivel."

I was just getting used to becoming an artist and already I was being exploited and driveled upon. I watched as he reached across the table and swapped his empty plate for mine.

"You don't mind do you? You're not going to eat yours are you Jerry?"

"Russia!!!" I barely managed with my jaw hanging open against my chest. This brilliant light of opportunity was quickly becoming a vanishing shooting star.

"A talent such as yours is a precious gift that belongs to all mankind."

My but he had a way with words and ideas. They always seemed to offer up a broader world in need of exploration or was it exploitation.

"In Russia," he continued, "such talent would be appreciated. You would be given an education for free and then, as an artist, you'd be supported for life and have the chance to create art that celebrates the nobility of all men."

"Is this why you called me at school?" I realized that he might just be another religious nut, only his heaven was Russia right here on earth. "Ah, just a moment," he said distractedly.

There wasn't quite enough ketchup left in the bottle to smother the second plate of hash. He spotted some several tables away and asked me to get it for him. As I returned to our table he looked up from my purloined food. "Ah, yes. That's it."

"About the phone call you mean?" I handed him the ketchup.

"No. I mean…thanks for getting the ketchup."

"What about the phone call? Why couldn't we talk over the phone?" Though it would have been terrible talking on the phone with the creepy boys' dean hovering over me.

"This is a serious thing. It needed to be done face to face."

"And the FBI thing too, right?" I added. He nodded as I sat down and watched him pour out a blanket of ketchup and mash in the cold stiff eggs.

"I'm very serious about this," he continued. "And I'm willing to sponsor your trip to Russia when you're ready to go."

I leaned forward resting my stomach against the cold, chrome edge of the table with my right hand cupped lightly over my eyes to shield against the sunlight streaming through the window. "You mean you'd pay for me to get there?"

"Yes, and clothes, an apartment, and before you go…whatever's needed."

There were two obstacles that occurred to me right then and there. If three months in Virginia nearly destroyed me with culture shock, what would a lifetime in Russia do to me? And second, I was presently failing Spanish. Russian had to be a lot harder. I did like the idea of becoming an artist though it seemed like a fantasy, like going to the moon or being rich.

"But how would making art for Russia be different from working for Hallmark?" I asked. Luck and I were now playing musical chairs.

He was ready and he was sincere. "In Russia you would be able to make art that reflected the values common to all people while in America you would either starve as an artist or work in commercial art seducing people into buying things they mostly didn't need or care about. In Russia you would bring people together." He concluded his inspirational talk by wiping the second plate of hash clean with a crust of, what should have been, my toast.

"You have any questions?"

My mouth said, "No. I have to think about all this I guess. I don't really know much about Russia." This is madness. It felt like an invisible hand had pulled the seat out from under my luck, and that my uncle had become the Mad Hatter in Wonderland.

"That's OK. We've got time," Uncle Phil said. "You need to learn to speak Russian and I need to save up money. By the time you graduate from high school everything should be ready."

I'm not sure where I was going to get Russian lessons in cow patch Virginia. Their idea of an enhanced educational experience was two and a half hours of religious instruction every day. The only elective courses offered which we had to take, were animal husbandry for the boys and homemaking for the girls, which included milking cows.

The waiter came to take away the dishes.

"You had enough to eat?" Phil asked, "You want anything else Jerry? Oh! No time. It's late. I've got to get up to the store."

We left Bickford's and crossed Market Street to a large newsstand that sold papers and magazines from all over the country and the world. Phil bought the latest Daily Worker, the American Communist Party newspaper and a copy of USSR magazine. "Here," he said. He handed me the magazine. "You should start learning about Russia." It was mostly pictures just like Life Magazine only thinner. There were no advertisements.

"I'll get you a subscription. It'll be sent to you at your school."

Oh, God, I thought. That's all I need. Now I would be known as the Communist, demon-possessed boy from Sodom and Gomorrah New York City.

When I got home I went right to the refrigerator and stood there hanging on the open door. The refrigerator, our first, was a huge double door commercial unit that Uncle Phil talked my father into buying. It was marked down because one side was crushed in. It took up a quarter of the kitchen, ran continuously, and had no freezer.

"You still hungry?" my mother asked. "I thought Uncle Phil took you out for breakfast?"

"We talked a lot and I got so interested in what he was saying... then it was time to go."

"Why did he want to talk to you?"

"Ah. He wants to help me go to college."

"Really! You'd be the first in your father's family."

"Except he thinks I should become an artist."

"What did you say? That's very generous of him, but art?

"I told him I'd think about it. I don't know. Art doesn't seem right."

"Don't say anything to your father. He doesn't trust Phil. We'll talk about it some more another time."

Well, when it came to food I no longer trusted him either after our sojourn at Bickford's. But, him sending me to Russia? He seemed really serious. I needed to talk to someone. Right then.

"I haven't seen Mary yet. Think I'll go next door, see if she's home."

"Be back by four thirty. Your father wants to talk to you."

Mary was home. We started a game of Canasta, not what I wanted to do but it was a way to ease into what was bothering me. Mary, I knew, would start asking me questions since we hadn't seen each other for three months.

"What's it like down there?" she said.

"Weird." I told her about all the school rules and having three religious meetings a day and lights out at nine, no radios allowed or magazines, that I had a hard time understanding the southern accent and their funny sayings, and they think I'm evil because I'm from New York City.

"But you're not from New York," she said.

"Yeah, I know, but there are some kids down there that think that way. The real religious ones."

"I'll bet you're glad to be home."

"Well not completely." I gave her a quick rundown—our Thanksgiving dinner was awful, my uncle wants to send me to college in Russia, and my father made an appointment to talk to me tonight. An appointment!

Mary was sympathetic. She had been dealing with the nuns in Catholic school for years, she hardly knew her father since he slept all the time when he was home, and she said everybody knew my uncle was crazy, which surprised me. And then she had the insensitive gall to win the game of Canasta.

It was 4:30, time for my second appointment of the day. My father and I sat at the kitchen table. This time there really was no food, nothing to drink just serious business. My mother was cooking supper.

"You'll be thirteen in three months…"

Was that a question?

"Do you know what that means?"

Ah, there's the question. I didn't stir. All my effort was going into being a non-participant, more like a visiting observer.

"It means you're of the age of responsibility. In the eyes of God and our church you are no longer a child. You need to get baptized. Your mother and I need to know that you have committed your life to the Lord. We are sacrificing to give you a good Christian education…"

"I don't like it down there." I interrupted. I didn't know I was going to say it. It just came out.

When I was leaving Mary's house her mother appeared in the open front door beside her daughter. I was standing three steps down on the edge of the sidewalk saying good-bye. My oldest and best friend was moving away from the neighborhood, to Hawthorne, in a couple of weeks.

"I didn't get a chance to talk to you. I guess Mary told you we're moving soon."

"Yes."

"You'll come see us at Christmas. I suppose you'll be home then. How's school going Jerry? Do you like it?" Mary's Mother asked.

A trace of tears started. "Not too good." I said in a whisper.

"Oh," she said. I wanted her sympathy. Somebody's. But good friends don't talk about religion or politics. They said good-bye and closed the door.

Ignoring my outburst my father clipped the end of my words "… but that sacrifice will be for nothing if you don't accept the Lord."

I didn't move.

"During Christmas vacation the church is going to offer baptismal classes for young people. We've signed you up. What do you say?"

"I don't know. I need to think about it?" I said for the second time that day.

It wasn't what he wanted to hear. He stiffened. My mother, working at the sink said nothing. I looked over at her back.

Supper came and went without a word from me. After I helped clear the table I went in to the dining room to work on a jigsaw puzzle, a huge 10,000-piece puzzle of Mount Everest I had started in the summer. And while I was preoccupied by my task I realized with some surprise that I was chuckling to myself. Some piece of my mind, perhaps the part that brings us dreams in the night, had made a whimsical leap. I saw myself wearing my uncle Joe Cerrone's ostentatious diamond ring that he had tried to bribe me with, carrying my grandparent's oversized, dust covered, oath taking bible to place my hand on while I promised to never become an Adventist. *Maybe they could teach the Baptismal classes in Russian.*

"What's so funny?" my mother called out from the kitchen.

"Nothing. I just found where a bunch of pieces fit together in the puzzle."

Two differing truths, two differing realities. If not more. To be endlessly continued?

28

Wherever You Go, There You Are

From the movie *Buckeroo Banzai*
9–12 Years Old

When I was a boy, alone, down at the river's edge, I watched seagulls circle effortlessly above the water, never once moving their wings to stay aloft. If I watched long enough I became one with them and then without my notice, nothing else mattered.

A S I CONTINUED TO work on the puzzle, my meandering thoughts took another unexpected detour, a kind of wondering about a thing to do, a way to get distance from all the thanklessness of Thanksgiving. I wasn't sure what that would be but knew that when the right time came something would present itself. Meanwhile I had to go to Friday night church. The next morning, I was back in church again, then home for the rest of the day. My mind kept returning to the clutter of demands from the past few days. I was angry, sullen, and terminally confused. In two days I would be making the return trip to school. I needed something to occur or change before I started the trip back south. My body felt as if it had been hollowed out. I took my muddled mind into the backyard just to get out of the house. Under the porch, buried behind our summer screens and lawn chairs, sat my dust covered three-speed English Racer. Though work, play or any other personal activity was not permitted on Saturday, the Sabbath, with sneaky defiance, I dug out my good friend, neglected since the summer. It's unlikely there was an electrical storm that November but lightning did suddenly strike my imagination as I extricated my bike and began to clean it off. I had never gone on that special bike ride that I had fantasized about when I first got the bike. Tomorrow I thought would be a good day to go on that ride. I had a lot to escape from.

Unable to sleep Sunday morning, I was up early, anxious to start my day but my mother, trying to smooth out all our differences, had made a large breakfast for all of us to eat together. Other than "pass the butter," we ate in silence.

"I'm going to try to get paid from that last job," my father said to my mother.

"Today?" she asked.

"Yeah, they said they'd have the money for me today. I'll be back in a little while." And with that he got up and drove off in his panel truck.

"I think I'll go up the hill to see Dougie today." I said, "Is that all right?"

"I guess so. But you have to be back by five. We're going to the Chinese restaurant tonight."

Of course I was lying. Why would I want to see an old friend that had turned his back on me? I knew my mother had no idea about Dougie or any of my old friends that wanted nothing to do with me since I went to the Adventist Church. Ironically, lying came easily to me now that I was living in a religious environment. It was becoming habitual. "How do you like school in Virginia?" "It's fine," I would say looking straight into the eyes of anyone that questioned me. What was the point of telling the truth? I'd just look wimpy and they would be uncomfortable or angry, depending upon who was doing the asking. I did like the cliffs and the caves and the mountains and the river. That made it somewhat truthful.

It was a gray day to match my gray mood, mild for November. I dressed for rain, made my usual peanut butter sandwiches to go, got on my bike and left the house. It was around eight o'clock. I still did not know where I was going. I knew I didn't want to be with anyone. Being free and alone was enough for the moment.

It took me several blocks before I realized where I had gone. I found myself passing over the Main Street Bridge. I stopped and looked down at my old friend, the river that had helped me, and taught me so much. I had begun to drop coins of thanks in the water each time I went to sit by the river's edge. It had been too long since I had thought of the river. I felt a longing twinge as I looked down into the water. The river felt remote and lonely. It was the same indifferent gray as the day. But today, a visit to this river would not be enough to overcome the madness of the last few days. I took a silver coin from my pocket and dropped it into the water, to let the river know I was still around, that I still cared. When I reached the other side of the bridge I continued up Main Street, passed by Ryerson Alley where Aunt Tyne's house stood dark and empty. At Broadway I felt I had to make a choice—go on up Main or turn onto Broadway. Straight ahead would take me into the heart of the city, too distracting for my mood. A right turn would quickly take me to the old factories and the falls that I loved. Not that those harsh factories or the precipitous river falls had been kind to my family that worked hard and stayed poor. I loved them for the safety of their knowable past—better to know the troubles of the past than face the trouble of the present. Too, too easy and comfortable for that day. I turned left on to Broadway, the only street in Paterson to flow like a leak out of the city from its heart. I didn't like Broadway, so aloof from the gritty city center as it transited through the self-satisfied middle class neighborhoods, so unreal to me. It had too many unpleasant associations for me, but it better suited my needs, and those needs were not diversion or comfort but navigating the dilemma of my uncle's and father's demands.

Twenty-three blocks from Main stood the Barnet Hospital where my mother and I struggled for three days to get me born, and Doctor Landau's office a few blocks away where I went with my chronic earaches and was anesthetized with ether on his office table to have my tonsils removed. "You can eat all the ice cream you want," he told me when I regained consciousness. But I couldn't. It hurt too much to even speak my refusal. And then there was the dentist that we only saw when something hurt. It was also down Broadway we traveled to visit my slimy Uncle Joe and victimized Aunt Lizzy in their smug comfortable house on East Twenty-Fifth Street with its oriental rugs, and the safe stuffed with money and the diamond bribe ring. It was all a part of what I didn't want in my life. Broadway felt like a grease gun symbolically squeezing me past all the old unwanted and unpleasant things I knew so I could deal with what I faced now.

Eventually Broadway, in its straight line rush to leave the city, meets the Passaic River, which wraps around the eastern end of Paterson in a serpentine embrace. I had never been to this area on my own. And while the river by my house felt approachable, at the city's eastern edge it seemed like a barrier. You can go this far but no farther.

Just before Broadway reaches the river it rises up into a gentle mound where I was now apprehensively looking down at the bridge that led out of town. I still did not know where this day was taking me, but knew that I needed to trust the moment, not worry it. If I kept going I would meet that place that would tell me what to do. There's nothing for me to decide, said the voice that wanted this journey. So I put my feet back on the peddles and let the bike's momentum carry me down the hill and over the bridge into East Paterson. And then I knew, by the feeling of excitement in my chest as I started to peddle away from the bridge, where I should go.

I was now on Route 4 heading east past another uncle's house. Austere, Holland—born Neil and his formal German wife, Mary, lived on the second floor of a white frame house that fronted the road I was on. They rented out the first floor for income. Since it was Sunday, they were probably home. I sped up to put this last reminder of my family behind me. Once the road left Paterson it widened into a four-lane highway. I passed a small shopping area, then a few vegetable truck farms, some open country with random clumps of trees and a sprinkling of indifferent buildings. The ride was just plain work now, nothing to see, nothing to think about. The morning's perversity, my discomfort with Broadway, my uncle Phil, the looming baptism class, and Virginia were at least, if not obliterated, tucked away. I was back to functioning in the moment, letting my body do the hard work while my mind took a needed rest. I had no real idea where I was, just a myopic suspicion of where I was headed, relying on the infallible hubris of youth to get me there.

A shatteringly loud noise brought me back to Route 4. I had blundered into the traffic circle where Routes 4 and 17 met. More horns and squealing tire sounds scared me onto the circular middle island of grass. Someone rolled down their window to yell obscenities while I stood mesmerized by the conveyor belt of cars merging into and out of the circle. There was no room in my feathery, euphoric feeling of freedom for inadvertent injury so I decided to eat one of my peanut butter sandwiches to calm down while I figured out how to get myself out of the middle of the traffic circle.

Route 4 had been quite level since I left Paterson. I was now in the suburban town of Teaneck peddling up a long gradient. At the top I stopped to rest. *Should I turn back? This is a bit crazy. My parents… not a chance.*

The air was sharp and damp. The road ahead flattened out. Traffic was now moving in an unbroken flow to the east. My speedometer indicated a travel distance of ten miles since leaving home. I shifted into low gear and started up the second long hill. As the ground began to flatten again I saw the top part of the George Washington Bridge come into view and then, my destination, New York City in the distance.

It felt like music was playing in the background of my mind, that I had just paid the price of admission to the best of all possible adventure movies at the Fabian, the best possible theater. I turned off the highway to get to the pedestrian walkway that led onto the bridge.

NO BICYCLES ALLOWED.

All this way and no bicycles allowed? "That's why I'm here," I said out loud. "I can't not go across the bridge." I had stopped before the sign. No one else was around. There were some police a long way off over by the tollbooths directing traffic. "I'm going! I came all this way and I'm going!" I said to the sign. *Oh no you're not, your parents would kill you if they knew what you were up to.* Then the guy on my other shoulder—*Don't be silly. Do you really care? They'll never know! You just have to get home by supper time. You're here. Just do it.*

A shiver went through me. I leaned on the bike for support and looked up at the sign. *I'll make a deal with you, Mr. Sign. I'll walk across the bridge. OK? I won't ride my bike. I've just got to do this. Otherwise this trip was for nothing.*

I took another look around. No one was on the bridge walkway. I glanced back up at the sign and in the spirit of the day, ran past it.

It's more than a mile across the GW to New York, a long naked mile and there didn't seem to be any one in sight. As soon as I stepped on to the bridge I felt energized and free once more. I started skipping as I pushed the bike toward the first cable tower. There was a couple hidden in the shadow of the huge tower where the walkway wound through it. They were hugging and kissing. I tried not to look at them but we glanced at each other. Why would two people want to hover in the chilly damp shadows of this place to kiss? I selfishly wished for the bridge to be mine alone but I had to admit, if I had to share the bridge, two people as crazy as I was was not so bad.

After I passed them I slowed my pace and felt the solid bridge quivering slightly like a living thing tickled by the fingertips of the traffic. The air was cooler now. The river and the sky both gray. My eyes locked on the swelling city skyline. It seemed dreamlike. Would I soon be in New York City? What was I doing? A confusing thought surfaced. Were there two mes, the outward boy that got good grades and went to church and did what he was told and the secret me that listened to a whispered internal voice that made me feel more alive than the other child ever did?

I reached the city, excitedly got back on my bike and rode through the city streets. Everything was busier and noisier than anything I had ever known. Everywhere I looked there were people and traffic and sounds and colors more intense than I could begin to imagine, buildings taller and bigger than big. If this was Sodom and Gomorrah, I was for it! It felt like a refuge. *And tomorrow I'll be on my way back to Virginia?* I felt constricted and apprehensive about those kids back there that were frightened by this place and suspicious of me. I'd no idea how long I had been exploring the streets around the bridge. I thought of my grandfather's pocket watch payoff. It would have been useful but I had no idea where it was. My internal clock said it must be time to go. I returned to the bridge, and keeping my part of the original bargain, walked my bike up onto the span and passed under another NO BICYCLES ALLOWED sign. On the way toward the city my attention had been totally focused on getting there, like finishing a race or winning a prize. The city was the reason for my secret journey, created out of an impulse. Yet, I also felt intuitively, it wasn't enough of a reason, or maybe not the reason for the trip at all. I walked past the bridge cable tower and looked down the tapering perspective of the walkway. It was empty. Conflicted feelings of who was right, what was right, or even real, blotted out the sounds of traffic. Even the quivering bridge vibrations were unnoticeable as I floated along in these jumbled thoughts. By mid-span I slowed to a stop, the adventure nearly over. At last I felt somewhat relieved that the pressure was lessened. Now only the work of peddling thirteen miles home remained. Still, this trip to the city felt vaguely anti-climactic. Not that it wasn't a crazy, exciting thing. It was. For the first time in months I felt unmolested there in the arms of Sodom and Gomorrah. But it also seemed, not unsatisfactory, but incomplete.

I stood at the railing looking down at the gray water far, far below disappearing into the heavy gray sky before it reached the sea. Had I not noticed the river when I crossed the bridge? To my left tiny silent cars were moving on the highway along the riverbank toward even taller buildings further south. From this height the Hudson River looked like a smooth ribbon with sea gulls, distant specks swirling freely through the vast space. I wondered if any of them had ever been to Paterson, had seen the river there or the new island where they might have fled for safety from boys throwing stones at them, or from me. And then I knew why this day was incomplete and how it could be made perfect. It was the reality of the river in its timeless flow through the crazy human world that I had almost missed. I stretched out my arms, spread my fingers like wing tip feathers to feel the wind high up on this bridge. The incongruity of everything evaporated. I reached into my pocket, took out all the coins I had and gave them up, to the perfect river and the perfect day. As I turned to finish my walk across the bridge, it began to drizzle. I had thought of everything that morning except a hat to keep my head dry and the rain off my glasses.

The reason for the trip to New York was not so clear to me at the time, most likely an escape, and it did make me feel better.

In some long forgotten movie about the sea, someone broke the tip off a knife and put it in the edge of the ship's compass to misdirect its navigation. My trip did not remove that tip but it brought me closer to the point of its discovery. I needed time.

Coda

"A man needs a little madness,
otherwise he will never cut the rope and be free."
—From Zorba the Greek

W E'RE ALL BORN PERFECT. I do believe this to be so. Even at an
early age—don't ask me how early—I knew this was true. Have
you ever in the fullness of adulthood, looked at newborn infant and
said to yourself, "Oh yeah! Born in sin?" We may be born ignorant and
trusting, but please, not in sin. More likely confusion, which may even
grow with passing years. Life is a jigsaw puzzle with no sharp finished
edges that can and usually does expand in unexpected directions with
no warning.

There are these three basic things I have come to believe about our
jigsaw human condition: that we are occasionally sentient beings, that
"we are," as Lilly Tomlin says, "in this together, all alone," and that we
have the ability to be introspective, but only if we're truthful.

My childhood was not particularly dramatic, no war, natural
disaster, or abusiveness. Just speckled with adults who thought they
knew how the world should and did work, 100 percent sure: my uncle
Joe Cerroni with his safe filled with seductive money, my mother's
parents, John and Ada Whitehead, with their dusty oath Bible, my aunt
Tyne's conscription of others into her unreal reality, Uncle Phil, who
believed whole heartedly in Karl Marx, my father's salvation by the one
and only True Religion. What was I to make of all these recruitment

efforts? They all sounded so reasonable. So convincing. So convinced they had my best interest at heart. If only I could blend them together, make them into a whole I might not need to choose. Over the years I have concluded that the only thing missing from this Pilgrim's Progress was a musical score to turn it into a humoresque.

When I rode my bike to the bridge I was twelve years old. That bike ride helped for the moment. There's nothing like a change of scenery and an exhausting activity to clear the mind. Then I toured the city, which was, I have concluded, a silent, secret revenge, and then I stood at the bridge railing and it all changed. As I looked out over the vast expanse, I felt connected, my mind filled with calm.

The next morning at five, I started back south to New Market, Virginia, and all the uncertainty I suspected lay ahead.

Acknowledgments

FOR CAROL STANLEY, MY editor, who was such a wonderful help, possessed of an unerring sense of what was needed to lead me to the heart of what mattered.